THE ONE YEAR®

Be-Tween You & God

devotions for girls

Sandra Byrd

Tyndale House Publishers, Inc.
Carol Stream, Illinois

Visit Tyndale's website for kids at www.tyndale.com/kids.

TYNDALE, The One Year, and *One Year* are registered trademarks of Tyndale House Publishers, Inc. The Tyndale Kids logo and The One Year logo are trademarks of Tyndale House Publishers, Inc.

The One Year Be-Tween You and God: Devotions for Girls

Edited by Erin Gwynne

Designed by Jennifer Ghionzoli

For manufacturing information regarding this product, please call 1-800-323-9400.

ISBN 978-1-4143-6245-8

Printed in China

19	18	17	16	15
7	6	5	4	3

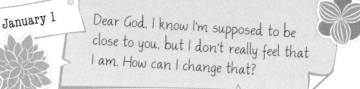

January 1

Dear God, I know I'm supposed to be close to you, but I don't really feel that I am. How can I change that?

CONSIDER THIS . . . No one wants to go to the movies alone. But almost all of us are eager to go places with people we love: a baseball game, a restaurant, the skating rink, the zoo—maybe even to a play or a concert. When we get there we want to sit or walk near people we came with, right? Then we can chat and whisper, enjoy one another's company, feel safe among a bunch of strangers, and share a laugh or a snack! If we had to sit apart or walk around alone, it would be lonely, maybe scary, and most of us wouldn't even want to go.

Being near each other and spending time together draws us closer to people. It's like that with God, too.

God loves you with his whole heart, and he wants you to love him back with your whole heart. He is eager to talk and listen, to guide and comfort, and even to have fun with you! But it's hard to share an experience with someone you're far away from.

The Bible tells us that when we come close to God, he comes close to us. Just like a magnet, he'll pull you right in. When you turn toward God, he draws closer, ready to walk with you through each day of your life, morning till night. No matter what happens, you can enjoy his company, feel safe with him, and go through both the good and the bad together.

Don't go to the movies—or anywhere else—alone. Save the seat right next to you for God!

GOD SAYS . . .

Come close to God, and God will come close to you. JAMES 4:8

HOW ABOUT YOU?

How will your life change when you and Jesus are not sitting rows apart or walking far away from each other? What are three things you can do right now to come close to God?

Dear God, Sometimes I feel too unimportant to do anything special for you. I mean, what can *I* actually do?

January 2

CONSIDER THIS ... Even though lots of girls dream of being a princess, or of marrying a prince, not many of us dream of being a servant. The word *servant* brings thoughts of scrubbing clothes on wooden boards, slopping a wet mop against a dusty stone floor, and ironing someone else's beautiful ball gown. But the truth is, in the real world of royalty, those who are chosen to serve actually have a lot of honor and power.

Even today, a queen chooses her ladies-in-waiting from among her very best friends. They are closest to her, after all, so they have to be trustworthy. And because they are friends, those servants get special benefits from being in a royal household. They get to do the most important jobs, share the best food, go to the best parties, and get the best gifts. Even if you're very rich, you can't buy your way into royal service. You have to be invited.

A servant's value isn't based on what her job is; it's based on the royal status of the person she serves. And that's what it's like to serve God, too. Our value isn't based on what we do—it's based on whom we serve. Because we are God's servants, he will give us special jobs and adventures that others won't get. We will get to go places we never dreamed of. We are important because he's invited us to serve him right now, and he will bless us when we do.

So put on your diamond tiara and prepare to serve the King!

HOW ABOUT YOU?

Do you believe that your value is based upon what you do or upon the one you serve? How could you serve Jesus this week?

GOD SAYS ...

Mary responded, "Oh, how my soul praises the Lord. How my spirit rejoices in God my Savior! For he took notice of his lowly servant girl, and from now on all generations will call me blessed." LUKE 1:46-48

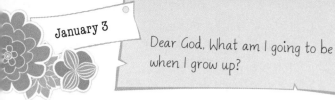

Dear God, What am I going to be when I grow up?

CONSIDER THIS . . . When Michelangelo started to sculpt his famous statue of the Bible's King David, the artist began with a large block of marble. It didn't look like a statue in the beginning. It looked like, well, a block of marble!

The artist took his tools and, over the passing years, chipped a little here, brushed a little there, carved a little in between. Weeks and months went by, and pretty soon people could begin to see more than a slab of marble. They could see a leg, and then two, and then a torso and some strong arms. Finally they saw a handsome face with a head full of curls. At the end, the whole statue, one of the most famous in the world, emerged from that block of marble.

Michelangelo said, "Every block of stone has a sculpture inside, and it's the task of the sculptor to discover it."

When God made you, he, too, knew there was a masterpiece inside you. Because who you are is already inside of you. It was created by him, instantly! Over the years God will allow life to chip, brush, and sculpt you into the perfect you-shaped statue. The Bible tells us that long ago God created good things for us to do. Do you like math or prefer art? Do you like children? Pets? Maybe you love sports. These may provide clues about what God has created you to be. It's not so much what you're going to be when you grow up; it's more that when you grow up, more of the real you will emerge and be given the chance to do wonderful things.

Get ready to grow into the masterpiece you already are on the inside.

GOD SAYS · · ·
We are God's masterpiece. He has created us anew in Christ Jesus, so we can do the good things he planned for us long ago. EPHESIANS 2:10

HOW ABOUT YOU?
What clues do you have about yourself that can show you who God created you to be and what he created you to do?

Dear God, There's a new girl in my class who still wears out-of-style clothes. If I make friends with her, I'll be stuck. What should I do?

CONSIDER THIS . . . One day at a fair a lot of different kinds of people walked around looking at booths, tasting food, and listening to live music.

A man with tattoos up and down his arms showed up. He had on black boots with studs on the sides, and his head was shaved. As he walked by, his T-shirt came into view. It said, "Body Piercing Saved My Life." Some people decided that this guy was scary and weird, and they wouldn't meet his gaze. When they looked up after he passed by, it was easy to catch the picture on the back of his T-shirt.

It was a picture of Jesus on the cross.

Jesus' hands and feet were pierced. The truth is, Jesus' body piercing saved *my* life too. But it's easy to make snappy judgments against people, some of whom may be your brothers and sisters in Christ, based only on their appearance.

The truth is, people judge others by the outside all the time. But the Lord teaches that what is most important isn't our clothing. It's our thoughts, our intentions, our deeds, our spirits, our hearts. God says that he cares more about what is inside than what is outside. Because he cares about his children treating one another with love, and because we are to imitate him, he shows us how to care for others too. When we do, we are more like him and closer to him. Give the new girl a chance. Before you make a decision, follow his lead and see what's on her inside.

You might be surprised!

HOW ABOUT YOU?

What kind of things are easy for you to judge other people by? Do you feel closer to or farther away from God when you judge other people?

GOD SAYS . . .

The LORD said to Samuel, "Don't judge by his appearance or height, for I have rejected him. The LORD doesn't see things the way you see them. People judge by outward appearance, but the LORD looks at the heart."

1 SAMUEL 16:7

January 5

Dear God, Sometimes January feels so blah. Back to school. No more presents. What can I do?

CONSIDER THIS . . . Every year we all look forward to December—lots of parties, school vacation, and visits from family and friends. Of course, best of all is Christmas. Christmas carols surround us in the car and at the mall; our homes and churches are decked out to celebrate the birth of our Savior. A tree with a growing pile of presents underneath it helps us look forward to a special day and night. But then afterward, nothing. The days after Christmas can all seem so . . . boring!

Some Christian traditions continue to celebrate after December with the twelve days of Christmas. You might think of it as that song with a partridge in a pear tree and six maids a-milking, but there is more to the tradition that starts on Christmas Day and ends today, January 5. Families take twelve whole days to talk about Jesus, celebrate his birth, and give little gifts to one another each day. Twelve days of gifts? Sign me up!

The good news is, whether you celebrate twelve days of Christmas in your home or not, you can celebrate Jesus every day, enjoy great music that is focused on him, and both receive and give gifts long after Christmas. The best gifts aren't wrapped in red and green paper and topped with bows. Sometimes these gifts are hugs, a good grade on a test, a compliment from a teacher, an unexpected snowman, or your favorite dessert.

Keep your eyes open and your heart ready; you'll find that the Lord faithfully brings you a good gift 365 days each year.

GOD SAYS . . .

Whatever is good and perfect comes down to us from God our Father.
JAMES 1:17

HOW ABOUT YOU?

Every night before you go to bed, think about what gift God, someone in your family, or one of your friends has given to you that day. It might be small or large. It might be something you can touch or something that simply touches your heart.

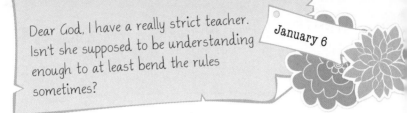

Dear God, I have a really strict teacher. Isn't she supposed to be understanding enough to at least bend the rules sometimes?

January 6

CONSIDER THIS . . . Toddlers can't understand the fence around the playground. Look at those great trees to climb—just across the street. And a pond—with ducks to feed! But toddlers don't know how to swim and can't safely cross a road. The fence is there for their protection. They just don't understand it yet.

Rules are like fences: *Don't go here. Don't turn this way. Danger over there.* Rules that protect you physically are easy to understand. Rules that protect your spirit and your mind are harder to understand, because you can't see your spirit or your mind like you can see your body.

When we cross one of God's boundaries, the Bible calls it sin. Sin leads us away from God. Following rules in one area of your life makes it easy to follow them in other areas of your life. Bending rules in one area makes it easier to bend them in another area.

God has put people over you (like your teacher or your parents) to set rules that are for your own good, not to steal your fun. They won't bend them to make it easier for you if it will really harm you in the end. They hold fast because they love you. Some fences will disappear as you grow older, but by then you'll be ready to run.

Even when you don't understand his rules, you can trust the one who gives them.

HOW ABOUT YOU?

Are there rules that are hard for you to follow or seem dumb or silly? Name one or two. Now think of something one of God's rules could be protecting you from—either preventing physical or emotional harm, stopping a bad habit from developing, whatever!

GOD SAYS . . .

He guards the paths of the just and protects those who are faithful to him. PROVERBS 2:8

Dear God, Do people really want to go to heaven? I kind of like it here.

CONSIDER THIS . . . At different times in all of our lives we have to leave home. Sometimes it's for something fun—a vacation or a visit with relatives. Sometimes we have to move. These new places are all enjoyable, but they never really feel like home. We grow up and go to college or to work, and some of us get married. And yet it's always fun to go back home again where we feel safe and taken care of.

God says the world that we live in is not really our true home—we're only here for a short stay as visitors. It's like starting in New York City on a really long road trip that stops at great places along the way—seeing Mickey at Disney World, climbing the Rocky Mountains, star-spotting on Hollywood Boulevard. But you don't live in any of those places. You stay in a hotel for a few days or weeks and then take off again. Once the road trip is over you finally make it back home, sinking into your own bed with your own pillow and blankets and eating your mom's best meals.

Most Christians who are dying understand they will leave behind people and good times from the "road trip" here. But Jesus promises that for all who believe in him, he has made a better place, the only place we'll ever feel really at home. Jesus tells us that he wants us to have a wonderful life here on earth. But we can be reassured that once we get to heaven, we will feel that perfect joy that only comes from being home.

No matter how long or short the trip, God's made a perfect map, with the best route to lead us back home.

GOD SAYS . . .
They were looking for a better place, a heavenly homeland.
HEBREWS 11:16

HOW ABOUT YOU?
Are you afraid to die? Why or why not? What great things can you look forward to experiencing in heaven, your true home?

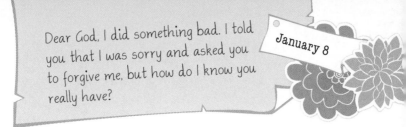

Dear God, I did something bad. I told you that I was sorry and asked you to forgive me, but how do I know you really have?

January 8

CONSIDER THIS . . . Once a girl hurt her friend's feelings by saying something mean. When she figured it out, she said she was sorry, didn't make an excuse for it, and promised to never say mean things again. She asked her friend to forgive her. The friend said she did forgive her, but she really didn't. She gave her rude looks and stopped hanging out with her. She didn't mean it when she said she had forgiven her friend, and the friendship died.

God isn't like that. When he says something, he means it. He tells us that if we ask him to forgive us, he will. He also tells us that after he forgives us, he completely forgets about the bad thing we did. He never holds a grudge against us, and he doesn't leave us out of his plans or his Kingdom because of it. He doesn't remind us about it the next time we do something wrong. He is happy that because of true repentance we can be close to him, and others, again.

If you have told God that you were truly sorry, you meant it, and you asked him to forgive you, you can be 100 percent certain that you are forgiven. If you've never done that, you need to go somewhere private and say, "Lord, I am sorry for wrong things I did. I never want to do them again, and I take all the blame myself. Please forgive me for those sins."

Feel that great big hug he's giving you?

HOW ABOUT YOU?

Have you ever told God you were sorry for your sins and asked him to forgive you, because Jesus died for you? Did you believe that he forgave you, or did you apologize over and over and still feel that he was mad at you?

GOD SAYS . . .

If we confess our sins to him, he is faithful and just to forgive us our sins and to cleanse us from all wickedness.

1 JOHN 1:9

Dear God, What do you mean when you call yourself our Father?

CONSIDER THIS . . . Because we can't actually see God with our eyes, he takes time in the Bible to explain himself a little bit by using words and relationships we do understand. That's why he sometimes calls himself our Father. The problem is, while God is perfect, people aren't. There are times when fathers make bad choices or mistakes, and then we think God is like that too. But he's not. So it's helpful to understand what a good father does, because that helps us understand our Father God.

- A good father works hard and makes sure you have food, clothing, and a place to live, because he wants you to feel cared for.
- A good father will go out and get supplies for a school project you forgot about because he understands you make mistakes too.
- A good father gives you some of the things you want besides all of the things you need because he knows fun is a part of life too.
- A good father gives you encouragement, love, and attention, because he knows that your needs aren't only physical.
- A good father disciplines you because he knows you need it, even though it's hard to do.

A good father will never bully you, or humiliate you, or make fun of you, or talk about you behind your back, or hurt you. A good father puts his children's needs ahead of his own desires. Why did your Father God allow Jesus to go to the cross? Because he was willing to undergo pain in order to give you all of what you need and some of what you want. That's a good father.

You know, you can also call God "Dad." Try it. It's kind of cool.

GOD SAYS . . .
Your heavenly Father already knows all your needs. MATTHEW 6:32

HOW ABOUT YOU?
No matter what your relationship is like with your earthly father, your heavenly Father is willing and able to give you everything you need. Tell him what you need, and ask him to help you see how he provides it.

Dear God, Sometimes I do things like hit my little sister because she's bugging me. How can I change?

January 10

CONSIDER THIS . . . It's terrific to have brothers and sisters, but sometimes it can be hard, too. All kinds of people and situations can make us angry, and when we're angry it's easy to lose self-control. In the end, we each have to decide what kind of person we want to be, even when we're mad. We have to make up our minds *before* we get angry in order to do the right thing the next time we are upset.

You've gotten a great start by deciding that you don't like how you react when someone is bugging you. Now think about what you're going to do instead of being mean or hitting. Could you go somewhere alone and cool off? Maybe whatever the person did won't seem so important in a few minutes.

If you feel like hitting someone, stuff your hands into your pockets. If you feel like saying something mean, go talk with your mom or call a friend. Think about all the fun times you share together, and remember that you can make people mad too. Make a habit of doing something right while you wait for your anger to cool down. Otherwise, it's hard to think straight when you're upset.

The Bible tells us that we have many blessings. God wants us to keep adding good things to our lives. Why not start with self-control and affection toward those you are angry with? They'll feel better, and so will you. Pray and ask God to help you with this.

He is always ready to help you do the things he asks you to do. Depend on it!

HOW ABOUT YOU?

What can you do right now to add these things to your life?
  Self-control:
  Affection (or love) toward your brothers and sisters:

GOD SAYS . . .

Supplement your faith with . . . self-control, and self-control with patient endurance, and patient endurance with godliness, and godliness with brotherly affection, and brotherly affection with love for everyone. 2 PETER 1:5-7

Dear God, I still feel embarrassed about some stuff I did in the past. How can I stop thinking about it?

CONSIDER THIS . . . When we have a bad hair day, it's easy to think everyone else is staring at us. It can make us want to run home and stay there until our hair looks good again! In reality, it's likely that nobody else notices our hair. Why not? They're too busy worrying about their *own* hair! We all tend to focus on ourselves. That's true not only with outward things, like our hair and clothes, but also with what's inside. When we make a mistake or say or do something embarrassing, we tend to focus on it a lot longer than anyone else does.

Have you ever tried to walk down the street backward? It's pretty hard to keep from bumping into trees, dogs, or other people, not to mention tripping over your own feet or not seeing danger just ahead. And it looks downright silly. How would you feel if your mom drove down the street while looking backward over her shoulder the whole time? You'd probably be screaming in fear, begging her to turn around and watch where she was going. You can't move confidently ahead if you're always looking back.

Instead of rehashing the past all the time, realize that everyone makes mistakes, leave those mistakes by the side of the road, and move on. In Scripture, God tells you that he has planned a wonderful future especially for you (Jeremiah 29:11). Isn't that delightful? But how will you be able to see it, to start looking forward to it, to plan for it and enjoy it if you're always looking back? You can't. He doesn't want you to worry about what you did or what happened before.

Look up! Look ahead! What's coming next?

GOD SAYS . . .

I [Paul] focus on this one thing: Forgetting the past and looking forward to what lies ahead, I press on to reach the end of the race. PHILIPPIANS 3:13-14

HOW ABOUT YOU?

What have you done in the past that still troubles you? What should you do about it right now?

Dear God, How am I supposed to do everything I'm supposed to do: school, homework, sports, church, family stuff? I'm stressed out!

January 12

CONSIDER THIS . . . Almost everybody eats a little snack before a sport practice, something light to keep them going through soccer, track, skating, or whatever workout they do. Snacks are good after school, too, when there's homework or chores to tackle.

But what should we eat for a pick-me-up? There are lots of options.

Lately, energy bars, which are supposed to be nutritious and chock-full of vitamins, look suspiciously like candy bars. You know—they're covered with chocolate and filled with caramel or fudge. They smell good. They taste sweet. But do they really give you the energy you need?

Face it, a candy bar masquerading as an energy bar can fool your taste buds, but when it gets down to giving you the energy you need to run up and down a field or power through twenty math problems, it's going to fall short. The strength you need just isn't going to be there, and you'll soon be out of breath or nodding off in an unexpected nap. You've got to build yourself up with good food on the inside in order to tackle the challenges on the outside.

There are a lot of "candy bars" in life that promise to power up your spirit—the Internet, a funny TV show, or gossip. But just like the empty calories in a fake energy bar, these won't give you strength. Instead, why not rely on an unlimited supply of true power that is available to you all day and night?

God!

HOW ABOUT YOU?

When the going gets tough do you tend to complain or distract yourself with games, TV, or texts, or do you rely on God? Choose one situation, and ask God to give you his power to make it through with victory.

GOD SAYS . . .

I [Paul] pray that from his glorious, unlimited resources he will empower you with inner strength through his Spirit. EPHESIANS 3:16

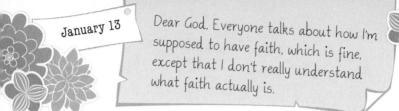

January 13

Dear God, Everyone talks about how I'm supposed to have faith, which is fine, except that I don't really understand what faith actually is.

CONSIDER THIS . . . God tells us that three things will last forever: faith, hope, and love (1 Corinthians 13:13). These three are bound closely together—like strands in a tight braid that overlap each other over and over again and work together to make a strong, permanent rope. Since they're so important, it's good to understand exactly what each really is.

We put faith in things every day. When you go to the doctor, she might prescribe a medicine for you. You take it without really wondering if it's poison, don't you? You drink water from your faucet trusting that it's pure. You get on a plane having faith that the pilot knows how to fly and the mechanics have taken care of the engine. You trust your teacher to mark down your correct grade in the grade book. Faith is trusting that people will actually do what they say they are going to do and that they have the ability to do it. We place our faith in people who have proved themselves to us and to others.

Imagine a long wooden bridge spanning a deep river. To get from one side to the other, you have to actually walk across the bridge, starting with one step. Someone can tell you that the bridge is safe, but until you take that first step, and then the next one, you won't know that the bridge is steady and secure. Faith is taking those steps.

The longer you know God, and the more you trust him with things you don't understand, the stronger your faith will grow. He does what is right, and he is able—meaning he can do everything he says he will do.

Put your foot out and take that step. Trust him!

GOD SAYS . . .

Faith is the confidence that what we hope for will actually happen; it gives us assurance about things we cannot see. HEBREWS 11:1

HOW ABOUT YOU?

How have you seen God's goodness toward you? How have you seen God's power in your life? What are you concerned about that you need to trust God to take care of for you?

Dear God, Is hoping for something the same as wishing for something?

January 14

CONSIDER THIS . . . Have you ever dropped a penny in a wishing well? You throw your money in, and you're supposed to get a wish. But there's no guarantee. Some people make wishes when the clock says 11:11. Does that mean anything? Doesn't seem to. When you wish, you can want something to happen, but there's no power or promise that it will.

Hope is different. When you hope something good is going to happen, you have reason to believe that it will. You hope you get gifts on your birthday. You hope there will be presents under the tree. You hope that the pizza at your favorite restaurant will taste good. You hope a book by your favorite author will keep you happily occupied for hours. You believe that these things will happen because experience has proved that the person you're hoping in follows through time and again.

People who love you do not mislead you into thinking that something great is going to happen but then trick you. When your birthday arrives, you know it will be a good celebration. You may not get everything you want, but many wonderful things will come to pass, and you may even get some things you couldn't have imagined. This helps us hope with confidence rather than wishing and wondering.

When we hope that God will bring good things into our lives, it shows that we trust in his goodness. We're telling him that we know he has the power and we believe his promise to bring good things into our lives. When we trust in his goodness, he is honored. And don't we want to honor God? He is worthy.

God keeps his promises. You'll see.

HOW ABOUT YOU?

What things are you hoping for? When you think about it, do you wish, or do you hope?

GOD SAYS . . .

Let us hold tightly without wavering to the hope we affirm, for God can be trusted to keep his promise. HEBREWS 10:23

Dear God, How do I know that you truly love me?

CONSIDER THIS . . . For weeks, excitement had been building at school. Posters taped up all over the hallways promised a show-and-tell visit from an amazing magician. He could make whole people disappear! He could turn a plate of green beans into a plate of chocolate cake.

The day came, and the magician arrived. Students stopped to talk with him in the hallway, and he confirmed that yes, he really could do those things. The hours ticked by till the assembly, and even the teachers could hardly wait. Once everyone was gathered, the magician appeared in front of everyone and did . . . nothing. Then he showed a film of himself performing tricks someplace else, although the movie was hard to see and no one could be sure that he hadn't changed the film to make the tricks seem real when they were not. On the way out of the gym, one girl said, "He's no magician. He didn't do any of the things he said he would do." He was all tell and no show.

People shouldn't be judged on what they promise, or what they say, or what others say about them, even if those things are exciting. The truth is shown only by what people do, not what they say.

God does not just *say* he loves you; his actions *show* he loves you. He demonstrates that love is patient and kind and isn't rude or jealous or boastful or proud (1 Corinthians 13:4-5). He is someone who loves you and doesn't hold a grudge. He sticks with you no matter what happens, good or bad. Most of all, God proved his love for you by giving you the most valuable gift—his Son.

GOD SAYS . . .
We know what real love is because Jesus gave up his life for us.
1 JOHN 3:16

HOW ABOUT YOU?
How has God shown you that he loves you today? How can you show him that you love him, too? Remember, don't just tell him. Show him!

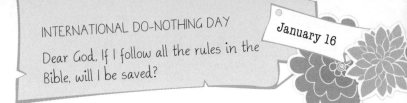

INTERNATIONAL DO-NOTHING DAY

January 16

Dear God, If I follow all the rules in the Bible, will I be saved?

CONSIDER THIS ... Even though it's no fun to be sick, there are a few things that are nice about it. You don't have to go to school or do homework. Usually you're tucked into a comfy bed, or you get the best couch in the house, with a fuzzy blanket and squished pillow to comfort you. You get to pick what to watch on TV or read some of your favorite books or nap. Usually someone will bring you whatever you want to eat—tomato soup with melted cheese in it or popsicles or ice cream or hot chocolate. When you're sick, people who love you do things for you because you're not well enough to do anything for yourself. You *can't* do anything for yourself.

This is true about being saved, too. Our sins make us sick in a way. Our spirits are not what God would want them to be: healthy, clean, and directed toward him and not toward the world or ourselves. We can't work our way out of this sin sickness on our own, no matter how many good things we do. Following the Bible and our parents and church teachings is good. Giving to others and loving other people and sharing are good. But these activities will not save us. Only God can save a person. And he does it by his grace—meaning it's a gift—when we believe.

So can you be saved without doing anything? Not exactly. You must do only one thing. Believe!

HOW ABOUT YOU?

Do you believe that God sent his one and only Son, Jesus Christ, to die on the cross and pay the penalty for your sins?

GOD SAYS ...

God saved you by his grace when you believed. And you can't take credit for this; it is a gift from God. Salvation is not a reward for the good things we have done, so none of us can boast about it. EPHESIANS 2:8-9

January 17

Dear God, Sometimes I wonder if you even notice the good things I am doing like going to church and reading my Bible even when I don't feel like it.

CONSIDER THIS . . . When you get your very first job babysitting, you get paid right after the job is done. Did you watch the kids from twelve to three? At three, then, when the mom returns, she'll pay you for three hours of work.

Your second job might be pet sitting while neighbors are away. Each day you'll go in and check to make sure that the cat has food and water and that her litter box is clean. The owners might be gone for three to four days, so you'll have to wait a bit longer to get paid. After they return, though, if you've done a good job, you'll get paid.

Later, when you grow up, you'll get a job working in a restaurant or a store or a doctor's office, perhaps. Then, even though you'll go to work every day, and work hard, you won't get a paycheck for two weeks—or maybe even a month. You'll be paid for a job well done long after you've done the job. Why will you keep working? Because you'll know that the company you're working for is honest. If they say they'll pay you later for work done now, you know that they will. One day soon you'll have a big check or a fat wad of cash to save, give, and spend!

Often when we do good, we see the reward right away. Sometimes we have to wait a little while—and sometimes we wait a long while! But we know that if we keep on doing the right thing, the Lord will reward us for our work. This payment isn't always cash, but God knows how to reward us in millions of delightfully different ways, and believe it, he does.

Keep working hard—payday is coming!

GOD SAYS . . .

Let's not get tired of doing what is good. At just the right time we will reap a harvest of blessing if we don't give up. GALATIANS 6:9

HOW ABOUT YOU?

What are you working hard at but seeing little reward for? Do you believe payday is coming?

Dear God, I have this friend, or so I think. Some days we get along, but some days she's really bossy. What should I do?

January 18

CONSIDER THIS . . . Friendships provide us with some of our *best* times. Sometimes, though, we give our hearts to friends who don't always treat us kindly. That can mean some of our *worst* times! One minute we can be talking to someone we think is our best friend till she treats us poorly. Later, she'll act nice again. That's when some decisions have to be made.

One choice you could make about your friend would be to do whatever she tells you to do. That would work for a while, but she'd get sick of you following her around and you'd get sick of her bossing you. You could stop being friends right away. But both of you might miss out on some good times if you did that.

Friends love each other, and the Bible says that love is patient and kind. How did Jesus treat his friends? He took time with his friends and had fun with them, but he also brought it to their attention if they did or said something wrong. He did not gossip about his friends, nor act meanly, nor turn his back on them. But he also realized that people who set out to harm him, or didn't have his best interests in mind, were not his friends, even if they pretended to be.

Tell your friend how you feel, and listen to see if you are hurting her, too. Quietly point out if she's hurt you, and listen to her if she says she needs you to act differently sometimes too. But if none of this works and being together feels like work more often than fun, it might be time to reconsider your friendship.

Be a friend, and choose friends like Jesus.

HOW ABOUT YOU?
Do you have a friend who treats you unkindly? What can you do? Is there a friend whom you treat unkindly? How can you change?

GOD SAYS . . .
Love is patient and kind.
1 CORINTHIANS 13:4

Dear God, Sometimes I ask you for things, things that are important to me, but time goes by and I don't feel like you're listening or answering. Are you?

CONSIDER THIS . . . Once upon a time there was a girl who loved all creatures, great and small, from the largest horse to the smallest bug. She asked her mother one day for an ant farm so she could watch as the busy little ants went about their day building and moving and eating and working. Her mom said, "Maybe. But not now."

"But I really want an ant farm," the girl insisted. "I have enough money to buy one of those ones with three rooms so I can watch the ants go from one room to the other and back again." When her mother didn't immediately agree, the girl pouted. "There's nothing in the Bible that says I can't have an ant farm," she grouched. "And I can pay for it myself." The girl wanted an ant farm, but her mom wouldn't agree right then. A cool distance grew between them because the girl wouldn't stop being angry about her frustrations and she couldn't understand why her mom had said no.

A few months later it was the girl's birthday, and guess what she got? Not an ant farm—an ant village! This version had more than three rooms; it had an ant bank, an ant store, an ant playground, and many tunnels. But when the gift was opened, the pleasure for both mom and daughter was a little sour because of all the angry words that had been spoken. The present had been bought months before and was stored under the mom's bed, waiting for just the right time to be presented: on the girl's birthday.

Sometimes we do not understand why we hear the words *no* or *maybe* or *not yet*. Wait patiently for God to surprise you with the desires of your heart.

GOD SAYS . . .

Be still in the presence of the Lord, and wait patiently for him to act. PSALM 37:7

HOW ABOUT YOU?

What is the thing you've asked God for, but he hasn't given it to you? Are you able to trust . . . and wait?

Dear God, I've started reading the Bible, but it's confusing. If you want me to read it, why is it so hard to understand?

January 20

CONSIDER THIS . . . We mostly get e-mail or texts, so it's exciting when we get an actual letter or a card or a package in the mail. It says, *I care!* If you speak only English, your family and friends won't write to you in Spanish. They'll write to you in English because they want you to understand what they have to say. If you don't understand what they're saying, you can ask them to explain and they will!

God cares about you too. He wants you to understand the things he has written in the Bible, his personal letter to you. It helps if you read a version that sounds like the language you speak rather than one with funny-sounding phrases or outdated language. Translations such as the New Living Translation are truly the Bible but put in words that sound just like you talk. Don't just pick and choose little parts to read—choose a book of the Bible and read it through from beginning to end. How much of a letter would you understand if you read only a few sentences here and there?

The Bible isn't a text message, something short to be quickly read and easily understood. It takes time and attention and quiet. You have to focus. Keep your attention on God, and he will make things clear. If you still don't understand, it's okay to ask for help. Sometimes God will make the meaning clear in your heart. Sometimes he will use someone else to show you. He is faithful to help you understand what he wants you to know.

Hey—you've got mail!

HOW ABOUT YOU?

How often do you read your Bible, compared with text messages, e-mails, or other books? Whom can you ask for help in understanding what God has to say to you in his Word?

GOD SAYS . . .

Open my eyes to see the wonderful truths in your instructions.
PSALM 119:18

Dear God, Sometimes I get picked on for my beliefs. How can I stop hurting about this?

CONSIDER THIS . . . When you're a nice and good person, it can be a shock to discover that there are some people around you who don't like you. Why wouldn't they be kind? Mind their own business? Leave you alone?

In Egypt, there are very few Christians, and they aren't thought of very highly. What do most of them do for a job? Pick up the garbage that no one else will touch. They used to own garbage-eating pigs that other Egyptians believed were dirty. But owning those pigs allowed Christians to make enough money for a place to live and food to eat. A few years ago, a sickness broke out that people mistakenly blamed on those pigs. In a panic, the Egyptian government killed those pigs. Then, many Christians didn't have any way at all to earn money. Their neighbors still didn't like them, and the garbage piled up.

All around the world, there are Christians who are looked down on for their faith in Christ. Many suffer in little ways, like being made fun of or left out, and a few, like the Egyptian Christians, suffer in big ways, like losing their homes and families. Jesus tells us that it's not *you* they don't like; it's him. And your brothers and sisters around the world feel that too. Knowing this won't make people like you. But understanding that all Christians sometimes get picked on for their beliefs helps you know that you're not alone.

And Jesus is with you. He draws near to his own when others are pushing them away.

GOD SAYS . . .
Be strong in your faith. Remember that your Christian brothers and sisters all over the world are going through the same kind of suffering you are. 1 PETER 5:9

HOW ABOUT YOU?
Has anyone ever made fun of you, or left you out, or teased you for your beliefs? Did you feel alone in that moment? . . . Are you alone?

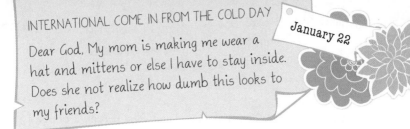

INTERNATIONAL COME IN FROM THE COLD DAY

January 22

Dear God, My mom is making me wear a hat and mittens or else I have to stay inside. Does she not realize how dumb this looks to my friends?

CONSIDER THIS ... Something happens to a woman when she becomes a mother. Normal people who sneeze and cough suddenly become "unsafe" because they might make her children sick. Stairs look steeper, bikes look more dangerous, and the bark chips under the playground swings don't look thick enough. The woman is now a mom—in charge of making sure that her children stay safe.

As kids get older, though, moms don't always realize that their sons and daughters are able to make good decisions themselves to stay safe and healthy. You might have a great sense of when it's safe to ride your bike to school, walk to a friend's house, or stay out in the cold. Most moms have provided good food and warm clothes for their kids for so long that they forget that kids can also make smart decisions for themselves.

Realize that your mom is only trying to protect you, even if it comes on a little too strong sometimes. Try to negotiate what is healthy and helpful to your mom, and what is workable and not embarrassing to you. There may be no need for wearing mittens or having to stay in all day, but maybe a warm coat is in order.

Just remember—the fact that you're still here means your mom's done a good job so far, right? The Lord has given you a mom who cares for you. Because he cares for you too!

HOW ABOUT YOU?

What would your mom like you to do that you do not want to do? Can you talk about it together and find a compromise? Does understanding *why* she's asking you to do it help a little?

GOD SAYS ...

She has no fear of winter for her household, for everyone has warm clothes.
PROVERBS 31:21

January 23

Dear God, Doesn't it seem a little unfair that pushy people always get to be first and patient people end up last?

CONSIDER THIS . . . One morning a wise Sunday school teacher asked her class to line up for a surprise. There was plenty of pushing and shoving and cutting to get to the front of the line. When they left the classroom, the students were surprised to find out that the "surprise" was that they were being led to the front of the church to sing. Those who had wanted to be first for a treat actually had to stand front and center and warble!

The next month, the teacher asked her class to line up again, and this time, no one wanted to be in front. Instead of pushing to get to the front, they dove behind one another to get to the back and pushed the weaker kids to the head of the line. Imagine their shock when she led them to the church kitchen for leftover cake. The kids at the front got to choose first.

Christianity is the upside-down, sometimes-backward-is-frontward faith. Scripture says that those who look out only for themselves will end up with less than those who look out for others, too. The person who sits down at the head of the table will be asked to move to the foot of it—to make room for the person who didn't push to be first.

Don't worry. Do the right thing, and be willing to be the caboose from time to time. God promises that even if we can't see it, the Teacher will turn the line around so that the caboose actually becomes the engine.

Cake, anyone?

GOD SAYS . . .

Those who are last now will be first then, and those who are first will be last. MATTHEW 20:16

HOW ABOUT YOU?

Do you ever feel like the pushers and shovers get the good stuff? What are some things you can do to look out for others instead of trying to get ahead in the line?

Dear God, Why don't people have a vote and put you back in the schools and government again?

January 24

CONSIDER THIS . . . Most democracies—that is, countries whose governments are chosen by and governed by their people—provide for a separation of church and state. That means the government can't dictate an official religion to any of its people; individuals get to choose their own religion or faith—even if they don't want one at all.

Long ago, in many countries, and even today in some countries, the king or government decided what faith citizens should have, and the people had no choice in the decision. As Christians, we know that Christianity is about someone choosing to follow God; no one is a Christian just because of where she was born. No one can be forced by a king or government to become a Christian.

Just because God isn't written into the laws of the schools, or the country, it does not mean he is not involved. The Bible says that God can turn the thoughts of kings like rivers of water (Proverbs 21:1). He can also turn the thoughts of judges and presidents and everyone else who makes decisions. The Bible tells us to obey the laws of our land (Romans 13:1) and to pray for our leaders (1 Timothy 2:1-2). Even if people in the government don't recognize God, leave him out of their decisions, or pretend he doesn't exist, God is still in charge.

No matter who is in charge of the government or the schools, remember that God is always in control.

HOW ABOUT YOU?

Do you feel more comfortable knowing that no matter what is happening in the government, God is always in control? What is the name of one person in government you could pray for right now?

GOD SAYS . . .

God reigns above the nations, sitting on his holy throne. . . . All the kings of the earth belong to God. He is highly honored everywhere.

PSALM 47:8-9

Dear God, Is it okay for my family to go out to eat when some people struggle to feed their families?

CONSIDER THIS . . . When you draw near to God, and he draws near to you, you begin to see people and things and situations more like he does, instead of like you always did.

There is nothing wrong with having a lot—even a lot of food! After all, God owns everything and talks about feasts in the Bible. But when you share his heart, and you begin to see that you have a lot of stuff and other people don't, you start to want to give some of that "a lot" away.

Your family can enjoy the blessings God has given you, and if that means a night out for burgers, have fun! But why not brainstorm ways that you can share your food with others? Some families choose to eat only rice and beans for one dinner per week because that is what many people in the world are limited to eating. Then they donate the money they've saved to feed the poor. You might ask a family who doesn't have very much to go out to dinner with you—your treat. Or you could sneakily mail a gift card to them so they can enjoy eating out together, like your family does.

The main thing to realize is that while eating out isn't wrong, when the Lord draws your attention to the fact that you have a lot and some others need a lot, it may be that eating out often, while others have little, isn't right for you. If the Lord has gently shown you that you might be gobbling up more than your fair share of the blessings he has passed along, perhaps it's time to share. He trusts you to do what is right.

Want fries with that?

GOD SAYS . . .
No food, in and of itself, is wrong to eat. But if someone believes it is wrong, then for that person it is wrong. ROMANS 14:14

HOW ABOUT YOU?
Do you have more than those around you? How can you creatively share what you have?

FAIRY TALE DAY

January 26

Dear God, I'm too old to want to be a princess anymore . . . but I kind of still do. Is that weird?

CONSIDER THIS . . . From the time they are little girls with pink tutus and pretty ballet slippers, many girls want to be princesses. What's not to like? There are fancy clothes, lots of jewelry, servants to do your chores, and a handsome prince who will love you no matter what. It sure beats going to school, wearing hand-me-down coats and shoes, and taking the trash out or loading the dishwasher.

Truth is, many of us wish our lives started out with "Once upon a time."

We need to remember the rest of those fairy tales, though. The life of a princess isn't perfect. There are hard times and disagreements. She's misunderstood! No one sees her for the beautiful maiden that she really is! Who can help?

There is someone who sees you as the beautiful princess you are. Nearly always, there is a handsome hero who comes riding in on a fine horse to save the princess—and the day. God is the King of kings! And because you are his child, you are a daughter of the King! No matter how others may treat you or how many difficult things you'll go through, in the end, you will have a Happily Ever After.

Why? Your very own hero, Jesus, will always ride in to save you at the end. Your story will include hard times and misunderstandings and people who do you wrong. But God will make sure that you, his princess, live Happily Ever After when all is said and done.

HOW ABOUT YOU?

If you could be any princess, which one would you be, and why?

GOD SAYS . . .

God knew his people in advance, and he chose them to become like his Son, so that his Son would be the firstborn among many brothers and sisters. ROMANS 8:29

Dear God, Does it really matter who my friends are?

CONSIDER THIS . . . When you're young, your friends are usually picked for you. Your mom arranges playdates or you hang out with kids in the neighborhood. When you get older, you begin to choose friends for yourself. It's exciting—and maybe a little dangerous. So many girls and groups to choose from. Who should your friends be?

Friends talk together, watch movies together, and go places together. If you choose a friend who goes to good places, reads good books, watches good TV shows, and talks about good things, that is where your conversation (and your mind) will be focused. If you choose a friend who uses nasty language, gossips, or is tempted to do wrong things . . . you will be too.

Consider the girl whose new friend wanted eye shadow that she had no money for. When the girls went to the drugstore, the broke friend slipped some eye shadow in her pocket. The police were called, and they held both girls—one for stealing, and the other under suspicion that she had helped. Both girls' parents had to come and pick them up.

When the girls first became friends, there was no indication that the one girl was a thief. But she did show signs of not following rules and being rude to those in authority. There may as well have been a sign that said, "Trouble, ten miles ahead." If only the other girl had stopped to read it.

God gives us choices rather than making all of the decisions for us. He shows us options, and then helps us to understand so we make good decisions. Think about the road people are walking before you decide if you want to jump on it and be their friend. Is it leading where you want to go?

GOD SAYS . . .
Walk with the wise and become wise; associate with fools and get in trouble. PROVERBS 13:20

HOW ABOUT YOU?
Are your friends walking on a path that leads to somewhere you want to end up? Why or why not?

CONSIDER THIS . . . Sometimes it's hard to tell who is a true friend and who is a false friend. Let's consider a few friendship facts:

1. Not all friends need to be your best friends. Some friends are really "acquaintances," people we like but who really aren't involved in our lives. It's okay to have lots of acquaintances.

2. Not all friends are good friends. Friends who try to control you or treat you badly really aren't friends. Sometimes we know that in our hearts, but we don't want to face it. Don't be afraid to leave bad friendships. God will replace them with good friendships.

3. True friends will allow you to put them first sometimes, but they will also put you first sometimes. Like a teeter-totter! Sometimes you're up when they're down. You give them a push, and for a while, you're balanced. Sometimes they're up when you're down. They'll give you a push, and then you're balanced for a while. Real friendships are equal friendships.

God knows we care about friendships, so in his Word, he shows us many examples of true and false friends so we know what to look for. Job, for example, had many problems. His friends didn't do and say everything right, but they came to be with him, and they focused on him when he was down. Sometimes they reminded Job of God's goodness and power. When Job was down, they pushed him back up again!

God, the very best of true friends, sticks by you in good times and in bad. He will help you find true friends if you ask him.

HOW ABOUT YOU?

What does true friendship mean to you? How does Jesus model what a true friend is like? Who is a true friend to you? Have you thanked her lately?

GOD SAYS . . .

When three of Job's friends heard of the tragedy he had suffered, they got together and traveled from their homes to comfort and console him. JOB 2:11

Dear God, Do I have to dress in fashion?

CONSIDER THIS ... Whether we like it or not, the clothes we wear say a lot about us—if we are modest or not, if we are daring or cautious, if we like attention or just standing in the background. People learn about us by what we are wearing before we even speak a word.

Why does that happen? Most people don't mean anything bad by learning about you through what you wear. After all, you choose your clothes, so your clothes give clues about who you are. Are you artsy? Sporty? Preppy? A one-of-a-kind fashionista? People want to get to know you better, and one way to do that is just to look at you. They aren't judging you; they're just getting to know you.

But some people only like people who seem rich or more fashionable because of what they wear. In the Bible, the Lord tells us that people who are nicer to those with better clothes or jewelry are making decisions using evil motives. Yes—evil! Pretty intense, huh?

If what you choose to wear says something you want people to know about you, wear it with pride! It doesn't matter if it isn't expensive or popular. No designer creates the same outfit over and over again; God created you to be individual, unique, and different from others. No matter what you wear, people will find out much more as they spend time with the real you, inside your heart and mind. The ones who judge you based only on your clothes aren't people you want to try to please.

Express your one-of-a-kind self!

GOD SAYS ...

If you give special attention and a good seat to the rich person, but you say to the poor one, "You can stand over there, or else sit on the floor"—well, doesn't this discrimination show that your judgments are guided by evil motives? JAMES 2:3-4

HOW ABOUT YOU?

What are you saying about yourself by the clothes you choose to wear? Is that what you want to say? How would you like to change it up?

Dear God, How does the Holy Spirit help us?

CONSIDER THIS . . . Christians understand God to be three-in-one: the Trinity. There is God the Father, God the Son (Jesus), and God the Holy Spirit. They are each the same, and yet also different. One way we can understand a little of this mystery is to begin to know them by their names. We know about fathers, which helps us understand God the Father. But what about God the Holy Spirit?

Imagine that you are in a classroom and, after you finish a test, you turn around in your seat to talk with a friend. The teacher calls you forward. She says you were cheating and must be sent home from school. You panic. You weren't cheating. And hadn't you been told that you could speak after finishing? Now you can't remember. You can bring one person with you to the principal's office to help share your side of the story.

You could bring the friend you were whispering with, but then you see that the assistant principal has been standing in the back of the room. He offers to go with you. He says he knows you were not cheating and, in fact, heard what you said. He also remembers that a rule was given earlier that okayed talking after tests.

Who would you bring to defend you, to help you, to be your advocate? The assistant principal, of course!

Jesus said that the Father sent the Holy Spirit to Christians for many reasons. One of them is to defend you, to help you, to remind you, and to speak up on your behalf. He's way more powerful than any assistant principal. And he's with you 24-7. That's one of the loveliest ways we know for sure that God loves us. He'll never leave you to stand on your own.

HOW ABOUT YOU?

When have you felt like no one was on your side? How can you remind yourself, next time, that someone is?

GOD SAYS . . .

I will ask the Father, and he will give you another Advocate, who will never leave you. He is the Holy Spirit. JOHN 14:16-17

Dear God, If there are so many missionaries, why are so many people still not Christians?

CONSIDER THIS . . . You're right. There are thousands of missionaries in this world—actually, hundreds of thousands. There are missionaries in almost all nations of the world, including the United States. Missionaries may move to somewhere far away, but sometimes people are missionaries in their own countries. For example, there are Americans who are missionaries to Americans, and there are Korean missionaries reaching out to people in Korea.

Even with all the missionaries in the world, not everyone who hears the Good News decides to become a Christian. In the book of Joshua, chapter 24, Joshua tells the people that they must choose whom they will serve. Some people choose to serve God, but other people choose to serve idols or even themselves! You can't make someone decide to be a Christian. That is between the individual and God. But they have to hear the Good News in order to choose.

That is where you and I and all missionaries come in.

Some missionaries are called to move away, but others are missionaries right in their own schools and neighborhoods. Did you realize that, in a way, you are a missionary too? A "missionary" is simply a person who has a mission, or a goal. Our mission as Christians is to share the Good News with those who need to hear it.

Just remember—it's your privilege to tell people about Jesus, and it's their choice how to respond.

God has given *you* an important mission. Are you ready? Get set . . . go!

GOD SAYS . . .

Not everyone welcomes the Good News.
ROMANS 10:16

HOW ABOUT YOU?

Who in your life needs to hear some Good News?

Dear God, Why does it matter what I am thinking about? No one but me hears my thoughts anyway.

CONSIDER THIS . . . When you turn on your tunes and slip your earbuds on, you enter another world. You might be listening to classical music or a pop song. Maybe you prefer country music about a dog gone wrong. Or something with a little spice and hip-hop that gives you some attitude. No matter what is coming through those earbuds, it's just between you and the music. Or is it?

Music that is cheerful makes you smile more often, even after the song is over. Down, depressing music makes the whole day feel gloomy. Praise music brings God to your mind as you face challenges throughout the day. It's true—what you listen to becomes a part of you and how you act.

Even more than music, what you listen to most often are your thoughts. What are they saying? Do they say that you're dumb? Do you replay the thoughts that say you're not pretty, not popular, not special? That you are no one's favorite? Those negative thoughts are going to change how you view every person who talks to you and how you feel inside.

Instead, tune in to the thoughts that say you are beautifully and wonderfully made. God's thoughts about you are precious, and he rejoices over you with singing. When you listen to these positive truths, you'll be cheerful, strong, and confident. No one but you and God may hear what comes out of your earbuds—or what's going on between those ears. But the Lord says it matters because YOU matter. What you listen to adds to and subtracts from the girl that you are becoming, and that's important to him and to you.

Is it time to consider a new playlist?

HOW ABOUT YOU?

What station do you keep tuned into in your mind's "radio"? What "songs" do you hear most often? Are they helping or hurting?

GOD SAYS . . .

Now, dear brothers and sisters, one final thing. Fix your thoughts on what is true, and honorable, and right, and pure, and lovely, and admirable. Think about things that are excellent and worthy of praise. PHILIPPIANS 4:8

Dear God, Sometimes I don't feel like reading the Bible. Why is that?

CONSIDER THIS . . . Eating out is so much fun, and one of the best parts is the bread basket served while you're waiting. The rolls are hot, the garlic butter is strong. Maybe the restaurant even has biscuits or corn bread. Fancy restaurants often serve olive oil and vinegar with spices for you to dip the bread in. And the best part? They'll refill the basket as many times as you want. For free!

But . . . there's a problem.

You place your order, something delicious and delightful that you've chosen from the menu as perfect for you. And then you eat some bread. And some more bread. Maybe just one more roll. By the time that delicious and delightful entrée arrives, you're full. You stick your fork in it and take a few bites, but it doesn't taste as good as you remembered. In fact, nothing does. The bread seemed like a treat at the time, but because you ate so much of it, you don't really want your dinner.

This happens in our spiritual lives too. We fill ourselves up on TV or movies or books or texting and use up our extra time and even our daily dose of concentration. By the time we realize we should spend some of our attention and energy on God's Word, well, we're stuffed. Instead of having a little of the bread and a lot of the meal, we've eaten a whole basket of garlic rolls, and there's no room left for the delicious and delightful Word of God.

Go ahead. Choose one biscuit: one TV show, or even two or three chapters of a great book. But be sure to save room for the main course every day.

God's prepared it especially for you!

GOD SAYS . . .

A person who is full refuses honey. PROVERBS 27:7

HOW ABOUT YOU?

Remember, Scripture tells us that people don't live by bread alone, but by every word from God (Matthew 4:4). Are you eating so much from the bread basket that you're not hungry for the Main Course?

CONSIDER THIS . . . One of the most difficult questions to face for people who know God is, if God is good, why does he allow bad things, both little and big, to happen? There is no quick or easy answer to that. I wish there were, but in truth, we won't know for sure till we see him face-to-face. We do know, though, that he promises to be with us no matter what, and that he will make all situations, easy and hard, work out according to his good and great plan.

It might be easy to think of this like your morning hair routine. Do you blow-dry your hair? Maybe you're a girl with straight hair, so you curl it. Or you might have curly hair and you straighten or flatten it. What do all of those have in common?

Heat!

Heat can burn, of course, if you let it get too hot or too close to your skin. But if it's controlled, heat shapes your hair the way you want it to go. Sometimes bad situations are like that in our lives. The heat from them could burn us if it were allowed to, but if it's not, that heat can shape us into the women God wants us to be. It will even shape you into the woman *you* want to be—strong, flexible, and lovely.

Next time you feel the heat, remember that God won't let the iron get too close. Ask yourself, how is he shaping and styling me into the young woman I am meant to be?

Flatiron. Curling iron. Girl iron!

HOW ABOUT YOU?

What hard thing are you going through right now, or have you gone through recently? Find two things that could come out of that situation to shape you for good.

GOD SAYS . . .

Do not be afraid. . . . When you walk through the fire of oppression, you will not be burned up; the flames will not consume you. ISAIAH 43:1-2

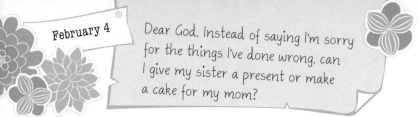

Dear God, Instead of saying I'm sorry for the things I've done wrong, can I give my sister a present or make a cake for my mom?

CONSIDER THIS ... When you hurt a friend's feelings, gossip, raise your voice to your mom, or say something to a sibling in anger, the first and most important thing to do is to understand you've done wrong. Then decide to change how you act. Next, you must apologize, and mean it.

Once everything is made right again, you may feel like giving a gift or a compliment to the one you've hurt. Maybe you want to invite that friend over to let her know that all is a-okay between you. Or maybe you want to write a note to your mom to let her know you love her. These are definitely good things! But kind words and gifts don't mean anything without repentance. You must feel sorry about the wrong you've done, determine not to do it again, and ask for forgiveness—first.

This is important in our relationship with God, too. Think about red nail polish. We can try many ways to get rid of it: washing it off our fingers or toes with water. Chipping it away. Covering it with another color. But the only way to get rid of that red completely is to use the product designed exactly for removing it: nail-polish remover. A few whisks with a cotton swab and voilà! The red is gone.

God has designed something perfect for the removal of your sins, the "bad things" you do and say: repentance, sorrow, and changed behavior. If you want to show your love afterward by doing good, well then, that's terrific! But don't forget that you have to remove the red polish before you can paint on some fresh pink. Otherwise you're painting over problems that are just going to show through again, and soon.

Whisk, whisk!

GOD SAYS ...

"Come now, let's settle this," says the LORD. "Though your sins are like scarlet, I will make them as white as snow." ISAIAH 1:18

HOW ABOUT YOU?

Do you try to act kindly or say nice things to people instead of repenting, asking for forgiveness, and changing what you do? Why can this never fix things?

CONSIDER THIS . . . Have you ever tried to draw a picture, maybe in an art class? You start by sketching.

Sketching involves using many short lines, made one at a time, in order to make a picture. At first when you're sketching, you can't see what the picture is going to be. It looks like funny hairs lying across the page instead of a picture! Sometimes lines are made in one place, then another, and they aren't connected for quite a while. Finally it's done. What started out as a bunch of disconnected lines turns into a picture of great clarity and meaning.

This is how your life is, especially now as a girl. You walk through your days making choices. What will I wear? How will I spend my time? Will I study my Bible and talk with God or not? Will I take care of my body? When I am offered the opportunity to do good, will I? If I'm tempted to cheat, will I? Each choice is a line that will connect with all of the other choices you make. Each choice may seem separate from other choices, but it's not. They all connect to make the woman you are becoming.

God has created certain things about you, but he also allows you to help draw the woman you are becoming. You are shaping tomorrow's woman out of the girl you are today.

When you're older, you'll be picture perfect.

HOW ABOUT YOU?

What one thing can you do today to begin to be more like the person you'd like to be when you're grown up?

GOD SAYS . . .

Happy are those who don't listen to the wicked. . . . They are strong, like a tree planted by a river. The tree produces fruit in season, and its leaves don't die. Everything they do will succeed.
PSALM 1:1, 3 (NCV)

Dear God, What does it mean to be the salt of the earth?

CONSIDER THIS . . . Have you ever gone through your spice cabinet? Try it sometime. Take out a whole bunch of jars and unscrew the lids. Then lean over and . . . sniff! When spices are new, they are fragrant and strong. Open cinnamon and it smells like . . . Christmas! Open nutmeg and it smells like . . . Thanksgiving! Chives smell like a garden, and pepper will just make you sneeze. Each spice has a distinct scent and taste, but spices are only good when they are fresh. After they lose their flavor, they all taste like . . . dust. And who wants dust in their cookies, their casseroles, or their cakes? No one!

Unlike spices, salt doesn't *change* the flavor of anything; it *enhances* the flavor. Food with salt sprinkled over it still tastes like itself . . . only better! A little bit of salt improves almost everything it touches. Try eating an egg without salt. Blech. Or french fries. Ick. Or salt-free potato chips. No thanks. Food without salt can taste bland and sometimes just plain gross!

As Christians, we're supposed to flavor our world like salt flavors food. Keeping your saltiness means keeping fresh the part of you that is different because you follow Jesus. Why? Because when you show up to class, or to a game, or a party, or even to chat, you can improve everything around you just by bringing Christ into the room. You do this by speaking good words, having love for others, being patient, and setting a good example. Add a little of his love, his insight, and his plan to everything you touch.

God made you to be wonderfully salty, and he wants to sprinkle you all over the world you live in. Will you let him?

GOD SAYS . . .
You are the salt of the earth. But what good is salt if it has lost its flavor? Can you make it salty again? It will be thrown out and trampled underfoot as worthless. MATTHEW 5:13

HOW ABOUT YOU?
Name two things about you that bring something special anywhere you go or to anything you touch. Can people see Jesus in you? Are you salty?

CONSIDER THIS . . . What's the first thing you do when you walk into a dark room? Turn on the light! Lights help us to see so we don't hurt ourselves or trip over furniture. Bright lights are used at the dentist's office to help diagnose if we have a cavity. Lights allow us to enjoy books. Soft light is pleasant at dinner. Night-lights help us not to be afraid of the dark in the middle of the night. Light makes everything feel safer and more enjoyable.

Very rarely do plain bulbs hang from the ceiling or shine from a lamp. There's almost always a cover—a beautiful etched glass, maybe. Or perhaps you have a pretty pink lampshade in your room, or one that looks like blue jeans. Maybe you have bling on yours, or you prefer pure white.

Before the light is turned on, that shade may look fine, but it's dull. When you turn the light on underneath it, though, its beauty shines through! You can see designs on fabric, or pleats, or little star patterns with peepholes for the light to shine through.

Like light, Jesus shines in dark places so they aren't scary anymore. He brings good and enjoyable things. He shows us when we sin. When he lives in you, you become his light too, and your life is like a lampshade. You're beautiful and unique, but you were made to look your best when the light of Jesus shines radiantly inside you and then flows out to brighten whatever room you are in. Then you help people see not only so they don't get hurt, can get well, and can enjoy life, but also so they see *you* at your awesome best.

Spend some time with your Lord and flip that switch!

HOW ABOUT YOU?

Do you realize that if Jesus lives in you, you light up a room whenever you walk into it? You have a beautiful design on your lampshade. Be sure to let everyone see it by turning your light a little brighter.

GOD SAYS . . .

You are the light of the world. MATTHEW 5:14

Dear God, Since I can't see you, how do I know you're really there?

CONSIDER THIS . . . All day, every day, we use our eyes to figure out what's going on around us because it's easiest: who's standing nearby, who may be in trouble, what people are wearing, what we're eating for dinner, when the bus is coming, who scored a goal, and who saved one. But at night, in the dark after we've gone to bed, we can't see much anymore. So we close our eyes.

We hear the soothing voices of family members murmuring down the hallway. We feel the winter wind sneaking through the window frame; its cool touch makes us burrow into our warm blankets. Maybe our mouths taste clean from a drink of cold water. Or the smell of peppermint still lingers from our toothpaste. Life is richer when we use all of our senses and don't only rely on one.

In the same way, we can learn to trust and love a God we can't see but must sense in other ways. We hear his voice, quiet and gentle, deep in our hearts and minds when we pray and wait for an answer. We feel his hand when he sends someone to hug us when we're worried or talk to us when we feel alone. We can sense his presence when we sing or listen to songs about him in church or in the car. He tells us stories and shares about himself through the Bible because he wants us to know him and to love him.

And when we close our eyes and use our spiritual senses, even though it's not always easy, we can hear him.

Shhh. What do you hear?

GOD SAYS . . .

You love him even though you have never seen him. Though you do not see him now, you trust him.

1 PETER 1:8

HOW ABOUT YOU?

What is God sharing with you or how did he reach out to you today?

Dear God, It seems like I'm always behind, especially in math. What can I do?

February 9

CONSIDER THIS . . . Did you know that people learn in different ways? Some people learn best by hearing, some by reading, and some by doing. Besides that, researchers have found there are many different kinds of intelligence. There is physical intelligence, which means you might do well in sports. There is social intelligence. (Does talking a lot in class count?) There is musical intelligence. There is artistic intelligence.

The hard part is that schools focus a lot on math and on language. People, of course, learn these at different speeds. But even the very best of teachers can't guess the individual needs of all their students. They need to know that you're struggling in order to help you. You can be sure that parents and teachers are eager to do just that.

God promises to give us wisdom when we ask him for it. That doesn't mean that he promises to suddenly make you smart in, say, math when he's already created you with strengths in other places. But it does mean that he will show you what you need to do in order to finish your work. Perhaps that means he will help you find a tutor. Maybe it means he will give you understanding and you'll "get" something you didn't understand before. It might mean he gives you extra energy to study. We don't know how he will work, but we do know that when he promises something, he keeps his promise.

Ask him for wisdom in how you can approach your schoolwork. Pray and ask, then listen for an answer. Let your teacher and your parents know about your struggles too. The answer might come through them! You'll learn a lot about how faithful God is when you see his answer at work in your life.

HOW ABOUT YOU?

Which subject do you struggle with? Pray and ask God for wisdom on how to approach the problem subject. What did he say?

GOD SAYS . . .

If you need wisdom, ask our generous God, and he will give it to you. He will not rebuke you for asking.

JAMES 1:5

Dear God, Why do some friends leave?

CONSIDER THIS . . . We are born into families, but for the most part, we get to choose our friends for ourselves. Usually we pick people who we have fun with, who we have a lot in common with, and who stick by us. And we try to be that kind of friend too.

Sometimes people just change and go separate ways because they don't have a lot in common anymore. But sometimes friendships are tested when difficult choices come along. Maybe a new group you're hanging out with wants you to do something you're uncomfortable with, like lie, cheat, or be mean to someone. Maybe someone who has been an old friend turns her back on you because she has become more popular. People might be jealous of you. Or, if you're a Christian, they might feel uncomfortable with some of the things you do and say as a follower of God.

This even happened to Jesus. He was speaking to a bunch of his good friends. He said some things that people didn't want to hear, and instead of changing their hearts, they changed their minds and left him. He asked his close friends, "Are you also going to leave?" (John 6:67). It's okay to out-grow friendships. Realize that even when you do and say the right thing, sometimes friends will leave you. It hurts, but it's okay. New, good friends will take their places. And you still get to be true to yourself—and to God.

God understands that it hurts when a friend leaves you. But he will never leave.

GOD SAYS . . .

At this point many of his disciples turned away and deserted him. Then Jesus turned to the Twelve and asked, "Are you also going to leave?" JOHN 6:66-67

HOW ABOUT YOU?

Have you ever had someone end your friendship? Why do you think she did? Have you ever ended a friendship? Why? Do you think there are people who don't want to be friends with you because of your faith?

Dear God, My brother and I just don't get along. Seriously. What should we do?

February 11

CONSIDER THIS . . . When God created us, he put us into bodies and then into families. We have a physical family: parents, siblings, grandparents, aunts and uncles. And if we've asked Jesus to be our personal Savior, we also have a spiritual family: other Christians.

Can't means you are not able. For example, boys can't be girls. Dogs can't be cats. Most twelve-year-old girls can't take ten thousand dollars out of their bank accounts for an all-day trip to the mall—because it's not in there! There is nothing anyone can do to change those facts.

Won't is a word that means unwilling. You won't clean your room, although you can, because you're unwilling. You won't be kind to the mean girl because she's not kind to you. You're unwilling, not unable. It's hard to take, but you probably "won't" get along with your brother, rather than "can't." If your brother is hurting you, either your body or your feelings, you need adult help right away. Otherwise, getting along means both of you making that choice that you *can* get along rather than *won't*.

It's not going to be easy. James 4 tells us that fights and arguments come from selfish desires—putting your own wants first. Let your brother take the first turn or sit where he wants in the car. Stay out of his room. Do something generous for him, expecting nothing in return. If he's hurtful, rather than hurting him back, ask your mom or dad to help you solve things in the right way. The amazing thing about living this way—a biblical way—is that it may not change your brother (though it might!), but it will certainly change you. For the better.

Now that's girl power!

HOW ABOUT YOU?

What is one good thing you can do for your brother or sister or another family member? What gentle response can you prepare in advance, ready to say the next time your brother or sister irritates you?

GOD SAYS . . .

A gentle answer deflects anger, but harsh words make tempers flare.
PROVERBS 15:1

February 12

Dear God, Why does it seem like every time I want to do something there's a roadblock?

CONSIDER THIS . . . A mother and daughter piled into the car early one Saturday morning to go for a hike at a nearby lake. They tied up their boots, filled their water bottles, and took off.

Halfway to the lake, a police officer had stopped his car in the middle of the road, allowing no traffic by. The road ahead was closed—it had been washed out, and had they not turned around their car might have slipped into a muddy ditch. Seeing the disappointment on their faces, the police officer told them another way to get to the hiking path.

They finally got to the trail and were told they had to wait before setting off. They waited. And waited! The park ranger finally came out to say that a cougar had been caught, but the trail was now safe to walk on. They got to their hike much later than they'd hoped. But they'd stayed safe and saw a beautiful sunset they wouldn't have seen if they'd arrived earlier.

There are roadblocks in life. Maybe you wanted to go to school but your parents prefer to homeschool you. You may have wanted to sleep at a friend's house but were told no because her parents hadn't met yours. Did you try out for a part you didn't get? It can all be disappointing. But the Lord often uses people and circumstances to protect us from dangers we can't see but are just ahead.

Remember, keep an eye to the sky for those beautiful sunsets you don't want to miss.

GOD SAYS . . .
God did not lead [the people] along the main road that runs through Philistine territory, even though that was the shortest route to the Promised Land. God said, "If the people are faced with a battle, they might change their minds and return to Egypt." EXODUS 13:17

HOW ABOUT YOU?
Have you been waiting for something for-ev-er and you can never seem to get it? Have there been any happy surprises during the longer-than-you-thought journey? Any dangers avoided?

INTERNATIONAL GET A NEW NAME DAY

February 13

Dear God, I don't like my name.
Can I pick a new one?

CONSIDER THIS . . . Your name is one of the most important things about you . . . and someone else picked it out! Most parents take great care in choosing their children's names. But sometimes you might feel something else is more fun, more serious, or more you!

What can you do if you don't like your name? How about a nickname? Try Beth, Bess, Betsy, or Lizzie instead of Elizabeth. Or use your name, but with a foreign twist: Rachelle or Raquel instead of Rachel. Some Christian faith traditions have people choose another name when they make a new step in their commitment to Christ. Even the apostle Paul did that—he was no longer referred to as Saul, only Paul, after he started following Jesus. If you don't like your last name, it may change when you get older. If you get married, you'll likely take a new last name: your husband's.

No matter what your name is, even if you change it again and again, God knows what it is. In fact, Scripture tells us that if you belong to him, your name is written on the palms of his hands (Isaiah 49:16). If you belong to God, your name is also written in the Book of Life, God's record of those who follow him and will go to heaven one day. Normally people write down things that they definitely, absolutely do not want to forget. Because they're that important.

You are so very, very important that your name is written not only on the palms of God's hands but in his Book of Life for all eternity.

HOW ABOUT YOU?

If you could change your name to anything at all, what would it be?

GOD SAYS . . .

Never again will you be called "The Forsaken City" or "The Desolate Land." Your new name will be "The City of God's Delight" and "The Bride of God," for the LORD delights in you. ISAIAH 62:4

February 14

Dear God, I want to have a kind-of boyfriend, but my parents won't let me. What should I do? It's Valentine's Day!

CONSIDER THIS . . . Babies aren't in this world very long before they figure out there is some pain involved in being a kid! When a baby is only two months old, she starts getting her first shots. If you were to ask those babies, "Hey, would you like this long needle poking into your chubby little leg?" the baby would answer, "No way!" But without those shots, babies are vulnerable to a lot of illnesses—some that could kill them before they ever get to be adults.

It's hard for parents to do the right thing for their kids when they know the kids won't like it. When they know the kids will find their answers to be hurtful. But they do it because they can look further down the road and see what is good for their kids in the long run.

Parents don't only protect us from physical pain. They also want to protect us from emotional pain. That might mean telling you you're not old enough yet to have a boyfriend, even a kind-of boyfriend. A teacher may like you, a neighbor may like you, a friend may like you, but your parents would give their lives for you. They are willing to suffer the pain of your unhappiness and anger now if they need to in order to guide you for your long-term good. Good parents try to love and protect like Jesus, the Good Shepherd, would.

He always does what's best for his sheep because his love is the best love of all.

GOD SAYS . . .

The good shepherd sacrifices his life for the sheep. JOHN 10:11

HOW ABOUT YOU?

In an area that you disagree with your parents on (boys, curfew, phone or computer use, etc.), respectfully ask your parents why they've set the guidelines they have. See if you can come to an agreement on how to proceed.

Dear God, I have a secret: sometimes I want to do things I know I shouldn't. What can I do?

February 15

CONSIDER THIS . . . It can seem like everyone else has an easy time doing what is right. That can make us feel ashamed or embarrassed when we feel tempted to do something wrong. Those temptations can be for little things or big things, and most people, even if they don't look like it, feel tempted to do or say something wrong every day. Even Jesus was tempted, though he did not give in to the temptation.

A few years back a circus came to town, and one of the most thrilling performances was the high-wire act. Way, way up in the air was strung a thin wire. The high-wire artist climbed a rope ladder and then, taking her balance bar in hand, walked from one end of the wire to the other. The most amazing thing? This brave woman used no nets beneath her. If she fell, she was going to get hurt. Although the crowd had been noisy all night, it was hushed and silent when she stepped onto the wire. No one wanted to distract her and cause her to fall.

Life is very much like that high-wire act. But the distractions in life don't quiet down like the audience did. The key to doing things right is to keep your eyes fixed ahead to the life you want: one that you will be proud of. When the temptations "call" to you from the left or the right with their distracting noises, keep looking ahead and walking step-by-step. Soon enough the tempting thoughts will shush, and you will have made it all the way across the chasm without falling or getting hurt. God has given you an excellent resource to help you keep steady.

Keep your Bible—your very own balance bar—in hand!

HOW ABOUT YOU?

What temptations do you face? How can the Bible keep you balanced?

GOD SAYS . . .

Look straight ahead, and fix your eyes on what lies before you. Mark out a straight path for your feet; stay on the safe path. Don't get sidetracked; keep your feet from following evil. PROVERBS 4:25-27

Dear God, What does it mean to become more like you? After all, I'm a human!

CONSIDER THIS . . . One of the most fun kinds of parties to attend is a dress-up party. No, not the kind where you wear fancy clothes—although those are fun. I'm talking about the kind of party where you come in costume. The more you want to "become" the person you're dressing up as, the more pieces to the costume you'll want. Long blonde wig? How about a beautiful satin gown and a crown? Add some slippers and jewels and it gets even better. What about a dentist's costume with a necklace of pulled teeth? The more pieces you adopt of the person you want to be, the more you disappear and she appears!

Isn't it fun to see what kind of person each of your family and friends choose to dress up as? Maybe there are a few partygoers whose costumes are so elaborate you can't tell who the person underneath it all really is! What do their costumes say about who they are inside?

Just as we turn more into the characters we're dressing up as, we become more and more like God as we grow in our relationship with him. The closer we draw to God—the more we imitate him, talk like he does, and make choices like he does—the more we change. Each good decision is like putting on one more item of godliness. The "old" you fades away and the "new" you begins to make a fabulous debut. It won't happen all at once; you will change bit by bit and piece by piece. But people will notice. And life, every day, will seem to be a bit more fun as you begin to show God, and others, the godly girl you are turning into.

Has anyone seen my stethoscope?

GOD SAYS . . .

Put on your new nature, and be renewed as you learn to know your Creator and become like him. COLOSSIANS 3:10

HOW ABOUT YOU?

What one piece of godliness would you like to add to tomorrow's outfit?

Dear God, So is godliness only what's on the outside of me and what others can see?

February 17

CONSIDER THIS . . . Everyone knows someone who is a faker. They pretend to be one thing on the outside but on the inside, they are very different. You can't hide what you really think and feel for too long! And you shouldn't do that anyway. To be healthy and filled with joy you must be free to express exactly who you are—while respecting yourself and others, of course.

God wants you to be authentic. Genuine. But he also wants you to be good.

Scripture tells us that "a good person produces good things from the treasury of a good heart, and an evil person produces evil things from the treasury of an evil heart" (Matthew 12:35). So that means in order to be who you are both inside and out, your heart needs to change. And God can definitely help you change things.

Think about a white daisy. You pick a fresh daisy and bring it into the house. You cut a little bit off the stem—to make it easier for the flower to drink water—and then you put it into a vase. Only the water you've put into the vase isn't clear because you've added some blue food coloring to it!

Over the next few hours and days, the petals on the white daisy (and even some of the leaves!) turn the same blue, just like the water it's drinking. Whatever the daisy is taking in will show on the outside. You are like that too.

If you want to be lovely on the outside, you also have to be lovely on the inside.

What color would you like to be? Pink or green or red or blue? You can choose the kind of girl you'll be. It all depends on what's inside of you.

HOW ABOUT YOU?
What kind of "water" do you take into your heart and mind every day? Is it pure, clean, and good?

GOD SAYS . . .
Create in me a clean heart, O God. PSALM 51:10

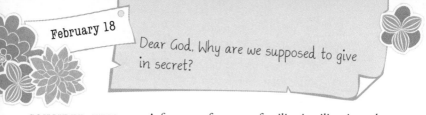

CONSIDER THIS . . . A fun treat for many families is piling into the car and going out for coffee. Some families stop by the local coffeehouse for hot drinks after church, or as a reward for shoveling snow or doing housework, or on their way to the mall. Everyone seems to have his or her favorite drink—mocha, caramel, with whipped cream, or without. But coffee drinks can be expensive!

One family decided to bless other families by "passing on" a coffee treat. When they pulled up to the drive-through window to pick up their own coffee order, they also paid for the order of the car behind them. When *that* car drove forward to get their drinks, they were in for a delightful, warm surprise. Their drinks were free!

By the time the family who had received the gift knew about it, the ones who had paid for their gift had driven on. There was no way to contact them or thank them. But the family who had received the gift decided to pass on the blessing in another way. The next time they went for coffee, they paid for the car behind them!

When people thank us for gifts we've given them, we are rewarded by their happiness and the looks on their faces as they open and enjoy the gifts. But when we give in secret, Scripture tells us that our Father, who sees everything, will be the one who rewards our generosity. Giving in secret is really a vote of trust in God. You know that if you are to be repaid at all, it will be only through him. But he is faithful to do just that and usually does it in a bigger, better, more surprising way than we can ever imagine.

Vanilla latte, anyone?

GOD SAYS . . .

Give your gifts in private, and your Father, who sees everything, will reward you. MATTHEW 6:4

HOW ABOUT YOU?

Plan, right now, one way to bless a friend, family member, or stranger in secret within the next two days. What will you do/give?

CONSIDER THIS . . . When a couple gets married, they stand in front of people who know them and the bride and groom promise to love and honor each other. They promise not to be interested in any other men or women from then on. Husband and wife will be set aside only for each other. The single life is over—married life is beginning!

Everyone in the room hears the bride and groom make those promises. When the going gets tough and a husband is angry with his wife or a wife with her husband, they will hopefully remind each other of those vows. And if not, hopefully one of those witnesses will gently remind them of the commitment they've made!

In the same way, when you are baptized in front of people, you are telling them that your old life as a non-Christian is over and that your new life as a Christian is beginning. You make a statement in front of all the people in the congregation and in front of God that you belong to him, and he to you, and that you want to live life following God—even when you're mad or angry or confused. Baptism is a public promise, a public celebration, and the way to show just what is most important in your life. Some people are baptized as babies—if so, their parents publicly promise to raise them in a Christian home.

Because baptism is so important, Jesus commanded his disciples to baptize other believers. Baptism is one way to honor him and show others around you whom your life is centered on.

Just do it!

HOW ABOUT YOU?

Have you been baptized? If not, would you like to be? What does baptism mean to you?

GOD SAYS . . .

Therefore, go and make disciples of all the nations, baptizing them in the name of the Father and the Son and the Holy Spirit. Teach these new disciples to obey all the commands I have given you.
MATTHEW 28:19-20

CONSIDER THIS . . . Although the Lord gave Adam the right to name the animals and the plants, and although he gave your parents the right to name you, God gave himself his own names. He chose those names with care; each one tells us something about him. One of the most important names he gave to himself was *El-Shaddai*—"God Almighty." This name means all-powerful, the strongest, in command.

Think about it this way: in the middle of winter, it's not unusual for some parts of the world to be covered by a deep blanket of snow. Has your family's car ever slid off of the road and into a ditch during snowy weather? Has it ever been stuck in a snow bank? Even if you don't live where it snows, you've probably seen cars or trucks get stuck in the mud. No matter how much gas you give the car, the wheels spin and the mud or snow flies. But the car still stays stuck.

It needs more help!

So when a tow truck shows up to pull a two-ton car out of a ditch, do you think it should be a little bigger than a tiny smart car? Or a Volkswagen Beetle? Of course it should be! Mighty tow trucks are large and powerful, and they have everything needed to get the job done. Nothing is beyond their ability to help. What about when a bully confronts you? Do you want a puny protector or a bodyguard with muscles standing between you? When a robber is breaking in, do you want a little cat for protection or a large, strong dog?

God is almighty, all-powerful, full of strength, and in command. He's here to protect and to help.

GOD SAYS . . .

When Abram was ninety-nine years old, the LORD appeared to him and said, "I am El-Shaddai—'God Almighty.' Serve me faithfully and live a blameless life." GENESIS 17:1

HOW ABOUT YOU?

Why would God want us to know that he is all-powerful? Does it make a difference to you? How?

Dear God, How am I supposed to know what is true and what is a lie?

February 21

CONSIDER THIS ... Sometimes when people have birthday parties, they tie balloons to their porches to show guests which house the party is at. One girl tied smiley-faced balloons to her railing to welcome her guests. After all, it was a happy occasion!

Her dog sure didn't think so. Every time the wind blew, those smiley-faced balloons would bob and sometimes even bump into the door or the window. The dog went crazy barking. It thought those smiley-faced things were real people on the porch, not balloons with faces drawn on them. People knew the difference. But the dog, who had never seen smiley-faced balloons tied to the porch before, did not. By the end of the day, though, the dog stopped barking and barely raised a paw when the wind picked up. She realized that the balloons weren't party guests.

Sometimes things appear to be real, but they are not. Someone tells you something that turns out to be a lie. A promise is made and not kept. A friend seems true and then is false. A five-dollar bill lying on the sidewalk turns out to be fake. There is only one way to know the truth about many things.

Scripture tells us that the truth will stand the test of time but lies will be exposed. Over time, everything and everyone is tested. If you try to spend counterfeit money, the cashier will refuse it. A real friend will be tempted to gossip but will remain true. A promise that is made will be kept. A smiley-faced "person" will turn out to really be a balloon.

Everything is tested and made clear over time. So don't be in a hurry, watch people, and test things. That's the way to tell the truth from a lie.

HOW ABOUT YOU?
Have you ever discovered that someone told you a lie? How did you find out?

GOD SAYS ...
Truthful words stand the test of time, but lies are soon exposed.
PROVERBS 12:19

Dear God, There are some girls in my class who whisper secrets about other people. What should I do?

CONSIDER THIS . . . Sometimes quiet sounds make a bigger impact than loud noises. For example, a doctor can tell a pregnant woman that her baby is okay by hearing the baby's heart beating through tiny sounds in a stethoscope. That's a good kind of quiet sound. A bad kind of quiet sound is gossip. That's what secrets sometimes are.

Some secrets—better called surprises—are good. It might be a planned gift or party. Another appropriate secret might be something you want to share about yourself with a trusted friend but not with anyone else.

One kind of secret that is *not* okay is when something has harmed you or could harm someone else. If someone has hurt you physically, touched you in a wrong place, or torn you down with his or her words, you need adult help. Those are secrets you must not keep. Ask a trustworthy adult to intervene.

Bad secrets share information that is mean or meant to be kept a secret. So why do girls say mean things secretly or share confidential information? Because they know it's wrong. It's a weak way to hurt someone who can't protect herself.

What can you do? A good rule of thumb when talking with friends is to talk about yourself, talk about the person or people you're with, talk about pets, or say anything kind or generous about anyone not present. That way you'll avoid gossip. If you happen to overhear these girls whispering, walk away. Someday soon the things they say will come to light. The friends who whisper with them will soon whisper about them. Don't be a part of any friendship group like that.

GOD SAYS . . .
Whatever you have said in the dark will be heard in the light, and what you have whispered behind closed doors will be shouted from the housetops for all to hear! LUKE 12:3

HOW ABOUT YOU?
We all are tempted to gossip. What can you do to fight the temptation?

Dear God, What does "eyes to see and ears to hear" mean? My eyes already see, and my ears already hear.

CONSIDER THIS . . . A lot of the words and phrases we hear inside church seem like they make no sense outside of it. This language is sometimes called "Christianese" and can occasionally be more confusing than helpful. Most of it, though, comes right from Scripture. So that means it's good and helpful. We just have to understand it.

As for eyes to see . . . have you ever been to a 3-D movie? You pay for your movie ticket, walk to the front of the theater, and give the attendant your ticket stub. In return, he or she gives you a pair of 3-D glasses. Once the lights in the theater are dim, you put the glasses on and all of a sudden—*wham*! The movie seems to jump out of the screen and come alive all around you.

This happens at amusement parks like Disney World, too. Once those 3-D glasses are on, the characters seem to sit next to you, Mickey walks beside you, and Cinderella may even dance alongside you. If you take those glasses off, the characters seem to disappear. The movie becomes flat again.

When we become Christians, God makes all things new inside us. Our hearts are made clean, our minds are renewed, and we begin to understand spiritual things we couldn't understand before. Even our eyes and ears are made new—we can see and hear things we couldn't before. We needed new "eyes" to "see" and "ears" to "hear" and understand the things about God.

Put on those Christian 3-D glasses and life will take on a whole new and exciting dimension.

HOW ABOUT YOU?

Are there things you see and understand that your friends who don't know Jesus do not?

GOD SAYS . . .

Yes, I am sending you to the Gentiles to open their eyes, so they may turn from darkness to light and from the power of Satan to God. ACTS 26:17-18

Dear God, How can I be unafraid of making mistakes, especially with new things I am learning, when I don't feel I'm very good?

CONSIDER THIS . . . The reason so many of us are afraid of making mistakes is that we are worried we'll look dumb to others—*What will they think?* Or because we are worried that it means we really *are* dumb—*I'm not performing too well, so I must be stupid.* But God doesn't expect you to be perfect; in fact, he already knows you won't be, not here on earth.

Have you ever thought about diamonds? Really, they're just rocks in the ground. They're really pretty when they're polished. But so are rose quartz, agate, and jade jewels. Why are diamonds more valuable, more sought after? Diamonds don't do anything. People who choose diamonds value them simply because they want to.

You are very much like a diamond. There is nothing that you have to do to be valuable. You are valuable because God made you. He loves you. He chose you. When you are certain about that, you will realize that you don't have to be the best in order to have worth. It doesn't matter what other people think about you. You are free to try anything God would approve of and then to either succeed or fail. Neither success nor failure makes you more precious to God. You are precious because you're the treasure of his heart.

GOD SAYS . . .

This hope will not lead to disappointment. For we know how dearly God loves us, because he has given us the Holy Spirit to fill our hearts with his love.

ROMANS 5:5

HOW ABOUT YOU?

What would you like to try but are afraid to because of fear of failure? What's the worst that can happen? What's the best thing that could happen? Are you willing to take a risk, knowing your real worth, in order to try?

Dear God, Which Bible verses will help me when I want to talk back to my parents?

February 25

CONSIDER THIS . . . The book of James says that your entire body is like a ship. The rudder on a ship isn't very big when you compare it to the size of the whole vessel, but it, and it alone, steers the ship. The sailor who controls the rudder controls the ship! If your body is the ship, your teeny-tiny tongue is the powerful rudder that steers it. Your tongue can either guide you through peaceful water or drive your ship into the sharp rocks. You'll hurt yourself and those around you if you're not careful.

The power of the tongue reminds me of the toothpaste challenge: offer ten dollars to anyone who can squirt all of the toothpaste out of the tube and then put it all back in again using a spoon. It can't be done! It's the same way with your words—once they're out of your mouth, they can't be taken back. No matter what.

You are a *smart* girl to figure out that you need some tools to help you control your tongue. You're even smarter to know where to go to get help. When we memorize the Word of God, the Holy Spirit will help us by bringing it to our minds at just the right time.

Stop your tongue before it stops you!

- "A gentle answer deflects anger, but harsh words make tempers flare" (Proverbs 15:1).
- "The wise are known for their understanding, and pleasant words are persuasive" (Proverbs 16:21).

HOW ABOUT YOU?
Which of these verses will you memorize to help you control your words?

GOD SAYS . . .
Those who control their tongue will have a long life; opening your mouth can ruin everything. PROVERBS 13:3

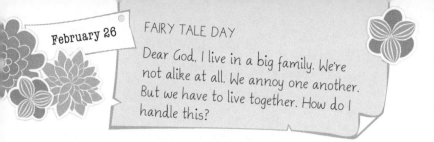

Dear God, I live in a big family. We're not alike at all. We annoy one another. But we have to live together. How do I handle this?

CONSIDER THIS ... There's a saying, "the more the merrier," and most of the time, that's true! But if you live in a big family, sometimes it can seem more like, "silence is golden," as in, please leave me alone for just five minutes!

Remember the story of Snow White and the Seven Dwarfs? Sneezy, Sleepy, Dopey, Doc, Happy, Bashful, Grumpy—all brothers—lived together when Snow White came to live with them, too, as a kind of sister. There was a lot to do in such a big household, and lots of different personalities. It's easy to imagine that Sneezy would get on your nerves during allergy season if you were trying to watch TV or that Sleepy would annoy you if he wasn't doing his fair share of the chores. Doc was a kind of know-it-all, and even happy people get on your nerves if they never chill out, right?

What about Bashful? Maybe you'd get tired of always having to order for him at a restaurant, or Grumpy would get on your nerves when you'd only asked a simple question. But in the end, they all worked together and found ways to enjoy one another too. Happy could balance out Grumpy, and Doc might find a solution for Sneezy's allergies!

It isn't easy to learn how to accept one another for who they are, but we hope that people accept us and our quirky personalities without getting irritated too. Families are made up of all kinds of people, and one of the ways we grow up is by learning to accept and love them as they are.

GOD SAYS ...

Love is patient and kind.
1 CORINTHIANS 13:4

HOW ABOUT YOU?

If you were one of the seven dwarfs, which one would you be? Would there be parts of you that would be difficult to get along with? Can you name one great thing about each of your family members?

Dear God, My whole body is changing, and my moods are too. What can I do?

February 27

CONSIDER THIS . . . You are beginning one of many times in your life when you will have major changes. You are changing from a girl to a young woman, and with that come some surprising changes to your body. Your moods are changing, too, because your hormones are shifting, whether you want them to or not! Can you believe they had the nerve to not even ask your permission? Your friends might be changing at the same time as you are. The whole process can seem so out of control. But it's really not.

Even though you can't control the changes happening in your moods or your body, you can decide how you feel about them and how you react to them. You are a wise girl for even seeing that these changes are happening. That's the first step to dealing with them! You can tell yourself, *I feel a little crabby today, but I can decide to talk to others more kindly anyway. My body is changing, but I can decide what clothes to wear. My face is changing, but I can choose what cleansers and astringents to use as it does.*

Life never stays the same; things will always change. If your happiness and security depend on things staying the same, you will be unhappy and unsure of yourself and of life. Our security must come from God, who never changes. The Bible tells us that he is the same today as he was yesterday and will be tomorrow (Hebrews 13:8). He is always good, always kind, always in control. He will be the same no matter what is happening in or around you.

Hang your hope on that when the ride gets a little wild!

HOW ABOUT YOU?

What changes are you worried about? What decisions can you make about how you will respond to these changes?

GOD SAYS . . .

Whatever is good and perfect comes down to us from God our Father, who created all the lights in the heavens. He never changes. JAMES 1:17

Dear God, Why do others always seem to come out better when I compare myself to them?

CONSIDER THIS . . . Have you heard the saying "The grass is always greener on the other side of the fence"? It means that when you look around the neighborhood, it always seems as though the other people have better lawns.

But looks can be deceptive. The reason grass looks greener at a distance is because you can't see the dirt as well. Up close, in your own yard, you can see the grass intermingled with the dirt, bare patches, and moss. From a distance you see only green grass tops. If you went to your neighbor's yard and looked from *her* perspective, your grass might look greener than *hers*. And you wouldn't be able to see your own weeds, either.

It's the same with other areas of life. Whatever you focus on seems to be bigger in your own life—which is why your problems often seem bigger than your blessings. You see the dirt close up! When you look at your friend, you may see her "green grass": good math grades, nice hair, cute clothes. But you don't see her weeds: reading trouble, nervousness in speaking, insecure friendships. You can bet *she* sees them, though.

Christians are made to cooperate, not compete. Your friend might be glad to help you with math if you'd help her with language arts. Show her how to pull her hair back into a new ponytail style, and she'll show you a new game. She'll be glad to know that you have problems, and she will feel better about sharing her own. The Lord made us to work together, and he helps us to do it!

GOD SAYS . . .
Share each other's burdens. . . . Pay careful attention to your own work, for then you will get the satisfaction of a job well done, and you won't need to compare yourself to anyone else. GALATIANS 6:2, 4

HOW ABOUT YOU?
Do you have a friend for whom certain subjects or skills come more easily? Will you ask for help? What help can you offer to her? *(Hint: if you don't know, ask her!)*

Dear God, Sometimes I don't want to make a decision because I'm afraid I'll make the wrong one and then something bad will happen. What should I do?

CONSIDER THIS . . . During the daytime, our homes are usually busy, bright, and full of noise. We hear televisions chattering or music playing. Our friends and families talk together and to us. We can see everything going on around us, too, because the sun shines in through the window. It's easy to make our way through a room without tripping over a couch or stepping on a little brother's Lego, because we can see where to step—and where we must avoid stepping! And if we don't, someone is sure to call out to us, "Watch where you're walking!"

Nighttime is different. The sun has left for the day. All of the lights are off. People are sleeping. It's dark and quiet. If you need to get up in the night to use the bathroom or to get a drink of water, you must walk slowly and carefully. What's even better is to think ahead and turn on a night-light or two before you go to bed. That way, when you get up at two o'clock in the morning and your head is fuzzy and it's hard to know where to walk, you've already made a way to safely see the path to where you want to go.

Just like day is always followed by night, easy decisions are often followed by hard ones. The good news is, God knew that there would be tricky decisions, and he made a way for you to see what you need to do without stumbling! If you spend time reading your Bible when things in your life are bright and sunny, he'll turn on a little night-light the next time you need one to see clearly in the darkness of a difficult decision.

HOW ABOUT YOU?

Do you rely on God's Word to show you the best choice when decisions need to be made? How can God's Word help you with a decision you need to make today?

GOD SAYS . . .

Your word is a lamp to guide my feet and a light for my path. PSALM 119:105

Dear God, Why am I supposed to forgive others?

CONSIDER THIS . . . The simplest, easiest, and yet hardest answer to this question is . . . because the Word of God tells us to forgive others. Jesus knows how hard forgiveness is. Remember, he had the weight of the sins of the whole world, from all time, heaped upon him. And he alone offered forgiveness for all.

But Jesus also knew that nothing good was going to come from letting unforgiveness make a nest in our hearts. The goal of being a Christian is to become more like Jesus—the Bible says God chose us to become like his Son (Ephesians 1:4). And his Son, we know, is forgiving.

Forgiving someone does not mean that you have to allow that person to hurt you over and over again, though. If you loan someone a dollar and she never pays it back, and then you loan her another one and she never pays that back, you'd be silly to keep loaning her money, right? You might say to her, "I forgive you for those two dollars that you never paid me back. But I won't loan you any more money."

In the same way, you forgive someone who has harmed you and don't hold it against that person anymore, trusting that God sees and will avenge you. (He says he will!) But that does not mean that you have to be friends with people who bully you or that you should hang out with people who hurt you. It's wise to step away from those kinds of people. God asks us to be wise as well as to forgive.

Jesus, after all, was both wise and forgiving. He leads the way, so you can be both too.

GOD SAYS . . .

Instead, be kind to each other, tenderhearted, forgiving one another, just as God through Christ has forgiven you. EPHESIANS 4:32

HOW ABOUT YOU?

Whom do you need to forgive, and for what? Will you let go and allow God alone to repay them for the hurt that they have done to you? How does that make you more like Jesus?

Dear God, Why does my brother have fewer chores than I do even though we get the same allowance? It's so unfair.

CONSIDER THIS . . . An easy trap to get caught up in is what is and what isn't fair. For most people, at least some tiny part of each day is spent thinking about what is not fair. It's not fair that someone else got a better grade than you did. It's not fair that a friend has a new phone and you don't. Inside our hearts we're often shouting, *No fair!*

But what about the fact that we get to have birthday parties when kids in other countries don't have clean water to drink? That we have warm homes when some kids live in their cars or in homeless shelters? That we get to go to school while some girls in other parts of the world cannot attend school and might even be working already? That's not fair either.

Jesus knows human hearts, and he knew we'd be fretting over what was and was not fair. So he told a story (found in Matthew 20:1-16), making it clear that the person in charge gets to decide what is and what is not fair. Maybe your brother can only handle a certain amount of jobs. Maybe you get more privileges, even if you don't get more money. Perhaps you're just really good at your work . . . and your brother is still in training. Your parents are trusting you with the greater part. Your parents have just decided that you're each doing exactly what is best for you.

Some kids get no allowance at all. They probably look at you and think, *No fair!* Right?

HOW ABOUT YOU?

What seems unfair in your life? Do you believe that God will make sure that in the end it works out to be all fair for you? Listen to him as he's calling you.

GOD SAYS . . .

Didn't you agree to work all day for the usual wage? Take your money and go. I wanted to pay this last worker the same as you. . . . Should you be jealous because I am kind to others? MATTHEW 20:13-15

Dear God, Even though I'm not supposed to think things like this, I wonder sometimes if you'll really keep all of your promises. Will you?

CONSIDER THIS . . . Have you ever shopped in a store that offered a "money-back guarantee"? The store promises that if you don't like its products, it will give you your money back. Would you be more likely to trust in such a promise from a person selling old clothes on a street corner, who may be gone tomorrow? Or would it be easier to trust a large store in a mall, one which has been in business since your grandmother was a girl? Of course you'd trust the one which had kept its promises for many, many years.

When God made people, he made us to be friends with him as well as to serve him. To be in awe of him, yes, but also to love him. And we can't love God if we're not honest with him about the heavy things on our hearts and minds. It's okay to share your deepest fears and worries with him, even if it doesn't "feel" right. He already knows what you're thinking!

The Lord makes a lot of promises to us: to love us, to never leave us, to repay those who wrong us, to care for us, to forgive us. He will never abandon us. Sometimes, when circumstances look iffy, it's easy to wonder, *Will he really do everything he said he would?*

The answer is yes. God is always good and always just, and he always does what he says he will do. God says his promises are backed up with something better than a money-back guarantee: the honor of his name. That has been found trustworthy for thousands of years.

Now that's something you can take to the bank!

GOD SAYS . . .

I bow before your holy Temple as I worship. I praise your name for your unfailing love and faithfulness; for your promises are backed by all the honor of your name. PSALM 138:2

HOW ABOUT YOU?

Which are your favorite promises of God? Do you 100 percent trust that he will honor them?

CONSIDER THIS . . . Whenever you go for a nature walk, you come across many opportunities to take one path or another. You could take the path that leads to the lake or the one that leads deeper into the forest. You might take the wide trail that has gravel on it or make your way up the narrow trail that you can barely see because the footsteps are so faint. Each time you come to a fork in the road, you have a decision to make. Only you can choose which path or trail you will take. It's best to make that decision based on where you want to end up. There's no sense taking the way through the woods if you want to get to the lake. Often, the path that seems like it might be the hardest, or least used, eventually leads to the most beautiful view.

Robert Frost, a famous poet, wrote a poem about choosing the path that is least taken. Here's part of "The Road Not Taken":

Two roads diverged in a yellow wood,
And sorry I could not travel both
And be one traveler, long I stood. . . .
I took the one less traveled by,
And that has made all the difference.

When it comes to going to heaven, we all have a choice to make: to believe or not to believe in Jesus. The Bible says, "If you confess with your mouth that Jesus is Lord and believe in your heart that God raised him from the dead, you will be saved" (Romans 10:9). If you do that, you will go to heaven. It is your choice to make. Be sure you pick the trail that leads to where you want to end up!

HOW ABOUT YOU?
Which path (or gate) do you choose?

GOD SAYS . . .
You can enter God's Kingdom only through the narrow gate. The highway to hell is broad, and its gate is wide for the many who choose that way. MATTHEW 7:13

Dear God, I always see these cartoons of people who, after they die, become angels with wings. Do we all turn into angels after we die?

CONSIDER THIS ... Even though it's lots of fun for cartoonists to draw pictures of people who have died and gone to heaven and turned into angels, that's not what happens. It brings to mind a certain set of friends who wanted their puppy to be a leopard. They took some safe food coloring and dotted little brown spots all over their beige pup. You can imagine how that canine felt! She turned and looked at them as if to say, "Get these dots off of me. It's below my dignity. I'm a mutt, not a leopard!"

Dotting a dog does not make it a leopard. Cats can't turn into rabbits. Fish don't become turtles if we throw them onto the land. All creatures were created to be just what they are, and they don't turn into any other kind of being.

God created angels to be a separate kind of being than humans. Simply drawing wings on a human won't make him or her an angel any more than dotting food coloring on a dog makes it a cat!

All through their lives, angels remain angels. And after you die, your spirit will still be one of what God created you to be—a human being, which he says he created just a little lower than the angels (Hebrews 2:7).

Sorry, there will be no wings unless you're in an airplane!

GOD SAYS ...

What are mere mortals that you should think about them, or a son of man that you should care for him? Yet you made them only a little lower than the angels. . . . You gave them authority over all things. HEBREWS 2:6-8

HOW ABOUT YOU?

Did you ever believe that human beings became angels? What do you believe now?

Dear God, What happens to us when we die if we don't turn into angels?

March 7

CONSIDER THIS . . . Have you ever looked forward to a sleepover at a friend's house? You went, and probably had a really good time. Maybe it was just you and one other friend, or maybe a group of you hung out together. You may have played games or watched movies together, or dressed up her unwilling cat in a ballerina costume. Maybe you ate pizza and then told secrets until late at night.

But when morning came, you probably were really, really glad to go home. Your own bed was there for you to catch up on sleep after a late night. Your own pet was waiting to greet you. Your parents or siblings were there to make you feel like all was well with the world. Even though you had a good time at your friend's house, you were happy to go back to the only place you really feel at home—which is, well, home!

Just as you spend only a little bit of time away from home and at your friend's house, life here on earth is short before it's time to go home to heaven. God made your body to last for a short time, your time here on earth. You take care of it and love it, and it becomes a part of who you are. But your body won't last forever. Your soul, the spirit within you, was made to last forever. If you are a Christian, when you die, that spirit will go to be with Jesus in heaven. Your human body will be left behind on earth, but your human soul will go to its true, most comfortable, best-place-ever home. Heaven.

HOW ABOUT YOU?

Do you wonder what heaven will be like? What does home mean to you?

GOD SAYS . . .

Yes, we are fully confident, and we would rather be away from these earthly bodies, for then we will be at home with the Lord.
2 CORINTHIANS 5:8

Dear God, If humans don't become angels after they die, then what are angels?

CONSIDER THIS . . . You know that man in the postal service uniform who delivers your letters? Or the lady who drives the brown truck up to your house to drop off a package? They're both messengers of a kind—bringing a note or a letter or a package from someone who wants to say or deliver something directly to you!

The word *angel* means "messenger." When God wanted to speak directly to Hagar in the desert, he sent an angel. When he wanted to speak to Mary, the mother of Jesus, he sent an angel. God used angels to speak to Abraham and Lot and Jacob and Paul and many, many others. They brought messages from God to those people God wanted to communicate with.

Angels aren't made like we are—they don't have bones and muscle and flesh. They start out as spirit and stay as spirit, although they can take the form of a person if they need to in order to do God's business. It doesn't seem like angels are the cute and cuddly cartoon version strumming on harps, either. When they appear in Scripture, they often have to tell people not to be afraid of them. They're powerful and bold.

Although angels have many other responsibilities—for example, guiding and protecting believers, being servants of God, carrying out judgment, and stamping out evil when God tells them to—the job they do most often is deliver messages. It seems like they often show up when people are in danger and need guidance or are sad and need comfort. The Bible tells us angels are all around us, even if we can't see them. What kind of messages do you think they might be delivering to different parts of our world today?

GOD SAYS . . .
Therefore, angels are only servants—spirits sent to care for people who will inherit salvation. HEBREWS 1:14

HOW ABOUT YOU?
What angels do you remember from the Bible? What did they show up to do or say?

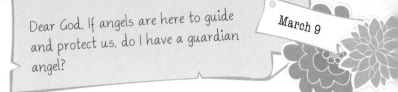

Dear God, If angels are here to guide and protect us, do I have a guardian angel?

March 9

CONSIDER THIS . . . If you've ever seen a famous person in public, you've probably seen a bodyguard nearby. Presidents and other politicians often have them too. Bodyguards are usually big, strong men who are in very good shape and know how to use a weapon. Their job is to surround, protect, and defend the person they are charged with taking care of. Bodyguards scan the crowd, looking for anyone who might be suspicious. Sometimes they dress just like ordinary people and blend in with the crowd so that they can hear if there are any plans going on that would hurt the person they are there to protect. Other times they stand right next to the person they're protecting to keep him or her from being hurt.

Angels are like bodyguards. The Bible doesn't say that each of us has one particular angel assigned to us, though that may be true. It does say that angels protect and defend us. Scripture tells us that angels surround, protect, and defend those who fear—that is, respect and love—the Lord. On rare occasions we'll actually see these angels—Scripture tells us they can appear as humans. But mostly we can't see them because they are spirits. They blend in with the crowd, as it were. But they are there doing an important job! From what the Bible says in Matthew 18, it seems that children's angels, especially, are close to God.

Good news for you!

HOW ABOUT YOU?

Have you ever sensed that one of God's angels had protected or defended you from something? Does it make you feel safer knowing that they are there?

GOD SAYS . . .

Beware that you don't look down on any of these little ones. For I tell you that in heaven their angels are always in the presence of my heavenly Father. MATTHEW 18:10

Dear God, How could everyone in the world really know that you're the real God?

CONSIDER THIS . . . Almost everyone has heard of the Seven Wonders of the World. This list, originally started about one hundred years before Jesus was born, contains the most impressive, amazing structures made by men. Because the list was written down in Greece, the wonders are mostly in the same area where the early Christians lived.

These wonders included a huge pyramid and a lighthouse in Egypt; hanging gardens in Babylon (what is now Iraq); and a temple, a tomb, and two statues—one of the god Zeus—in Greece. Religion was important to ancient people, just as it is to many people today. The lighthouse in Egypt was dedicated to "the savior gods." In fact, many of the wonders were built in honor of gods. The people who built these magnificent structures knew that gods could save. They just weren't quite sure who the real God was.

Paul, when he went to speak to the Greek people on behalf of Jesus, did not make fun of their belief in other gods, though he knew those gods were false. Instead, he praised them for knowing that there was a god, even though they weren't sure who the real one was. And then he told them about the One True God they'd been looking for all along.

Deep in the hearts of all men, women, and children, we know that God exists. Some of us know him. Some of us do not. God has asked all of us who know him to respectfully share the Good News with everyone else in the world. This is how people will know that there is one true God.

After all, we're the only wonder in creation that bears his image and will last forever.

GOD SAYS . . .
[Paul said,] "Men of Athens, I notice that you are very religious in every way. . . . One of your altars had this inscription on it: 'To an Unknown God.' This God, whom you worship without knowing, is the one I'm telling you about." ACTS 17:22-23

HOW ABOUT YOU?
Do you treat other peoples' beliefs with respect even if you don't agree with them? Why or why not?

Dear God, My mom says I need to have more friends than just my best friend. But why?

CONSIDER THIS . . . One favorite hairstyle with girls around the world and with all different kinds of hair is the braid. From basic braids to Heidi braids to French braids to tiny braids to cornrow braids, we girls love our braids.

When a young girl first tries to braid her own hair, she often separates her hair into two strands and then just wraps one around the other until she reaches the end, tying it off with a ponytail holder. Unfortunately, she soon finds out that kind of braid doesn't hold well—but it sure does unwind quickly!

An experienced woman or older girl will then show her how to braid with three pieces of hair. Two pieces are twisted at a time, sure, but she alternates the sections. If she tightens the braid at the end and holds it together with an elastic band, her braid will stay put, keeping her fashionable all day, or even longer.

The key to both strong braids and strong friendships is in the threes.

You may get along well with your best friend. But even your best friend can't be available all the time, won't like all the same things you do, and will have weaknesses. Just like you do! When you add more friends to the mix, you'll discover that you balance one another out even more. Perhaps two of you like soccer but one doesn't. Maybe another friend likes to read but one doesn't. Three or four people are likely to have more ideas and interests than just two.

It's okay to have a best friend. It's even better, though, to have two or three.

HOW ABOUT YOU?

Do you have more than one close friend? Is there someone you'd like to be friends with?

GOD SAYS . . .

A person standing alone can be attacked and defeated, but two can stand back-to-back and conquer. Three are even better, for a triple-braided cord is not easily broken. ECCLESIASTES 4:12

Dear God, Why did you make us so we can cry?

CONSIDER THIS . . . When someone we love dies or a friend decides she doesn't like us anymore or our parents divorce or our cat runs away, we're sad. Mostly we feel sad because we love the thing or person that has made us sad. We have feelings for them, and they are feelings that can be hurt.

One family decided to buy one of those robotic pets. You know—the ones that work on batteries and will roll over or do tricks on command. They make purring or barking sounds but are pretty cold. They don't have cuddly fur. They don't come up to you for a pat on the head. They don't nuzzle you to see you jump. They don't sense when you're sad and lick your tears away. These robotic pets don't love you, and you don't love them.

The family got tired of the fake pet pretty soon and put it away. But when a real dog passes away because it is old or it's been sick, people cry for days or months. They keep pictures of the pet. They talk about and miss it. People do all these things because the pet was loved. If we don't love, we don't feel loss. When we feel loss, we're sad. When we are happy, we laugh. When we're sad, we cry. It's good to express how we feel.

God made us in his image, and we know that he has emotions because the Bible tells us that. Among other feelings, God himself feels love, anger, and sorrow. When Jesus was here on earth and he lost a friend, he cried.

None of us likes to cry. Even crying when we're happy can feel a little uncomfortable, though it's perfectly okay, too. But it'd be a whole lot worse to never love anyone or anything, feel neither sorrow nor joy. When we love, there will always be a loss. But that is *real* life, not robotic.

GOD SAYS . . .
When Jesus saw her weeping and saw the other people wailing with her, a deep anger welled up within him, and he was deeply troubled. "Where have you put him?" he asked them. They told him, "Lord, come and see." Then Jesus wept. JOHN 11:33-35

HOW ABOUT YOU?
What has made you cry?

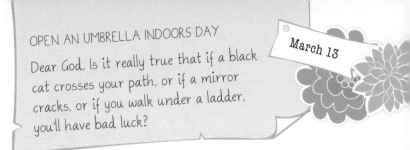

Dear God, Is it really true that if a black cat crosses your path, or if a mirror cracks, or if you walk under a ladder, you'll have bad luck?

CONSIDER THIS . . . One of the things we all realize, even as toddlers, is that we have no power! Want to buy a piece of candy, but you're a kid? Someone has to buy it for you or give the money to you; you can't get it on your own. Want to stay in your house, but your parents say you're moving? Too bad; it's off to Nebraska for you! Want to make the team, but the coach cut you from the roster? Sorry, but it's time to pick another sport. It can be frustrating to have no power!

Having no power is one reason why superstitions were created. People started to believe that if they did certain things, or didn't do certain things, they could stop bad things from happening to them. For example, people thought that if they stepped on a crack in a sidewalk they would break their mother's back. Lots of hopscotching goes on when you believe things like that and want to protect your mom. And guess what? Sometimes it worked. Only it worked because of chance, not because of obeying a superstition. But not everyone believed that.

If you're a Christian, you know the only one who has the true power—Jesus. You can step on as many sidewalk cracks as you want, use a broken mirror to put on your lip gloss, and ignore man-made horoscopes. Jesus has got the power, and he's got your back.

Go ahead. Open that umbrella indoors today. Just don't poke the dog!

HOW ABOUT YOU?

Do you believe in any superstitions? Have you ever knocked on wood or crossed your fingers to make something come true? Why have you done that, and what will help you stop?

GOD SAYS . . .

Don't let anyone capture you with empty philosophies and high-sounding nonsense that come from human thinking and from the spiritual powers of this world, rather than from Christ. COLOSSIANS 2:8

Dear God, How do you treat your followers?

CONSIDER THIS . . . A favorite movie of many girls, both the original from 1971 and the remade version, is *Willy Wonka and the Chocolate Factory*, also known as *Charlie and the Chocolate Factory*. Not only are there mountains of marshmallows and gumdrops galore in the chocolate factory, but there is also an entire river of chocolate that runs through it! Who wouldn't want to swim in that? Or at least dip a mug into it? (Augustus Gloop certainly couldn't resist!)

You may have seen a popular treat at weddings and parties that is very much like the chocolate river: a chocolate fountain. In a chocolate fountain, melted chocolate streams out of the top and gently falls over layers of glass plates. At the base of the fountain are dipping delights like marshmallows, pretzels, cut up strawberries, bananas, bites of pound cake and cheesecake—and, of course, lots of dipping forks to keep hands from getting messy. Guests put a treat on the fork and then slide it under the flowing chocolate, turning the fork until the sweet treat is completely coated. The best part? The chocolate never runs out. You can dip as many berries, marshmallows, pieces of pound cake, or other treats as you like.

God, too, has an unlimited store of sweetness and goodness. Although there are times when he withholds things from his children in order to teach or to discipline them, he delights in showering them with love. Reach out to your heavenly Father with an open hand. Dip your cup in, and watch him fill it to overflowing with his goodness.

It's sweet!

GOD SAYS . . .

You prepare a feast for me in the presence of my enemies. You honor me by anointing my head with oil. My cup overflows with blessings. PSALM 23:5

HOW ABOUT YOU?

What is one thing God totally, unexpectedly, knock-your-socks-off blessed you with?

Dear God, Why don't adults treat us kids with more respect?

CONSIDER THIS . . . One twelve-year-old girl's family was trying to figure out how to tie some bundles of luggage to the top of their car before setting off on a trip. She made a suggestion for how to make it work. Did anyone listen? Nope. They ignored her. Then they kept trying and failing with their own plans. Later, the girl's uncle came out of the house and made a recommendation. He told them the exact same thing that the girl had suggested. This time, because the idea came from an adult, they tried it. Guess what? It worked.

Sometimes adults are too busy to listen to kids. Sometimes they are too proud. That's sad but true. Because adults are sometimes too busy or too proud, they don't always realize kids have a lot of wisdom and great ideas. If you keep sharing your thoughts and ideas, the adults in your life will eventually listen. How you speak will prove to them that you are respectable and wise, even if they themselves aren't always acting that way. How do you do that?

By being an example!

You can choose to speak with respect toward others, make good choices on your own, act with love, be faithful in hard times, and live the way God tells you to live in the Bible. So many people *don't* do this (both kids and adults) that even the most thickheaded adults will start to see the difference between your life and others' lives. This will set a great example for them and earn their respect.

Even if you are a young Christian, you are as important in the Kingdom of Heaven as Christians of any other age.

HOW ABOUT YOU?

Are there times when you feel disrespected because you are young? How can you set a good example for adults?

GOD SAYS . . .

Don't let anyone think less of you because you are young. Be an example to all believers in what you say, in the way you live, in your love, your faith, and your purity. 1 TIMOTHY 4:12

Dear God, In the Bible, all the talk about Jesus' blood is a little gross. How can I think about it in a way that doesn't creep me out?

CONSIDER THIS ... Most of the time when we see blood, something bad has happened. Small things that bleed might be a paper cut, or a bloody nose, or a skinned knee. Big things that have a lot of blood might be a collision on the soccer field or basketball court, a car accident, or something tragic that we see on television. When a lot of blood is flowing out, it's not usually good news.

God tells us that the life of a being is in its blood. In the Old Testament, an animal had to be sacrificed to pay for sins. This wasn't because God was mean, but because he wanted people to understand that sin causes something awful: death.

Sometimes when someone loses too much blood in an accident or during an operation, he or she gets a blood transfusion. That means someone has donated some of his or her own blood so the sick or injured person can have it to get well. The healthy person will make new blood soon to replace that which was lost. But it still comes at a cost to her. It hurts to put the needle into her arm, and she might feel weak, or woozy, or tired until she makes enough new blood.

When Jesus came and died for us, the blood of his sacrifice paid the cost that God had set up—a life. His blood, the life of his being, paid for your sins, which required death. He gave you a blood transfusion. Life! This time the blood *is* good news.

In this case, blood is not creepy, but it shouldn't be totally comfortable, either, because it came at a cost. The cost was one that Jesus was willing to pay, though, because he loves you very much.

GOD SAYS ...

Now you have been united with Christ Jesus. Once you were far away from God, but now you have been brought near to him through the blood of Christ. EPHESIANS 2:13

HOW ABOUT YOU?

How do you feel knowing that Jesus gave you a blood transfusion?

Dear God, My dad is very sick. I feel scared and alone, and I wonder if you have left us.

CONSIDER THIS . . . A group of young campers was enjoying the woods near their campground. By day, it was easy to race through the woods and jump into the nearby lake without any fear of danger. The campers didn't run the risk of falling off the nearby cliff and into the water—or worse—because they could see where they were going. But one night, in the pitch black of no moon, their counselor woke them up and told them to get dressed. It was time to earn their navigating at night badge.

After getting dressed, each girl lined up single file, holding the hand of the girl ahead of her, and took off. Only the leader had a compass—with glow-in-the-dark headings. She would find the way, and the campers would follow along behind her. Because none of them could see where she was going, each girl had to hold on to the hand of the camper ahead of her.

The trail was long. There were animals just off the path. There were those cliffs—and the long drop if anyone fell off. In order to make it safely, each girl had to trust that the group's leader and the girl ahead of her were walking in the right direction. The girls were unable to see on their own.

Life is sometimes like that. Dark. Scary. Full of dangers. And we're not able to see where the path heads. The only way to get through those times is to trust that your guide, God, has the compass pointing in the right direction and will lead you to the best place. Hold on to the people around you who are following him too.

God doesn't ask you to walk alone; he holds your hand as he leads the way.

HOW ABOUT YOU?

What frightening situation or circumstance do you face? Who has the compass? Who can you hold on to?

GOD SAYS . . .

Do not be afraid or discouraged, for the LORD will personally go ahead of you. He will be with you; he will neither fail you nor abandon you.
DEUTERONOMY 31:8

Dear God, I have a situation. I know the right thing to do, but I'm afraid to do it. How can you help?

CONSIDER THIS . . . Each year schools around the country, and maybe around the world, conduct a fitness test for their students. They want to see what kind of shape their students are in so they can help them to become even more fit. The tests usually include sit-ups, push-ups, running, and stretching. They also include one test that almost everyone hates—the pull-up, or flexed-arm hang.

When you do the flexed-arm hang, you're supposed to climb up onto a stool, grab a bar, and pull your head up above it. At the same time, a coach or teacher is taking the stool out from under your feet. The teacher counts how many seconds you can "hang" there, holding up your own body weight. Most people can't go very long. It's hard! It hurts! So they let go and drop to the floor.

But what if the coach or teacher didn't take the stool away?

Why, then you could stand there as long as you like with your head above the bar, your arms flexed, and something else holding up your body weight.

This is what God does for us. He still puts us through tests—to see how fit we are and to build our spiritual muscles—but he helps us. He does not make us do right things on our own; instead, he literally says he lends a hand. He's there to hold us up. If you pray and ask him to help you, he will, and you can do the right thing.

GOD SAYS . . .

I will strengthen you and help you. I will hold you up with my victorious right hand. ISAIAH 41:10

HOW ABOUT YOU?

Can you think of two things that you know you should do but are afraid to do, or feel they are too hard for you to do? How can God help you?

Dear God, If I'm having a party and someone I didn't invite asks if I'm having a party, what should I do?

March 19

CONSIDER THIS . . . Honesty really *is* always the best policy. You need to understand in your own heart, first, that this party is *your* party. You are not required to invite everyone to your party. But you should remember other people's feelings. If you haven't invited a person, you should still be honest, kind, and considerate. Here's how: If someone asks you, "Are you having a party?" first, simply answer yes. Then try to change the subject. If that person persists and asks, "Why am I not invited?" you might try saying, "I couldn't invite everyone, but perhaps you and I could do something another time." Then change the subject. You will have been honest, kind, and considerate. Understand her hurt feelings, and don't hold them against her or gossip. But if she isn't a good person to hang out with, don't give in, either.

Life is full of peer pressure. It's better to learn how to say yes and no right now instead of waiting until you're older! Anyone who is going to punish you for saying no politely is probably not a good friend anyway. Paul reminds us in 2 Corinthians 1 to make sure we say yes when we mean yes and no when we mean no, and to leave nothing between the lines. That means being straightforward with your thoughts and feelings. It's okay. He tells us why, too. Because Jesus was straightforward and honest with others.

Whom should you invite? Old, good friends are always a wise choice, but so are a couple of people you'd like to get to know better. Celebrating with old friends will make it special, and inviting someone new to a party will make it even more fun!

HOW ABOUT YOU?

When is it hard for you to tell people no? What response can you prepare ahead of time and practice, so when the sweaty-palms moment comes you'll be prepared?

GOD SAYS . . .

Just say a simple yes or no, so that you will not sin and be condemned. JAMES 5:12

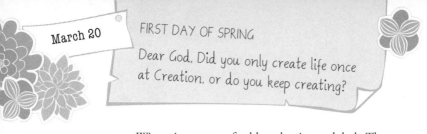

FIRST DAY OF SPRING

Dear God, Did you only create life once at Creation, or do you keep creating?

CONSIDER THIS . . . Winter is a season of cold, and quiet, and dark. The trees have no leaves, and the grass is brown and does not grow. While there are some plants that have fruit and flowers, most are waiting patiently for spring. Spring is a beautiful season. It's a season of new life! But creating life, while lovely, isn't easy.

Tiny plants, their stems thin and weak, struggle to push themselves through hard or soggy ground. Baby chicks must peck, peck, peck for a whole day sometimes to free themselves from their shells. Babies being born have a stressful time too. They've been warm and safe inside their mothers for as long as they have been alive, and now, they must come out and face a cold, bright world! It's not an easy process for the mom, either.

Although God created the very first human beings, and the very first plants and animals, he didn't stop there. He told people to be fruitful and increase. That means people should have children so the earth's population will grow. He created the land to keep making plants and trees and fruit. He made animals so they could make more animals. He set things up so that he, and we, would keep creating.

God didn't just stop with physical life, though. For humans, who have a spirit within them, he created life to go on after the body dies. This new life, a life in Christ, makes it possible for you to belong to him forever. It wasn't easy for him to give this life to you, but he did it so you would have a beautiful season even after your time on earth ends.

No shell pecking required!

GOD SAYS . . .
Everyone who belongs to Christ will be given new life. 1 CORINTHIANS 15:22

HOW ABOUT YOU?
Have you found your new life in Christ? If not, talk to a trusted adult about how to receive new life in Christ.

Dear God, I don't understand the Trinity. How can God be Jesus' Father if they and the Holy Spirit are one?

March 21

CONSIDER THIS . . . This is one of the hard questions Christians have to deal with, and it's not something that can be completely answered here on earth. Because we don't fully understand it, there is no example that exactly shows how the Trinity works, so maybe we can just describe what we do know.

The word *Trinity* isn't in the Bible. It's just the word we use to describe that God is *three* distinct persons but one God. The Father, the Son, and the Holy Spirit all have many different roles—Creator, Savior, and Counselor are three of them, for example—even though they are all one. It's also clear they work together to achieve all that they want to. They are one unit, but they are also separate. The Father sent the Son to save us. Jesus told us that he was sending the Holy Spirit to help us. The Holy Spirit helps us pray to the Father so we can be close. Each is fully God, and they all work together because, actually, they are one. We are humans, and God is God. He is superior to us, and because he is God we cannot understand everything about him.

Some people say it's like an apple peel and apple flesh and apple seeds all being the apple, when we really think of them as all those parts put together. That's a pretty good picture, even though it's not exact.

It's exciting to know you will have eternity to ask God these things, isn't it? First Corinthians 13:12 tells us that now we know things only in part, but one day we will know things in full, as fully as God knows us. What a wonderful day that will be!

HOW ABOUT YOU?

What questions will you ask God when you see him face-to-face?

GOD SAYS . . .

Therefore, go and make disciples of all the nations, baptizing them in the name of the Father and the Son and the Holy Spirit.
MATTHEW 28:19

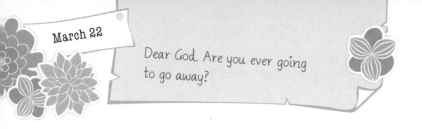

Dear God, Are you ever going to go away?

CONSIDER THIS . . . Almost everyone has a stuffed animal or a doll that is special to them, one that is so loved-on that it might become fragile and lose some fluff. Sometimes these are called "love objects" because we love on them, cuddle them, and take them wherever we go. When we're sad, they stay right beside us, always listening, helping us to stop feeling bad. When we're worried, they're cushy to hug and make us feel like everything is going to be okay. When we have a secret that we absolutely, positively can't share with anyone else, we whisper it in their soft ears. They keep on smiling but will never tell. They are faithful, no matter what.

Some of us may outgrow our stuffed animals, but we never outgrow our need for love objects. We'll always need someone to feel safe with, to share our deepest secrets with, to come with us when we go to new places and want to feel safe. And when you know God's Son, Jesus, you can have all that and more.

Not only is Jesus always there for you, but he's always strong and he loves you back, unlike other love objects. You never outgrow him. In fact, as you get older, he can grow closer and more important to you than ever. You can talk to him inside your head and your heart; Jesus always listens, helping you to feel better and reassuring you that everything will be okay and that with him, you'll never be alone.

He's faithful, no matter what.

GOD SAYS . . .
And be sure of this:
I [Jesus] am with you
always. MATTHEW 28:20

HOW ABOUT YOU?
Do you have a special doll, stuffed animal, or blanket? How is the Lord like your love object? How is he unlike it? As you fall asleep tonight, think about the fact that you will always be a focus of great love from Jesus.

Dear God. There are a lot of things I am waiting for, but it seems like they're never going to happen. Will they?

March 23

CONSIDER THIS . . . One of the best smells in the world can be smelled on Saturday or Sunday mornings. Sometimes you can get a whiff of it at the food court at the mall. Often, grandmas are behind this delicious breeze. What is it? It's the smell of cinnamon rolls baking in the oven. It's only fair, then, that it should be followed by one of the best tastes in the world: soft, gooey rolls (with butter!). But cinnamon rolls don't just magically appear, even if you buy them at the mall. Someone has to bake them.

After getting all of the ingredients mixed together, including that delightful cinnamon, bakers have a goopy ball of speckled white dough. This dough isn't like cookie batter; it doesn't taste good if you sneak a bite of it raw. The baker has to divide the dough into pieces, roll it out, brush cinnamon sugar and butter on it, roll up, and let the rolls sit on the cookie sheet to rise. And rise. And rise!

If you put the rolls into the oven before they are done rising, you'll get a disgusting flat disk instead of a puffy roll. But if you wait the full time, then after baking . . . *mmm!*

This is what life is like. There are many good things ahead for you. God has promised you a future and a hope (Jeremiah 29:11). But each event in your life, each privilege, each good time will come at just the right moment, if you wait for it. Look forward to it! Plan ahead for it. But don't force it too soon, unless you like disgusting flat dough disks instead of the tasty pillows you'll get if you wait for God's timing.

HOW ABOUT YOU?

What are you oh-so-eager for? Do you believe God wants to bring good things to your life?

GOD SAYS . . .

[Jesus said,] "God blesses you who are hungry now, for you will be satisfied."
LUKE 6:21

Dear God, Why don't people say, "I'm sorry," when they should? I have to admit, I don't like to either.

CONSIDER THIS . . . Hey, who *does* like to admit they are wrong? No one! We worry that the people we have wronged won't like us anymore. We worry that we will lose their respect. We worry that there will be consequences, and sometimes there are! Sometimes, though, we just don't think that what we did was a "big deal." It's one way of saying that our sin really wasn't so bad.

It's humbling to have to say you're sorry when you've done something wrong. *Humble* means meek, modest, and low. It means you don't place yourself above, or higher than, or more important than the person you hurt. You lower yourself down to say you're sorry. You admit you were wrong without saying, "But you . . ." afterward. You realize what you said or did was wrong and wish you could put all that toothpaste you squeezed out of the tube back into it. But you can't. The best thing you can do is clean up your mess and promise not to do it again.

We all make mistakes and must say we are sorry and ask for forgiveness. Both parts are important. Saying you're sorry is great, but it doesn't restore the relationship. God says that he forgives others when they repent of their sin and ask him for forgiveness, and he teaches us to forgive the way he does. Only when forgiveness is asked for and granted is that relationship made right. Next time someone sins against you and is truly sorry, forgive him or her, too.

Is there anyone you need to tell that you are sorry? It's okay to do it. Remember, God loves the humble.

GOD SAYS . . .

Be kind to each other, tenderhearted, forgiving one another, just as God through Christ has forgiven you. EPHESIANS 4:32

HOW ABOUT YOU?

When you say you're sorry to someone, do you always ask for forgiveness, too? Why or why not? What happens inside of you when you truly forgive someone?

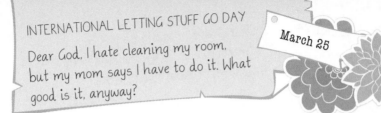

INTERNATIONAL LETTING STUFF GO DAY

March 25

Dear God, I hate cleaning my room, but my mom says I have to do it. What good is it, anyway?

CONSIDER THIS . . . One of the toughest jobs in the world is spring cleaning. You know that there are unknown jumbles stuffed under your bed, chaos in your drawers, and clutter lurking in the corners of your closet. Things you haven't seen in months! So put some music on and go drawer by drawer, sorting your clothes into piles.

- These clothes don't fit or aren't my style anymore. Give them away.
- I like this one, but it has a button that fell off. Needs to be fixed.
- Hey! I forgot I had this shirt. I can't wait to wear it again!

Once you've sorted your clothes, go through the rest of your things, sorting them into piles for giving away and keeping.

Even though the process isn't fun, it does feel good to have a tidy room and also—bonus—room in the drawers and closets for new clothes and things. Life is like that too. From time to time we need to sort through and see which sports, or activities, or even friendships need to be changed. Ask yourself these questions about your activities and friendships:

- Have I outgrown them?
- Do they need a little tender loving care?
- Have I rediscovered something or someone I really like but had forgotten about?

When you allow the Lord to move activities and relationships out of your life that are no longer the best for you, he will move new activities and friendships in to bless you. Don't dread spring cleaning, or cleaning up at any time. You'll see that there's room for something wonderful, now.

HOW ABOUT YOU?

What stuff, or attitudes, or people do you need to allow God to clean out to make room for something new? Will you trust him to bring something even better?

GOD SAYS . . .

I am about to do something new. See, I have already begun! Do you not see it? ISAIAH 43:19

March 26

Dear God, In fairy tales, there's always a knight in shining armor who comes to rescue the damsel in distress. Does that ever happen in real life?

CONSIDER THIS . . . One of the reasons that so many fairy tales have heroines who are in trouble is because we girls often feel like there is a lot of trouble in our lives. We may not have an evil stepmother, but we do have mean girls. We may not eat poisoned apples, but we listen to people gossip and backbite with poisoned words. We feel lost and unsure how to travel . . . with no bread-crumb trails to show us what to do. We find that even if we haven't pricked our fingers with a needle, bad things happen to us through no fault of our own.

How we long for someone to come and rescue us, to make it all go away, to make everything work out right in the end.

Most of us have one or more good men in our lives. We may have a good dad, or grandfather, or brother, or uncle. You will grow up and hopefully marry a really good man who will love God and take care of and protect you. But even the best men can't solve all things at all times. Because they are only men.

Scripture tells us that Jesus, Faithful and True, has not only the power to protect us, but the desire to do so, because he is good. He sees when bad things happen, and though he may not charge in right away to scoop you onto his horse, he will make all things right for you in the end. He loves you, and he can be your knight in shining armor today and every day.

GOD SAYS . . .

Then I saw heaven opened, and a white horse was standing there. Its rider was named Faithful and True. REVELATION 19:11

HOW ABOUT YOU?

How can Jesus be your knight in shining armor today? What can you ask him to help you with? What kind of husband would be good for a Christian woman?

Dear God, It's sometimes hard to understand the Bible, or when I read it I get bored. Then I feel guilty. What should I do?

March 27

CONSIDER THIS . . . Spring is a season for planting. While the ground is still hard, we take tools and loosen it up some, breaking big clumps of dirt into soft mounds of black and brown soil. Once it's softened, we place a seed or a little plant in it, and then we cover up the seed or the roots. Even though the plant doesn't look like much at that point, we know it will grow into something beautiful.

What people often forget to do when they plant is to water right. Too little water and the seed or plant dies. Nothing can live without water. It can hang on for a little while, but it eventually shrivels up. Some people do the opposite—they give the seedling too much water. The ground can't absorb a gallon of water at once! What happens is the water rolls away, down into the grass or on the sidewalk, which does the new plant no good. Or it drowns the plant, or lifts it out of its new bedding.

Scripture is like that. It is water for your soul, and your spirit cannot live without it. But if you try to take too much in at once, your mind wanders and the good that it can do doesn't really happen; the "water" rolls down the sidewalk. Or lifts you out of the bedding, making it hard for you to remember what you just learned.

You are a lovely seedling developing into a beautiful flower. Make sure you get a little "water" each day, but don't feel bad if it's not a lot. You don't need a lot to grow and see the beautiful plan God has for you be fulfilled.

HOW ABOUT YOU?

Do you water your soul every day? Reading the Bible is important not only to teach you, but to give you encouragement and hope. How can you make sure your soul is getting enough water?

GOD SAYS . . .

Such things were written in the Scriptures long ago to teach us. And the Scriptures give us hope and encouragement as we wait patiently for God's promises to be fulfilled. ROMANS 15:4

March 28

Dear God, I want to do big things with my life. But I am only one person, and a kid at that. How can I do anything important?

CONSIDER THIS . . . The beginning of spring can find those of us living in cooler climates putting away our winter clothes and bringing out the clothes that are made for warmer weather. Away with the ski hats with the puff balls on top; bring out the sunglasses instead! Away with the heavy coats; bring out the bright pink and yellow hoodies. Away with boots; time for flip-flops. Okay, maybe not flip-flops yet. But it's definitely time to put away the mittens and the gloves.

A glove sitting by itself looks odd. It's the shape of a hand—we see the palm and the fingers and thumbs. But it doesn't have anything inside it, so it can't do much. A hand can pick up and move things, it can give a pat on the back, or a hug around the shoulders. A helping hand can be lent to someone who needs it. A hand can do work. And hands can show love. A glove on its own is not very powerful.

God designed you to be a beautiful young woman. You are not exactly like a glove, of course. You can do things, you can show love, you can help. But there are limits to what one person can do. God doesn't have any limits. And he loves to work with you, and in you, and through you. His Spirit, alive inside of you, is like the hand inside your glove. The two of you work together to do everything that pleases him. And when you love God, doing things for him pleases you, too.

Seasons may change, and so may clothing, but every day of every year, you and God can be working together to do exciting and important things.

GOD SAYS . . .
God is working in you, giving you the desire and the power to do what pleases him. PHILIPPIANS 2:13

HOW ABOUT YOU?
What do you want to do with your life? What can you do with God's help today to make a difference?

Dear God, How can a butterfly come from a caterpillar? A caterpillar is so ugly, and a butterfly so beautiful.

March 29

CONSIDER THIS . . . Caterpillars may have a charm of their own, but mostly . . . they're awkward. They have a lot of creepy little feet that move at once, and they're very squishy in the middle. They have to scrunch their bodies into awkward shapes in order to move. They come in some pretty colors, but usually, they're kind of a greenish gray—you know, the color of dirty water. They munch on leaves. And they often have a lot of fuzz all over their bodies. When it's time for them to become butterflies, they split their skin. Ouch!

But they do turn into butterflies, somehow. And though the process seems like it might be painful, when it's done, the caterpillars have turned into beautiful and unique creatures. They fly freely, gracefully. They alight on branches and twitter and flitter through the air. Their wings are many colors, swirled with beautiful designs, and when the sun shines through them it's like looking through stained glass. No more leaf munching for these beauties. They only sip nectar.

In some ways, human lives are like caterpillars. We all go through our "caterpillar" times. Bad things happen to everyone. Hard things. Awkward stages and ugly words or tough situations. But somehow, God says he takes all the difficulties and unhappiness we undergo and makes something lovely out of them. He takes our ashes and turns them into a crown of beauty. Sometimes the more difficulties we undergo, the more delightful our reward.

When hard times come, hold on. God is getting ready to transform them into a masterpiece.

HOW ABOUT YOU?

What are the ugly or difficult things in your life? Do you believe that they, like the caterpillar, can be transformed into a thing of beauty?

GOD SAYS . . .

To all who mourn in Israel, he will give a crown of beauty for ashes, a joyous blessing instead of mourning, festive praise instead of despair. ISAIAH 61:3

Dear God, I'm beginning to wonder if my friend is a Christian.

CONSIDER THIS . . . When we grow up in a family that loves Christ, it is easy for us to think that everyone who is nice is a Christian too. Many people think they are Christians when they may not be. When I was a girl, I thought I was a Christian because my family went to church on Christmas and Easter and because we weren't Jewish or Buddhist or another religion. I was a nice girl. If someone had asked me if I was a Christian, I would have said yes, because I thought I was. But I wasn't . . . at least not yet.

Why not? A person becomes a Christian only when she has trusted Jesus Christ for salvation. It's a two-way deal. When someone holds out a gift to you, it's not yours until you decide to reach out and take it. In the same way, Jesus offers himself as Savior, but you are not a Christian until you decide to reach out and accept the offer. That is what calling on his name means in Acts 2:21. When I was a girl, I didn't understand that I needed to. Your friend might not understand that either.

When you are a Christian, the Holy Spirit helps you tell the difference between someone who has faith and someone who does not. Maybe you're sensing that your friend believes she's a Christian but isn't. Perhaps no one has told her that Jesus has made the offer but that she herself has to reach out and make a decision to accept it. Most exciting of all, maybe God has put you together as friends so *you* can help her understand!

GOD SAYS . . .
Everyone who calls on the name of the LORD will be saved. ACTS 2:21

HOW ABOUT YOU?
Will you pray to ask God if you have any friends who might need to know just what it means to be a Christian? Who can you tell about the salvation that Jesus wants to give them?

Dear God, I'm really shy around people I don't know. And whenever I want to make friends with somebody, I can't figure out what to say.

March 31

CONSIDER THIS . . . It's hard for anyone to speak up. Even people who seem much braver than you struggle with talking to other people, especially people they don't know. We might be worried that they won't accept us or that they will think we're weird. What if we don't know what to talk about? What if they reject us? It's especially hard when you want to make new friends. One thing is true: when life is especially hard, that is the time we must rely on God. And he is faithful to help us.

Normally the one who wants the friends must make the first move—so unfair, and yet still true. So pray and ask the Lord to help you. He knows that you need new friends. He is here to help us with everything we need. But God also wants us to trust in him and try to do the hard things. If you never try anything hard while trusting in God to help you, you'll never prove to yourself that he is there to give you strength.

Remind yourself that it is normal to be shy—the apostle Paul even said he was much braver when writing letters and more shy in person. Ask the Lord to help you be strong and brave, to help you speak clearly, and to give you some good ideas about what to say. Ask him to prepare a kind heart in the person you're going to speak with. Then go for it!

The only way to have friends is to make friends, and you have to do at least half of the making! Don't give up if it doesn't go perfectly at first. Keep trying until you get to just the right new friend.

HOW ABOUT YOU?

Whom would you like to talk with but have been too shy to speak to?

GOD SAYS . . .

As soon as I pray, you answer me; you encourage me by giving me strength. PSALM 138:3

APRIL FOOLS' DAY

Dear God, I like jokes! If I play a prank, or fall for a trick today, does that make me a fool?

CONSIDER THIS . . . Today, whether you like it or not, is a day full of jokes and laughter and pranks and tricks. April Fools' Day was first started hundreds of years ago when nations changed the first day of their year from April 1 to January 1. Some people were hardheaded about it and didn't want to do things the new way. They stubbornly refused to agree to a new calendar! The hardheaded people continued to celebrate the new year on April 1 while everyone else moved their celebrations to January 1. So other folks decided to play tricks on them by inviting them to parties and meetings . . . but on the wrong day. Because the fools hadn't listened, they missed out and were made fun of. Did it change their hearts? Nope. They still didn't listen.

Through the years the day has turned into one in which people play kind tricks and lighthearted jokes on one another. Playing fun ones, in which no one's body or feelings get hurt, is just fine. Try layering a sheet of bubble wrap between the toilet rim and seat. Or put fake bugs in the bathroom sink so it looks like they're crawling up out of the drain. Ask your mom to buy you the special hamburger for left-handers. (It doesn't exist.) Or just store up on knock-knock jokes to share with your family and friends.

The Bible has a lot of things to say about who fools are, including people who don't listen to advice, who deny there is a God, who insult others, and who turn away from wisdom. But there's nothing at all wrong with having a good time.

You'd be a fool not to have fun!

GOD SAYS . . .

Fools have no interest in understanding; they only want to air their own opinions. PROVERBS 18:2

HOW ABOUT YOU?

Which behaviors are fun and which are foolish?

Dear God, I get asked to do a lot of chores, and I think they're boring and too hard for me. Can I get out of doing them?

April 2

CONSIDER THIS . . . Most people don't look forward to Saturday so they can clean their rooms or mow the lawn. Not too many girls rush home from school hoping to unload the dishwasher. Allowance, if you receive one, is great to spend. Vacuuming the stairs in order to earn it—not so much. Often it feels like the jobs we're given are just too hard!

When it feels that way, step back. Is it too hard? Or do you just not want to do it? Most of the time, the chores are within our abilities, just not within our desires. If something is too high to reach to clean well, get a step stool. If the room is too messy, clean one corner at a time. If loading the dishwasher is a hassle, slip on some music to listen to while you do it. It will make the task more fun.

Many people feel that the Bible is boring and just too hard to understand too. Some parts of it are difficult to understand, for sure, which is why we have teachers. And there's never anything wrong with asking for help. But most of us, if we're honest, will admit that it's not *really* too hard to understand; it's that we just don't feel like

- obeying our parents;
- forgiving people who hurt our feelings; or
- giving some of our money away.

God knows that there will be difficult things in life, but just like muscles, our spirits don't grow unless we do things that we might resist at first. God's there to help with an encouraging word, a hand up, and even good music!

HOW ABOUT YOU?

What feels too hard for you to do? Is there someone who can lend a hand?

GOD SAYS . . .

This command I am giving you today is not too difficult for you to understand. . . . It is on your lips and in your heart so that you can obey it.
DEUTERONOMY 30:11, 14

Dear God, Why do people sometimes lift their hands in church?

CONSIDER THIS . . . Have you ever been to a play? The performers all do their parts, and then at the end they make a final appearance on the stage as the audience applauds. One by one they come, from the least important player to the most important. As each one comes onto the stage, she casts her hands up and out to welcome the next highest—and more important—level of performers. Finally, at the end, all the supporting cast hold their hands in the direction of the most important member of all. When they hold their hands toward the star, it brings glory and praise to that person. They recognize who deserves the highest honor.

When we lift our hands toward God, we are giving him the honor due to him as the ultimate Star of the universe. We are praising him for his work in creating the world and his love for us. We hold our hands up to him, open, as if to say, "We have nothing to give to you except our love, but we offer that to you." We raise our hands at the mention of his name to show the respect due to him. The Bible tells us to raise our hands to pray from the heart, to praise the Lord, to bless him, and to show that we are holy, too. Raising our hands directs all the attention his way.

You don't have to lift up your hands to praise him, of course. You can think of other ways to do that, too, like telling others about the great things he has done or remembering to give him credit in front of others. When you do, you'll feel closer to him.

GOD SAYS . . .
Lift up holy hands in prayer, and praise the LORD. PSALM 134:2

HOW ABOUT YOU?
What does it mean to bless the Lord or praise him?

Dear God, Are you going to ask me to try new things—things I might not like?

April 4

CONSIDER THIS . . . Now, almost everyone likes candy—Jelly Bellies, M&M's, and Nerds are some favorites. A local store sells lollipops that have scorpions in them. But do you know what could be the weirdest kind of candy at the mall? Chick-O-Sticks.

Chicken candy? Who are they kidding?

Does it taste like chicken nuggets? Are you supposed to dip it in ranch dressing? No thanks. It sounds kind of weird. But the candy store cashier might insist, "It's good. It doesn't taste like KFC or Church's. It tastes like peanut butter. Taste it and you'll see . . . you'll like it."

Now, peanut butter is good! And the cashier looks trustworthy. She wouldn't try to trick her customers, or they wouldn't come back. She hands over a Chick-O-Stick. "Just taste it. You'll see."

The wrapper is peeled back. A nibble is taken. It's good! It's great! Trying something new can be uncomfortable; it involves taking a risk. We don't know what to expect, and we're afraid of getting a nasty surprise. You may have known Jesus for a while, but when you first begin to truly trust him with the day-to-day living of life, you will be trying something new.

We may wonder if he will ask us to do a new thing, like share our faith, join a youth group, or go to a Christian camp. Maybe he'll ask us to speak first with him instead of paying back someone who's done us wrong. The good news is, well, Good News. Christ is trustworthy. He won't trick you. And while he's going to keep asking you to try something new, to take risks, and maybe be uncomfortable, it will always be only for good.

Even if you don't like chicken.

HOW ABOUT YOU?

When have you been hesitant to try something new—a food, an activity, music—and were surprised at how much you liked it? What new thing might God be asking you to try?

GOD SAYS . . .

Taste and see that the LORD is good. PSALM 34:8

April 5

Dear God, Is everyone in the whole wide world able to find you?

CONSIDER THIS . . . A favorite party game, Blind Man's Bluff, is played by covering the eyes of one person who is "it." One of the other people at the party spins the blindfolded person around a few times, to confuse him or her, and then the people in the party call out. "I'm over here!" one might shout, and then pull away or quickly step in another direction. "Hey, you!" someone might say, drawing close to the blinded person and then moving backward. The idea is to "bluff" or fool the person who is "it" into believing that you are nearby.

This game might seem like fun . . . unless you're "it." And then it just seems mean. After all, you're reaching out for the person who spoke to you, and that person is trying to trick you into thinking he or she is near, instead of out of reach.

God does not trick anyone. In fact, he works in just the opposite way. He tries in many, many ways to draw our attention. A beautiful tree, ocean, or sunset might be God drawing your gaze to something too beautiful to be man made. Have you ever prayed for help, and someone came alongside to talk? What about people who befriend the lonely, or care for the sick? God is talking through them, too. When you share the Good News, the gospel, you are helping God speak to everyone.

Jesus is much closer to us than we realize. In the same room. In our hearts and minds. He doesn't trick us into thinking he's close when he's far away, or speak to us and then jump out of reach. Instead, he's close, hoping we'll stop moving around long enough to see him.

Go ahead. Take off your blindfold!

GOD SAYS . . .

His purpose was for the nations to seek after God and perhaps feel their way toward him and find him— though he is not far from any one of us. ACTS 17:27

HOW ABOUT YOU?

Do you sense God around you? In what ways? Are they always the ways that you expect to see and sense him?

CONSIDER THIS . . . Grandpas can be so fun. Some might let you pretend to drive the car when it's parked in the driveway—and even use the steering wheel! Others might cook with you, or let you watch football with them on TV. Good grandpas are kind, and they cheer you on at school or sports or when you're in a play. They love you. They love your parents. But because they are older, they are sometimes the first important people in your life who die. That can make you feel empty and sad.

Everything God created on earth has a life cycle. Plants start out as seeds, become shoots, grow into plants, bear fruit with seeds, and wither away. Even nonliving things, such as cars and computers, work well for a time, then eventually break down and don't work well any longer. This book will eventually turn yellow and fade, then crumble away. Stars are born—and die. Everything, and every person, has a time to be young, to be fresh, and to be energized, but then everything and everyone eventually grows older and tired. At some point people's bodies wear out, and they die.

The good news is that God created humans to have a spirit that lives on after the body dies. Ecclesiastes 12:7 says that when the human body dies, the spirit inside returns to God, who made it. The human body may pass away, but if the person is a Christian, his or her spirit will spend eternity in heaven. Plants decay back into the soil, computers and cars are crushed and recycled, books fade away, and bodies die, but human spirits live on.

HOW ABOUT YOU?

How does it feel when someone you love dies? Does it make you feel any better to know that his or her spirit, the real person, lives on?

GOD SAYS . . .

For everything there is a season, a time for every activity under heaven. A time to be born and a time to die. ECCLESIASTES 3:1-2

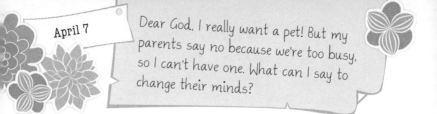

Dear God, I really want a pet! But my parents say no because we're too busy, so I can't have one. What can I say to change their minds?

CONSIDER THIS . . . Most kids, if they're not allergic, would like a pet. Some girls want a puppy, cute and wiggly, to cuddle and to hold. Some girls are afraid of dogs; they'd rather have a tiny kitten that curls up in their laps and purrs softly. Other kids prefer little pets, like guinea pigs or hamsters or mice. Or birds!

Pets aren't like stuffed animals, though. They have physical needs. Unlike stuffed animals you can leave alone for days, real animals need to be fed and watered and groomed. This takes time and patience. They cost money to care for; food and vet visits, for example, aren't cheap. Pets also need attention. Some dogs need to play or be walked for an hour per day. All animals have emotional needs. They all need love and attention.

Your mom and dad have said that your family is too busy to give a pet the affection and care that it needs. Although it may not seem fair, your parents are really keeping your family's needs in mind, and they are also being kind to a pet, which wouldn't like to be neglected. That would be a cruel thing to do. Maybe there are concerns about how much a pet would cost right now, because money is tight.

If you've talked respectfully to your parents and they still say no, you might need to give up the idea of having a pet for now. You might ask about fish, or care for pets with a friend. Ask if you could start a neighborhood dog-walking business, or volunteer at a local animal shelter. There are lots of ways to show love to pets, even if you don't have one of your own.

GOD SAYS · · ·
The godly care for their animals, but the wicked are always cruel.
PROVERBS 12:10

HOW ABOUT YOU?
If you don't have a pet, what could you do to care for an animal? If you do have a pet, how could you help take even better care of it?

Dear God, Sometimes adults lie. That confuses me, because then I don't know what the truth is. How can you tell?

April 8

CONSIDER THIS . . . Kindergartners think that fourth graders know it all. Seventh graders think that fourth graders know absolutely nothing. It's all a matter of perspective, isn't it?

When you're a kid, it can seem like adults know what's right and will always do the right thing. But being an adult, or a fourth or seventh grader, doesn't guarantee good character. Good character means telling the truth, considering others before yourself, being kind, etc. Lots of kids do those things. Some kids don't. Lots of adults do those things. Some adults don't.

In the book of Acts, Paul talked to people every day about the right things to do. Some of the people he talked to, the Bereans, would go home and check with the Scriptures to make sure the things Paul was saying were true. They wanted to make sure, before they acted on anything, that they were hearing the truth. The Bereans didn't believe Paul only because he was a person in authority. They checked with other reliable sources, too, to make sure they knew the truth.

When an adult tells you something, it's okay to go to a second reliable source to make sure it's true and to make sure that adult is a good person. Scripture, of course, is the best place for truth. Just ask the Bereans! Going to your parents, your Sunday school teacher, or the Christian parent of a friend is a good idea. Be open and willing to be taught. But be wise, and if something doesn't sound right, or if it sounds dishonest, respectfully check it out. Seventh graders tell the truth most of the time. Most adults do too. But sometimes bad choices or mistakes are made. It's okay to verify.

HOW ABOUT YOU?

Who are three good people you can go to in order to make sure you know the truth?

GOD SAYS . . .

Honesty guides good people; dishonesty destroys treacherous people. PROVERBS 11:3

Dear God, There are a lot of people who have different religions. How can I know which one is right?

CONSIDER THIS . . . Have you ever visited a new city, or even a new country? Some things might look just like home. For example, there are roads and houses and electricity and water. But some things are very different. You won't know where anything is because it's all new to you. What is the best restaurant? Where are the safe neighborhoods? You don't want to spend your money at a place with bad food. Or worse—wander into a neighborhood where you wouldn't be safe!

What's the best thing to do when you're new? Get a tour guide! If you're visiting family or friends, your tour guide might be someone you know and love. Surely they know the best sites to see and the most delicious pizza to eat in their own hometown. They're also pretty aware of the places you'll want to stay away from.

If you're in a completely new town without any friends or family nearby, you can look up a reputable company to show you around, guide you to the right places, and keep you safe.

This world we live in was created by Jesus. Scripture says that all things were created through him (Colossians 1:16). As the creator of heaven and earth, Jesus knows all the ins and outs. He certainly knows what's good and what's safe. He definitely knows the right way to live while we're here, and then the right way to get "home" to heaven. Jesus says that he is the Way, the only way, to the Father. There is no other way besides him, even if people who seem good and kind insist that there is. If you choose Jesus to guide you through life, you are a Christian and you will never be lost.

GOD SAYS · · ·

Jesus told him, "I am the way, the truth, and the life. No one can come to the Father except through me."
JOHN 14:6

HOW ABOUT YOU?

Do you believe that Jesus is the only Way to the Father? Why or why not?

> Dear God, Why did Jesus have to come and die for us? It seems cruel.

CONSIDER THIS . . . In the Bible, the Lord gives himself many names and shows how he plays many roles in order to help us understand many parts of his character, his being, his intentions, and his love for us. One of those roles is our ransom.

Nowadays, there are lots of movies about pirates. Usually, the pirates are attractive, funny, smart, and even sweet. In some strange way, they are the heroes of the movies. In history, however, and even today, there are many pirates who are not heroic at all. They can actually be cruel thieves and murderers. Here's how they work:

Pirates lurk about the open oceans, where unsuspecting ships sail through. When an innocent ship is away from all help, the pirates attack. They steal the goods on board and then they take some of the passengers—usually the most important ones—as captives. In order to get those captives back, their families have to pay a ransom—money in exchange for the lives of their loved ones.

Satan, and sin, lurks about waiting to steal and destroy too. Satan hates most what God loves best, and through his temptations he tries to, like pirates, rob and deceive God's children. A penalty had to be paid in order to rescue you and me from sin. A ransom was paid so we could go free. Jesus willingly paid that ransom with his own life.

Although it was certainly painful, Jesus willingly went to his death. Not because it would be pleasant. But because it would free his loved ones. You.

HOW ABOUT YOU?

How valuable must you be for Jesus to have paid his life as a ransom for you? How does knowing that make you feel?

GOD SAYS . . .

Even the Son of Man came not to be served but to serve others and to give his life as a ransom for many. MATTHEW 20:28

Dear God, I have some questions about important things, but I don't want to ask my parents. Is it wrong to write to someone to get advice?

CONSIDER THIS . . . There have been "advice" columns around as long as there have been newspapers. Letters to the Lovelorn first appeared in newspapers and magazines in the eighteenth century. Two of the most popular columns in America have been Dear Abby and Ask Ann Landers. In England, advice columnists are called "Agony Aunts." Why? Because there are some things you want to tell someone you love and trust to get their advice, but maybe you don't want to ask your parents right away. An auntie is someone you can often confide in. And usually the things you worry about have you in agony! Now, in addition to newspaper columns, there are advice-givers online.

There is nothing at all wrong with going to a trusted adult and asking questions or sharing your concerns. If you have a close relationship with your mom or dad, you might be surprised to find that they will not react badly to whatever questions you have. In fact, they likely had worrying questions themselves when they were your age. If you have an aunt, or a grandma, or a friend's mom that you can confide in, that's okay too.

But don't forget that the Lord is near to you too. He willingly gives wisdom and guidance to all who ask, and he isn't angry with you for asking. He won't write the answer in a newspaper column, like Dear Abby. But he does give advice through Scripture, through circumstances, through wise counselors, and even through whispers in your heart. He doesn't want you to be in agony.

So go ahead—ask away!

GOD SAYS . . .

If you need wisdom, ask our generous God, and he will give it to you. He will not rebuke you for asking. But when you ask him, be sure that your faith is in God alone. JAMES 1:5-6

HOW ABOUT YOU?

Do you have an important, embarrassing, or fear-filled question? Whom can you talk about it with?

Dear God, Do you really care about my schoolwork?

April 12

CONSIDER THIS . . . God cares about every little thing about you. The Bible tells us that God knit you together in your mother's womb (Psalm 139:13). Have you ever seen someone knit?

First, the knitter envisions her product. She decides what she wants to make—a sweater, a scarf, a blanket. She determines what color would be best. Will it need to be lightweight yarn so it can be used all year? Heavier, for winter only? Next, she keeps her supplies in a safe, clean place to protect them. She wants the final product to reflect her forethought, her concern, her care, and her craft. When she finishes her knitting, it will be beautiful. The creation reflects the maker.

In the same way, *you* are God's creation. He thought about you before you were created. He planned you with a special beauty in mind. He wants everything you do and everything you are to reflect him and his intentions for you. Similarly, your work reflects who *you* are. When you work with forethought, concern, and care, it tells about you as a person. You do good work. You care about what kind of reports you turn in. You study for tests because it shows that you are diligent and prepared. When you make a mistake, you go back and fix it.

Not everyone can get an A for achievement, but we can all get an A for effort. A knitted blanket reflects the care of its creator. Your attitude and effort show what kind of a person you are. Your diligent work reflects honor to your Maker.

HOW ABOUT YOU?

What subjects do you try really hard at? What subjects are you tempted to slack off in?

GOD SAYS . . .

Work willingly at whatever you do, as though you were working for the Lord rather than for people. Remember that the Lord will give you an inheritance as your reward, and that the Master you are serving is Christ. COLOSSIANS 3:23-24

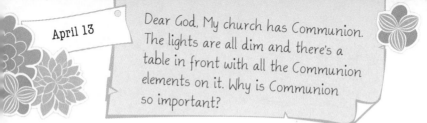

April 13

Dear God, My church has Communion. The lights are all dim and there's a table in front with all the Communion elements on it. Why is Communion so important?

CONSIDER THIS . . . Different Christian churches around the world celebrate many kinds of sacraments, that is, things we do on the outside to show holiness, grace, and spiritual life on the inside. Most Protestant churches believe there are two sacraments: baptism and Communion. Sometimes Communion is referred to as the Lord's Table, because it recreates and celebrates what Jesus said at the Last Supper.

The Last Supper was the one Jesus ate with his disciples right before he was crucified. He, of course, knew what was going to happen soon, even if the disciples weren't certain how it was all going to come about. The Lord knew that the most important part of his ministry, his coming to earth, was about to unfold—the sacrifice of his body so that the consequences for our sins would be paid through him.

He knew that the days and years ahead would have confusing moments and difficult times for all his disciples—including us. He knew that we might forget how much he loves us, or forget that his death made a way for us to live and to be forgiven.

Sometimes it's easier to recall important things if we have something physical to help us to remember. We tie strings around our wrists or write notes. Celebrating Communion is a physical way to help us remember again and again, whether we observe it every week, every month, or a few times a year, that Jesus loves us, and that he willingly allowed his body to be broken for us. Breaking the bread, and then taking it in to be a part of us, is such an important way to do that, he told us to do it until he returns.

GOD SAYS . . .
As they were eating, Jesus took some bread and blessed it. Then he broke it in pieces and gave it to the disciples, saying, "Take it, for this is my body." MARK 14:22

HOW ABOUT YOU?
Have you taken Communion? What does it mean to you?

Dear God, What does the wine, or grape juice, part of Communion mean?

April 14

CONSIDER THIS . . . Within the past few years there have been many more strange weather events on the earth. More earthquakes rattling more cities, big and little, and then the tragedies of disease and death that follow them. A huge tsunami swept over Japan and then furiously washed lives out to sea. But perhaps one of the most touching deaths—and the saving of a life—happened during a tornado in Massachusetts.

As the winds picked up and the swirling funnel drew closer to one house, a mother looked out of the window and saw that her home was directly in the path of the terrible twister. There was no time to escape. She grabbed her daughter and took her into the bathroom. After placing her daughter in the safety of the bathtub, the mother laid on top of her daughter, to protect her from all sides. The tornado flattened the house, but the daughter was saved. Her mother died. The mother's death, her blood, was shed to save her daughter's life.

Have you ever heard the phrase, "I'd take a bullet for you"? That means someone loves you so much that he or she would step in front of the path of a bullet heading right for you, sacrificing his or her life to save yours. That's what Jesus did—he took a bullet for us, the bullet leading to death. His blood was the payment for our eternal life. When we celebrate Communion, and drink the wine or grape juice, we're remembering the new covenant, or plan: Jesus' blood sacrificed for our lives.

HOW ABOUT YOU?

How much must a mother love her daughter, or a Savior love his child, to die for her?

GOD SAYS . . .

He took a cup of wine and gave thanks to God for it. . . . He said to them, "This is my blood, which confirms the covenant between God and his people. It is poured out as a sacrifice for many." MARK 14:23-24

CONSIDER THIS . . . Nearly everyone texts. Who doesn't? It's fast, easy, and fun. In only a few seconds your mom or dad can text you from work. A friend might text to see if you want to hang out. Your grandmother can picture-message you a snap of her by the pool on vacation.

Some of the most important messages we receive from friends and family are said in a few words:

- I love you, and I'm glad you love me.
- Good work—I knew you could do it!
- Be home soon . . . can't wait to see you!

But what about when we hear from God? When we think about what God has to share with us in the Bible, we can be overwhelmed by how much there is to read. There are wonderful longer stories. Think of the story of the Good Samaritan, who helped a stranger he found lying wounded in the road. Another favorite is when Peter walked on the water, but then nearly drowned as he took his eyes off of Jesus. We can learn great things about God through those stories. But he also says amazing things in only a few words, too.

- I have loved you with an everlasting love.
- I will never fail you. I will never abandon you.
- Trust in God, and trust in me!

In his Word, God speaks to us in long stories and letters and medium-size psalms, but also in verses that are easy to read and to the point, just like a text. There's nothing wrong with keeping it short and sweet.

GOD SAYS . . .

God spoke many times and in many ways. HEBREWS 1:1

HOW ABOUT YOU?

If you were to text a short message to God, what would you say? What might he reply back with?

INTERNATIONAL HIGH FIVE DAY

Dear God, What do you really think of what I'm doing with my life?

April 16

CONSIDER THIS . . . For some reason, a lot of people have this feeling that God is stern and forbidding. They picture him in heaven, sitting around with his heavenly binoculars, watching all of us here on the earth and waiting for us to mess up so he can zap us. They think that he's never happy. They believe that when we get one thing wrong, he's waiting to throw some more rules at us. People imagine him saying, "I'm so disappointed," or "You could have done better." Why do so many people think of God that way? His enemies must be floating rumors. . . .

Instead, here's the true picture of God: he loves you. He's not up in heaven looking down on you. He's right beside you, cheering you on no matter what's going on. Are you taking a test? He's there. Playing a sport? He's there. Giving a presentation in class? He's on it. He says things like "Good job!" and "I knew you could do it" and "You're the best!" He's not looking for your mistakes; he's watching for your victories. When you make one, he's right there to give you a fist bump or a high five.

Yes, he's holy. But he's also our friend.

Live like Christ. Today, be on the lookout for people you know to do something right. Cheer them on. Give them a fist bump or a high five and watch their faces light up with a smile.

HOW ABOUT YOU?

If you close your eyes, do you imagine God wagging his finger at you in disappointment, or do you see him offering a fist bump or a high five? Keep your eyes closed till you see him smiling . . . at you.

GOD SAYS . . .

The master was full of praise. "Well done, my good and faithful servant." MATTHEW 25:21

Dear God, Why do some Christians have fish symbols on their cars?

CONSIDER THIS . . . We live in a world that is comfortable using symbols to convey a message. When you text someone and you place two exclamation points at the end of your sentence, you're telling them that you're very happy—or angry!! Including emoticons is a quick way to show people how you feel instead of typing it all out. When you put a :) in the message, you're telling them that you're happy. Adding ;-) at the end of a sentence means you're being sarcastic or playful. And :(means you're sad. A few little images can convey a deep meaning.

When Jesus was here on earth, a lot of his disciples were fishermen. Jesus used fish as a symbol when he talked to his followers—he called us to be fishers of men. He miraculously fed a crowd of five thousand with a boy's lunch of five loaves of bread and two fish (John 6:1-13). After Jesus was crucified, there were years when it was dangerous to be a Christian. Christians began to draw half of a certain kind of fish in the sand, or on their hands, and if the person they were talking to was another Christian, they'd draw the other half. This kind of fish is called an ichthys (pronounced ICK-thus), or in Greek IXΘΥΣ.

In Greek, the letters stand for words that mean Jesus (I), Anointed (X), God (Θ), Son (Y), and Savior (Σ).

When Christians place the fish on their cars, they are declaring their faith to those around them with one small symbol. Hopefully, it encourages other believers to know that their brothers and sisters are close by in troubled times. It also helps remind us to set out our nets!

GOD SAYS . . .
Jesus called out to them, "Come, follow me, and I will show you how to fish for people!" MATTHEW 4:19

HOW ABOUT YOU?
What other symbols remind you of God?

April 18

Dear God, Is it okay to be a goof-off?

CONSIDER THIS . . . There is a time and a place for everything. When you're at someone's birthday party, you definitely don't want to be Dora Downer or Catfighting Cate. Right? But if you're at a funeral, or if your friend's pet has just died, you probably shouldn't tell the funniest joke you've ever heard. Those are the times when you need to be serious and respectful. Usually when people say they're "goofing off," they mean they are acting up in the wrong place. Maybe in class they're whispering with friends when the teacher is talking or people are still taking a test. In that case, it's better to be Silent Savvy and not Chatty Chelsea.

The world can sometimes seem like a hard place where bad things happen. Some people focus on all that is going wrong, the bad that might happen, or the work that lies ahead. But the blessed among us focus on the good in the day, the pleasant things that are on the horizon, and the fun that the next week is sure to bring. These people make life light and fun, full of laughter for everyone around them.

If you're a goof-off in a good way and at the right time, you'll show all those around you that God has filled you with joy. Your happiness will show others that God is good and that he turns dark nights into bright mornings.

So go ahead. Be Gabby the Goof-Off. Just make sure it's not in the middle of an exam!

HOW ABOUT YOU?

Are you more likely to look at the good side of things or the bad, the happy or the sad? Which attracts more followers to Jesus?

GOD SAYS . . .

When the LORD brought back his exiles to Jerusalem, it was like a dream! We were filled with laughter, and we sang for joy. And the other nations said, "What amazing things the LORD has done for them."
PSALM 126:1-2

Dear God, I'm afraid something scary and unexpected is going to happen to my family. Will it?

CONSIDER THIS . . . Last week a really big storm blew into my town. The electricity kept flickering on and off, and the howling wind made me think of all the unfriendly things that could be outside. And then a terrible cracking noise stopped us in our tracks. My family stood absolutely still before running to the window to see what had happened.

A beam from a flashlight told the news—a huge tree had cracked and fallen, just missing our house. The tree could have smashed the roof in and perhaps hurt one of us badly. We thanked God for keeping us safe.

The next day, when it was light again, we walked onto the patio to see what had happened. Perhaps the largest tree in our backyard had broken nearly in half. All that was left was a jagged, sharp-edged stump. The rest of the tree had thudded into our yard and spilled over into our neighbors' yard. The squirrel friends, who had been faithfully storing nuts in that tree in preparation for winter, looked as confused as we did.

Why that tree? they seemed to ask. *It felt so strong. We didn't expect this.* But then we watched as they carted their stash out of that tree and into another one standing firmly nearby. They were busily starting over, in an even stronger tree trunk—one that had proved its superior strength by surviving the storm.

Life is often like that. Things happen that seem scary and dangerous. The "tree" we don't expect to fall does tumble. And we scratch our heads and wonder why. While it may not be what we planned for, with God's help we are able to move forward with a new plan and stash our acorns somewhere new, stronger, and even better.

GOD SAYS . . .

If you make the LORD your refuge, if you make the Most High your shelter, no evil will conquer you; no plague will come near your home.
PSALM 91:9-10

HOW ABOUT YOU?

Have you ever been afraid of a situation that seemed at first to be terribly bad for your family, but in the end it wasn't? What unexpected blessings did the Lord bring out of that?

Dear God, Why won't my parents allow me to do what other girls are allowed to do, even if the other girls and their families are Christians?

April 20

CONSIDER THIS . . . Have you ever noticed how your parents know things about you that no one else does—like how your mom never puts gobs of peanut butter on your sandwich because you like only a little bit? Or how your dad never teases you in front of other people because he knows it embarrasses you? Lots of things are special about you, and lots of things are unique to your family. Every family is one of a kind. Each family is different.

When God set you in a family, he gave your parents an awesome—and fearsome—responsibility: to raise you in the way he requires. Your parents are responsible to God for that. When they meet God face-to-face, they will have to answer to him for the choices they made for you.

God has given your parents wisdom in raising you and your one-of-a-kind family. Their rules may be different from what other families have decided. That's okay. If you'd like your parents to think again about a decision on a movie or a TV show or clothing, you certainly can ask them to do so. But if they say no again, don't pester them or grow bitter. Be thankful that you have parents who truly understand you, even when you are *sure* that they don't. They seek to do the best for you. The Bible says their teaching is like a light, to keep you safe and show the right way during dark times, and it helps you to have life.

HOW ABOUT YOU?

What rules do your parents have that are hard for you to follow? How do you think your parents might be trying to protect you with these rules that bug you? (Hint: if you don't know, ask!)

GOD SAYS . . .

Obey your father's commands, and don't neglect your mother's instruction. . . . For their command is a lamp and their instruction a light.
PROVERBS 6:20, 23

Dear God, I have a friend who always needs help with everything. I don't want to help anymore. But aren't I supposed to help everyone?

CONSIDER THIS . . . This was the day—the field trip that the whole class had been looking forward to. Each person had emptied his or her backpack of schoolbooks, paper bits, pencils, and half-eaten candy bars. Instead, they were supposed to bring a small lunch, a bottle of water, a notepad, and a compass.

Most of the class did just that, but one girl felt that she wanted to bring more. Even though the day was warm, she packed a jacket. The ground was dry, but she threw in an extra pair of boots just in case. She wanted to take pictures, and since cell phones weren't allowed, she brought a camera. Her backpack was heavy.

As soon as the class arrived they began to hike into the woods, and it wasn't long before the girl with the overstuffed backpack was lagging behind. Her friend helped her carry it for a while, but then she got tired out too. "I can't help you carry it any longer," she said, "because I am getting too worn out to carry my own pack now, and I'm not enjoying the trip. You have to take some stuff out. Or carry it on your own."

This is how it is in life sometimes too. We are definitely asked to share the burdens of our friends and fellow Christians. And yet they are also called to make wise decisions about the choices they make—so their backpacks, and lives, aren't too heavy to bear.

The Lord doesn't expect anyone to buckle under the weight of someone else's choices. Help others, but don't feel bad when you say no so you don't overdo it.

GOD SAYS . . .

Share each other's burdens, and in this way obey the law of Christ. GALATIANS 6:2

HOW ABOUT YOU?

Do you have a friend who relies on you too much? What part can you help with, and what part do you have to politely say no to?

Dear God, Why are people trashing the environment? Don't Christians care about the world we live in?

April 22

CONSIDER THIS . . . Alongside a highway sat hundreds of blue-and-white garbage bags. They were not just on one highway on this particular weekend, but on every highway in the state. Sometimes there were ten bags stuffed with litter every few feet. Dump truck after dump truck was eventually loaded with this trash, and after emptying their loads, the trucks came back for more. How did all this garbage get there? It mostly came from adults tossing it out of car windows. Who was picking it all up? The signs along the way said, "Youth Ecology Working Here." In other words, kids!

So often we take for granted the things we are given. What if you gave someone you love a birthday present and they trashed it? You would be hurt! You spent a lot of time planning for and picking out that gift, and you want it taken care of and appreciated.

The earth is a gift that God has given to us, and we are to take good care of it. Some people don't think about or believe that it is a gift. Maybe that's why they trash it. Just because the earth is important, though, doesn't mean it's as important as some people think. After all, the earth was not made in God's image. People are. Still, we are to treat the earth with respect so that other people can enjoy it too.

Be a good caretaker of God's good gifts. Don't litter. If you see some trash, pick it up. Spend a day each spring and fall cleaning up the area around your house or your favorite park. Encourage others to do the same. Christians, maybe even more than others, should tend to and watch over the gifts God has given us.

HOW ABOUT YOU?

What things in the environment concern you? What can you do about it in the next month?

GOD SAYS . . .

The LORD God placed the man in the Garden of Eden to tend and watch over it. GENESIS 2:15

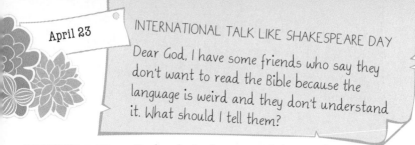

INTERNATIONAL TALK LIKE SHAKESPEARE DAY

Dear God, I have some friends who say they don't want to read the Bible because the language is weird and they don't understand it. What should I tell them?

CONSIDER THIS ... For hundreds of years, people have spoken of what a wonderful playwright and author William Shakespeare was. People refer to him as one of the best storytellers of all time. Five hundred years later his plays are still performed all over the world. So when you sit down to dig into one of his better-known stories, like *Romeo and Juliet*, you might scratch your head as you read, "What, art thou drawn among these heartless hinds? Turn thee, Benvolio. Look upon thy death."

Huh?

One publisher decided to take these terrific plays and put them into the kind of language we use today; the series is called No Fear Shakespeare. When "translated" to today's words, that same section reads, "What? You've pulled out your sword to fight with these worthless servants? Turn around, Benvolio, and look at the man who's going to kill you."

Better! Now I understand.

When the Bible was first translated into English, people used words like *thee* and *thou* and *ye* and *forthwith*, but we don't use those words anymore. That makes reading an older translation of the Bible hard, almost like reading a foreign language. There are very good, true translations, though, that use words just like you do. God gave us the Scriptures so we could better understand him. There are missionaries all over the world translating those Scriptures into the languages of every people so they can "hear" him for themselves and believe that Jesus came from God.

GOD SAYS ...

His disciples said, "At last you are speaking plainly and not figuratively. Now we understand that you know everything, and there's no need to question you. From this we believe that you came from God."

JOHN 16:29-30

HOW ABOUT YOU?

Do you have a copy of the Bible in easy-to-understand words that you can have handy to give to a friend? If not, how can you get a copy?

> Dear God, Why does the Bible say that I become a brand-new person when I become a Christian? Aren't I okay just as I am?

April 24

CONSIDER THIS . . . One day a mom was fixin' to bake up a batch of brownies for her family. She poured the brownie mix powder into a large bowl and then stepped over to the refrigerator to get the butter and eggs. While she did, her small daughter climbed up on a stool and looked into the bowl. Seeing the brown dust within, she reached over, grabbed a handful of soil from a plant on the counter, and threw it into the mix. When the mom came back, she stirred in the rest of the ingredients and put the brownies into the oven.

When she served the brownies, though, they just didn't taste right. Her little daughter finally piped up. "I helped you, Mommy. I put some of that in!" She pointed her finger to the potted plant. When the mother looked closer, she could see that a scoop of dirt was missing. Even though there was only the tiniest amount of dirt thrown in, it had ruined the whole batch. The next batch—made without any dirt—tasted chocolaty and delicious!

We humans are kind of like that brownie batter. God designed us perfectly, with all of the right ingredients. But when sin came into the world, and into our lives, it was like throwing the tiniest bit of dirt into the mix. You can't pretend it's not there, and you can't put a lot of whipped cream or frosting on it to cover up the taste. You have to remake the batch. When you become a Christian, you give God the old self, and he makes you new. It's still you—just without the dirt inside.

HOW ABOUT YOU?

Have you been made new? If not, you can ask God to make you new. Talk to your parents or another trusted adult about becoming a Christian.

GOD SAYS . . .

This means that anyone who belongs to Christ has become a new person. The old life is gone; a new life has begun!
2 CORINTHIANS 5:17

Dear God, I'm afraid my grades will start to fall if I get one bad grade on a test, even though I'm usually a good student.

CONSIDER THIS . . . You have a common, hurtful condition called perfectionism. A perfectionist is someone who has extremely high standards for herself and is unhappy with anything less. Such a person spends a lot of time being sad. Why? We all make mistakes—we come in second or last place, or we do things we wish we hadn't done. Perfectionists are disappointed when those things happen.

Now, if anyone were to ask you, "Do you think you can be perfect?" you would answer, "Of course not!" In your mind, you know you can't be perfect. But in your heart, you expect yourself not to make mistakes. If you do make mistakes, you're really hard on yourself, right? You say things like "I am so dumb!"

The Bible tells us that we are to continue to grow in our faith and in Christlikeness. But it's also clear that we won't be perfect before heaven. In fact, once we realize that we *can't* do everything just right on our own, *then* we realize how much we need help! Does a perfect person—who does everything right, knows all the answers, and can save herself in every situation—show how much she needs God? No! But a person who knows she has weaknesses knows she needs God.

When we tell God we can't do it on our own, we admit that we are weak. When we are weak, his power is made perfect in us. How? Because then we show others and ourselves the power of God at work. They know *we* can't do everything on our own, so we must be relying on Someone Else. Relax. God knows exactly who you are and what you can and can't do, and he loves you just as you are.

GOD SAYS . . .

Each time he said, "My grace is all you need. My power works best in weakness." So now I am glad to boast about my weaknesses, so that the power of Christ can work through me.
2 CORINTHIANS 12:9

HOW ABOUT YOU?

What are some times when you are hard on yourself? How could God's grace be at work in that situation?

Dear God, It doesn't feel like you're always helping me, even though I know you are. How does that work?

CONSIDER THIS . . . Do you remember the story of the three little pigs?

Three brothers, all pigs, were sent out into the world to make their fortunes and build their homes. The first pig was lazy and unwise; he decided to build his house out of straw. The second pig, a little smarter, constructed his house out of wood. And the third pig worked hard, worked smart, and crafted his home out of sturdy brick.

Soon after the pigs had finished building their houses, their enemy—a wolf who wanted to eat them—came around and visited their homes. He easily blew down the first pig's straw house. That pig had to run to the second brother's house. That house, made of wood, soon caved in under the wolf's breath too. Only the third house, built of brick by the wise pig, withstood the wolf over and over again, saving the little pigs' skins!

When we choose to build our houses on the rock of Jesus, rather than the sand of the world, we're doing the same thing. Hard times and difficult situations will blow into our lives, but because we've listened to Christ's teaching and obeyed his instructions we'll remain safe through each storm. The person who has built her house of straw, wood, or on the sand—that is, human wisdom alone—will not do so well. The person who uses sturdy brick on the Rock will withstand even the fiercest tornado—or wolf puffs.

HOW ABOUT YOU?

What steps can you take to make sure your house is built on the Rock and not on the sand?

GOD SAYS . . .

[Jesus said,] "Anyone who listens to my teaching and follows it is wise, like a person who builds a house on solid rock."

MATTHEW 7:24

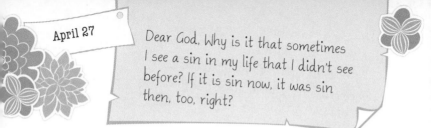

Dear God, Why is it that sometimes I see a sin in my life that I didn't see before? If it is sin now, it was sin then, too, right?

CONSIDER THIS . . . After a long, dark winter, one of the best things about spring is the sunshine that begins to appear more often. First, the sun appears just a day or two more than usual, and then three days, and pretty soon the sun is out almost every day as spring moves into summer. When the sun shines in through the windows in your room, it does more than spread cheery light. It reveals dust, dirt, smudges, and smears in places that you couldn't see in the winter gloom.

When the Lord draws near to you and gently whispers or convicts you about something in your life that is wrong, he's bringing light on an area that he wants you to see again. It might be a habit that needs to be dusted off, like using bad or sassy language. Perhaps it's an attitude that smudges the pure beauty of your heart, like laziness or anger. You may not have been mature enough or strong enough to have heard his whisper before. Or maybe you hadn't been close enough to hear or feel his quiet direction.

In any case, the time to clean things up is as soon as you can see that they need to be worked on. His bright light isn't shining on you to condemn. It's there to bring that cheery light into your life every day and to bring you closer to him.

GOD SAYS . . .
I could ask the darkness to hide me and the light around me to become night—but even in darkness I cannot hide from you. To you the night shines as bright as day. Darkness and light are the same to you.
PSALM 139:11-12

HOW ABOUT YOU?
Can you feel the Lord allowing light to fall on some dark places in your life? What is he telling you? Be quiet and sit still for a few minutes. Can you hear him?

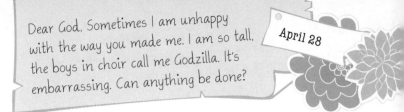

Dear God, Sometimes I am unhappy with the way you made me. I am so tall, the boys in choir call me Godzilla. It's embarrassing. Can anything be done?

April 28

CONSIDER THIS . . . Boys aren't always the most sensitive creatures, are they? Thankfully, they get better as they get older. But in the meantime, you still feel unhappy with the way you look!

Have you ever looked really closely at a baby? Usually we just look at them and think, *Oh, how cute*. Soft, fuzzy hair and a darling little toothless grin. Next time you look at a baby, though, notice how large his or her head is compared with the rest of his or her body. The head is much larger—or what you'd call "disproportionate." It means that parts of the body still have some catching up to do in order to be the right size to balance with the rest of the body.

Body parts don't all grow at the same rate. Heads grow large first, which is why babies have such large heads compared with their tiny bodies. Your "big" feet aren't going to end up being too big at all. Your nice long legs are already catching up with them. Boys and girls don't grow at the same rate, either. Girls grow sooner, and usually stop growing sooner, than boys do. That makes girls bigger than a lot of boys for a while. Most of those boys who are teasing you are probably just jealous of your height! Soon the boys will begin to catch up, too, and most of them will grow taller than you.

Ask the Lord to help you see all of the wonderful and amazing ways he made you. Then hang tight for a few years until the boys catch up—and grow up. When you have finished growing, all of your parts will fit together exactly and perfectly, just as God has planned. You will be a completely balanced young lady.

HOW ABOUT YOU?

What parts of yourself are you happy with? (Pick at least two!)

GOD SAYS . . .

You made all the delicate, inner parts of my body and knit me together in my mother's womb. Thank you for making me so wonderfully complex!

PSALM 139:13-14

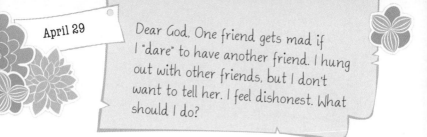

April 29

Dear God, One friend gets mad if I "dare" to have another friend. I hung out with other friends, but I don't want to tell her. I feel dishonest. What should I do?

CONSIDER THIS . . . There are two types of dishonesty—one is lying, which you have not done, and one is withholding necessary information, which you have not done. Be at peace. You haven't been dishonest.

Your friend made you feel as though you owe her an explanation for every move. The people who have legitimate control over you need to know where you are, with whom, and for how long. They would include your parents, a grandparent in charge, a day care provider, your school during the school day, and Sunday school teachers on Sunday or at a youth event. Not friends. Friends are to exercise *self*-control, not *other* control.

Your friend has made a condition on your friendship—you do things her way or she's not going to be your friend. That's controlling you. You don't feel free to be honest, to be yourself, because of that control. These types of friends generally are very nice and kind for a while. They can be fun to be around. But when you decide to do things your way and not their way, they make you "pay" emotionally.

Tell your friend that while you enjoy her company, you also have other friends. Encourage her to do the same, and if she can't, find a new friend. The Lord, who knew we'd need friends, took time to show us what a real friend is so we'd be wise and know the difference. Check out what a 1 Corinthians 13 friend would look like.

GOD SAYS . . .

Love is patient and kind. Love is not jealous or boastful or proud or rude. It does not demand its own way. It is not irritable, and it keeps no record of being wronged.
1 CORINTHIANS 13:4-5

HOW ABOUT YOU?

Do you have a friend or friends who punish you emotionally (ignoring you, leaving you out, getting angry with you) if you tell them no or do things your own way?

Dear God, I just go to school, do my homework and chores, and go to church. I really don't see how you can use me. Can you?

April 30

CONSIDER THIS . . . Of our five senses—touch, hearing, sight, taste, and smell—the one that we don't think of as powerful is smell. But it is! Did you know that if you can't smell things you can't really taste things? You probably learned this the last time your nose was stuffed up with a cold. Or do this little experiment—plug your nose with one hand and try taking a bite of food with the other. Doesn't taste too good, does it?

When you light a pumpkin spice candle, the little bit of light is pretty, but what's even better is the scent it sends throughout the room. If someone sprays too much perfume on herself, it's hard to keep your eyes from stinging or starting a domino effect of coughing! But when someone gently applies perfume, then it is a delight. Two favorite perfumes for girls are Love's Babysoft and Pink Sugar. Used lightly, when the girl enters the room, a hint of a sweet fragrance arrives with her or remains after she leaves.

Scripture tells us that we Christians are used by God to spread the knowledge of Christ everywhere, like a sweet perfume. It doesn't mean we have to race into a room, spray a bottle, and then leave. Rather, it means that when we come into a situation, if Jesus lives in us, we bring a bit of him everywhere we go. The kindness we offer, the words we speak, the affection and help we bring without even thinking about it shares our faith.

Just be wonderful you. It's an effective but gentle and sweet way to partner with God.

HOW ABOUT YOU?

What reaction do people have when you enter a room or a group, and when you leave it? Why?

GOD SAYS . . .

Now he uses us to spread the knowledge of Christ everywhere, like a sweet perfume. 2 CORINTHIANS 2:14

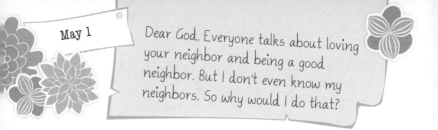

Dear God, Everyone talks about loving your neighbor and being a good neighbor. But I don't even know my neighbors. So why would I do that?

CONSIDER THIS . . . In days past, people depended on their close families and their neighbors for much more than we do now. They kept one another safe during dangerous times—kind of like our "block watch" or neighborhood watch programs. They knew one another better. You could borrow a cup of sugar from your neighbors or stop by to enjoy a cup of coffee with them. Kids rode bikes together, explored the neighborhood together, played with dolls together, or organized a game of Wiffle ball or kickball together.

As our world has become busier, and less connected, most people don't know very many of their neighbors. Even if they know some of their neighbors, they don't know them well. People would rather spend time inside watching TV or playing video games or working on the computer. But we still have a heart need to know a little about those people we live close to, those whose lawn mowers we hear, whose Christmas tree lights we see blinking from our windows.

There's a fun May Day tradition, always on the first day of May, that involves hanging a little posy of flowers on your neighbor's door. It's a way of bringing a bit of beauty and cheerfulness to your neighbor's day. You don't have to do posies—you can draw a pretty picture in front of your neighbors' house with sidewalk chalk, or offer to weed their garden plot, or bring cookies by with your mom. The idea is just to reach out and offer friendliness in a world that's not very friendly anymore.

GOD SAYS . . .

In the same way, let your good deeds shine out for all to see, so that everyone will praise your heavenly Father. MATTHEW 5:16

HOW ABOUT YOU?

What are two things you could do for your neighbors that would be small but pleasant, and let your good deed shine for them to see and bring praise to God?

Dear God. When I tried to share about you with one of my neighbor friends, she totally shut me out. Her parents even got mad. What happened?

CONSIDER THIS . . . It can be so hard to share our faith—we often feel nervous that other people will think we're weird or snobby because we tell them that Christianity is the only way to heaven. And then when people reject us—or get mad at us—it really stings. We think, *Why did this happen? I thought I was doing the right thing!*

The truth is that you did exactly the right thing. Jesus tells us in Mark 16:15, "Go into all the world and preach the Good News to everyone." That is exactly what you did! Jesus also tells us in Luke 21:17 that some people will hate us because we follow him. Some people just want to live their own way, not God's way.

Those words you shared with your friend may end up being very powerful in her life later on. Did you know that some seeds stay inactive and almost unseen for many years before they are ready to sprout and grow into plants? This might be true with your friend, too.

Sometime when she is in trouble or lonely or looking for an answer, the words you spoke to her heart may sprout and grow into a search for faith in Christ. Keep on sharing the Good News. You can share the Good News when God does something in your life, you can pass along a Christian book to a friend, or you can invite someone to a fun church outreach.

God will bless you, and he knows which seeds will sprout!

HOW ABOUT YOU?

Do you know someone who needs to hear the Good News? When can you tell him or her? How will you do it?

GOD SAYS . . .

He told them, "Go into all the world and preach the Good News to everyone. Anyone who believes and is baptized will be saved. But anyone who refuses to believe will be condemned." MARK 16:15-16

Dear God, Sometimes when I walk into a room, everyone looks at me and then gets quiet. Are people talking behind my back?

CONSIDER THIS . . . Although shouting is loud, and yelling can make you want to cover your ears, one of the most unsettling sounds of all is very, very soft. It's a whisper.

When we believe people are talking about us, it hurts. We know that what they are saying is not nice, or else they would say it aloud. We understand that we won't like what they are saying, or they'd feel free to tell us, or keep talking once we arrived. Whispers, like gossip, make us feel unloved, unwanted, and unwelcome. Your back doesn't have to be turned for people to talk behind it. Sometimes they do it right in front of you, by text, or online.

If you ask the whisperers, kindly, if they were talking about you, they may deny it. Go ahead and ask anyway. You will know you've done what you're called to do—kindly confront people. If they have nothing to hide, they'll tell you. If they do have something to hide, well, you'll know that, too.

You can't do anything about those who choose to sin. You can, however, choose the kind of person *you* are. You can choose to speak sincerely, which means without any deceit or falseness. Most of the time, we think that means just not straight-up lying. But it also means you shouldn't speak in whispers what you'd feel uncomfortable saying out loud. Soon, other girls with good hearts and clean mouths will see that you don't whisper, and they'll entrust you with their friendship.

It helps to remember that God hears even the smallest whisper. He hears not only the ones against you, but also the ones you speak.

GOD SAYS . . .

Listen to me, you who know right from wrong, you who cherish my law in your hearts. Do not be afraid of people's scorn, nor fear their insults.
ISAIAH 51:7

HOW ABOUT YOU?

Have you ever been hurt by someone talking behind your back? How did that make you feel? Have you ever whispered about someone else? How can you stop the whispering?

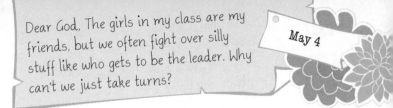

Dear God, The girls in my class are my friends, but we often fight over silly stuff like who gets to be the leader. Why can't we just take turns?

May 4

CONSIDER THIS ... Preschoolers are grabby—they take what they want no matter who else wants it. They cut in line and don't care who sees. They play with a toy for a long time, even if someone is waiting. Usually, a parent or a teacher steps in to make them share.

When kids are older, like you are, being selfish isn't so obvious. A group leaves you out because you didn't play by the leaders' unspoken rules. People pout and punish if their ideas aren't followed. As you get older, the adults around you tend to see less, because selfishness is happening under the surface. You're not supervised as much. But that can actually be a *good* thing. Why? Because it allows *you* to be a leader by making Christlike choices rather than being forced to by an adult.

Christianity is the upside-down faith. The world says, "Get as much as you can." Jesus says, "Give away your coat." The world says, "Keep away from the unpopular." Jesus says, "Visit the sick and those in prison." The world says, "Get your turn." Jesus says, "Those who are first will be last." Choose friends who aren't going to be bossy all of the time. Those kinds of people don't easily change. But within a group of friends, start leading upside down. Let others choose the game. Sit quietly until you're asked what you'd like. Go to the back; take the smallest prize. You'll be surprised. When you stop looking out for yourself and are interested in others, many people will rally around to be interested in *you*! Think of it like a snow globe. When it's right-side up, it looks okay. When you turn it upside down, you can see beautiful things you didn't see before.

HOW ABOUT YOU?

What are three ways you can be an upside-down leader in your group of friends?

GOD SAYS ...

Those who exalt themselves will be humbled, and those who humble themselves will be exalted. LUKE 14:11

Dear God, I heard my pastor say that Scripture is alive and powerful. How can the words in a book be alive?

CONSIDER THIS . . . The Bible is a book, of course, and it's a book with many different kinds of writing in it. The Bible has poetry, and stories, and parables. It is a history book. It is a science book. It contains biographies. It's a law book, and a love story. The Bible is also full of mysteries!

One of the mysteries in Scripture is how the book can be made up of words that lie flat on a piece of paper that will eventually decay, but it can still be considered alive. Maybe one way to look at it is like seeds. Seeds stay in their packet for years and years not growing at all. If water is never added to them, they won't grow, but they will decay. If you add water, sunlight, and food, then the seeds will grow into a plant.

The words in the Bible may be flat for some people, but once the Holy Spirit is added to the words they come alive. The Holy Spirit in you will help you understand what the words mean, not only for everyone, but especially for *you*. You can read a verse one time and, while the meaning won't change, what you're supposed to do with it might. Each time it's new. The words in the Bible may not change, but you do!

Don't worry. God will help you understand what you need to know each time you open the pages of Scripture.

GOD SAYS . . .

All Scripture is . . . useful to teach us what is true and to make us realize what is wrong in our lives. . . . God uses it to prepare and equip his people to do every good work.
2 TIMOTHY 3:16-17

HOW ABOUT YOU?

What has the Lord shared with you through Scripture lately?

Dear God, What is the Fall? I hear people talking about it all the time, but I'm not sure what they mean.

May 6

CONSIDER THIS . . . Right after God made man and woman, they lived in the Garden of Eden. It was a perfect place where there was no sin, no sickness, no pain, and no shame. There was one rule, though. It was for Adam and Eve's protection. They were not supposed to eat fruit from the tree of the knowledge of good and evil. And they were fine with that.

But even if people don't go looking for sin, it comes looking for them.

Satan found them one day, and he asked, "Did God really say you must not eat the fruit from any of the trees in the garden?" (Genesis 3:1). This was not what God said, of course. But Satan takes the truth and twists it just a little, enough to confuse, and tempt.

You know how the story goes: "'You won't die!' the serpent replied to the woman. 'God knows that your eyes will be opened as soon as you eat it, and you will be like God, knowing both good and evil'" (Genesis 3:4-5). So Adam and Eve ate the forbidden fruit and sin entered the world. The world, and people, "fell" from their perfect setup to one which now had sickness, pain, and shame.

But there is good news. If you fall on a concrete sidewalk, you might have a twisted ankle or even a skinned knee. It definitely hurts, but you're not dead. You can recover. Because of Jesus, the Fall in the Garden of Eden doesn't have to be deadly either.

HOW ABOUT YOU?

When has someone lied to you and you believed him or her? What were the consequences?

GOD SAYS . . .

[Eve] saw that the tree was beautiful and its fruit looked delicious, and she wanted the wisdom it would give her. So she took some of the fruit and ate it. Then she gave some to her husband, who was with her, and he ate it, too.
GENESIS 3:6

Dear God, I became a Christian last year. The other day, I was trying to explain this to my friend, but she didn't get it. How can I explain it?

CONSIDER THIS . . . Many people have a favorite drink they enjoy in the morning. Some drink orange juice. Other people drink coffee, and some drink hot tea. In the summer, iced tea is delicious and refreshing any time of the day. Have you ever watched how tea is made?

Tea is actually dried leaves from a certain plant. The leaves are broken up into small pieces, kind of like spices and herbs are. Then the leaves are usually placed into a little pouch. You put the pouch into a mug, pour hot water over it, let it sit for a little while, and . . . voilà! You have tea.

So . . . is the water still water at that point? And if not, then where did it go?

When the water was poured over the tea bag and left to steep in the mug, the water was transformed into tea. It's not water anymore. No one would look at it and say, "Wow, look at that delicious mug of brown water." No! They'd call it what it is now: tea.

When you became a Christian, you were transformed by God from one person into, kind of, another. The parts of you that made you who you are still remain. (You can test for H2O in tea, too, and still find it.) You're still you. But you've also been transformed into something new. Plain water no more. You're now . . . chill.

Iced tea!

GOD SAYS . . .

Don't copy the behavior and customs of this world, but let God transform you into a new person by changing the way you think. Then you will learn to know God's will for you, which is good and pleasing and perfect. ROMANS 12:2

HOW ABOUT YOU?

Do you remember when you first decided to follow Jesus? If you were young, do you decide to follow him every day, still? How are you different because of that?

Dear God, How do I know that the Bible is the true Word of God?

May 8

CONSIDER THIS . . . Whenever we want an answer we can trust, we can always turn to the Bible. But how do we know for sure that the Bible is the true Word of God?

The Scriptures that make up the Bible have been copied over thousands of years, from the first person who wrote down the words by hand to the person who is helping to make new translations today using a computer. In Old Testament times, if a scribe (the person copying the Scriptures) made even one mistake, he had to start the entire page all over just to make sure it had no mistakes. Today, many people who love the Lord and have studied his Word go over each new translation before it is published to make sure it is correct. The Bible does not disagree with itself, and although stories in it can be told from different points of view, we can be sure it is true.

God told people like Jeremiah and Moses to write things down so his people would know what he wanted them to know. Paul tells us in 1 Corinthians 14:37 his writings are a "command from the Lord." And most important of all, the Bible itself tells us that Scripture is "God-breathed." Stick out your palm and breathe on it. Your breath came from inside you. The Scriptures came from inside God.

There is, of course, a point at which you must have faith. Do you believe that God is powerful enough to create the entire universe just by speaking it into being? Then isn't he powerful enough to make sure that the words he wanted written down for his people stay pure and whole throughout time?

Of course he is!

HOW ABOUT YOU?

Is God powerful enough to make sure that the Bible says just what he wants it to say? Do you believe he watched over the words being written in his book? Why?

GOD SAYS . . .

All Scripture is God-breathed.
2 TIMOTHY 3:16 (NIV)

Dear God, A lot of people think the Bible is a big rule book and that Christians just want to take away everything fun. Why did you make rules?

CONSIDER THIS . . . Whether you live in the country, or a small town, or a large city, you've surely seen stop signs—and red lights. One day, when you begin to drive, you'll pay even closer attention to them.

Red lights ask us to stop, for our safety. If the light is red for us, it means there might be traffic crossing in front of us. Have you ever been in a car where someone raced through a red light by mistake, or went ahead and drove through one anyway, tired of waiting? If you have, you'll know how scary it felt. You might have even squeezed your eyes shut. If the driver goes ahead and drives into the traffic anyway, it's very likely that one or all of you, and the people in the other car, will be hurt. Most people don't ask why the light is red. Inside, they know why. They must not go forward or they, and others, will be harmed.

If a person really looks through the Bible, they will see that there are very few sections that are telling people what NOT to do. And when there are passages that say no, it's because God knows that moving forward with that activity will cause harm to us, or to someone else, or to both, even though it may seem like a good idea at the time! We may want to do wrong things sometimes, because we're still here on earth and can make bad choices. Don't be afraid to read God's Word, or share it with others. God's not trying to kill anyone's pure fun any more than a red light at a busy intersection is trying to hold back good times!

GOD SAYS . . .

The sinful nature is always hostile to God. It never did obey God's laws, and it never will. ROMANS 8:7

HOW ABOUT YOU?

What are some things that you know for sure God has said no to? Why do you think he has said no to those specific things?

Dear God, If there are red lights in the Bible, are there yellow lights too?

May 10

CONSIDER THIS . . . Yes! There is an old joke that a yellow traffic light means, "hurry up, speed, and get through!" If you watch how drivers behave when approaching yellow lights, you might think that's exactly what it means. But it doesn't. A yellow light indicates the following:

> caution
> pay attention
> potential danger
> be warned and alert

In life, too, there are definitely times where there is no clear "No. Stop!" red-light answer, but there's also not a clear "It's okay to go ahead" green-light answer, either. These are times when it's important to go to the Lord in prayer, and to also ask the advice of people who care about you and are known for making wise decisions. There are also times when you *can* do something—meaning it's not a sin—but it may not be wise to do so. For example, you could eat only chocolate all day every day. That's not a sin, but it wouldn't be wise. You could only play one kind of game all day. That's not a sin, but it would be boring and likely bad for your brain! You could choose to be friends with someone who isn't kind to another friend of yours. Again, it's allowable, but it may not be the best choice.

Sometimes, it's even easier to make a decision when the light is red rather than when it's yellow. You need more wisdom at yellow lights. Thankfully, God will provide it for you and help you to do just the right thing.

HOW ABOUT YOU?

Is there anything in your life that it might be smarter to say no to than yes? If so, what is it?

GOD SAYS . . .

You say, "I am allowed to do any-thing"—but not everything is good for you. You say, "I am allowed to do anything"—but not everything is beneficial. Don't be concerned for your own good but for the good of others. 1 CORINTHIANS 10:23-24

Dear God, There must be green lights in the Bible, too, right? I've been waiting to hear what we can do!

CONSIDER THIS . . . Yes—there are lots of green lights! When you read through the Bible you'll see that the Lord laughed and ate dinner with his neighbors. He went fishing. He taught. He slept. Jesus went to parties and spent time with his friends. He had many friends, and they had good times together too. One surprising thing you'll find is that when you do what *is* good, you will actually *feel* good. People who don't know or follow God don't understand that, and so it's easy for them to assume all the fun will be taken away. But just like a good meal makes you feel healthy, a good night's sleep refreshes you, a good movie makes you laugh, or a good friend fills your heart with love, good is good.

Scripture tells us many things that are good, among them the kind of "fruit," or actions, attitudes, and activities, that spring out of a person who is closely following Jesus. When you live for God, you'll see love in yourself, for yourself, and for others. You'll have disappointments, but they will soon turn to joy. Even when you're worried, you'll find that you can have peace. When you're out having a good time, you don't mind if people go first. And if someone needs help or a good word, you're there to assist. Your gentle spirit will help make sure that people enjoy your company, and you'll get to go more places than those who are bossy. Your self-control will help you pay attention to yellow lights and stop when they're red. But mostly, you'll just drive into the great life God has planned for you and . . .

Go . . . go . . . go!

GOD SAYS . . .

But the Holy Spirit produces this kind of fruit in our lives: love, joy, peace, patience, kindness, goodness, faithfulness, gentleness, and self-control. There is no law against these things! GALATIANS 5:22-23

HOW ABOUT YOU?

What things do you most enjoy doing, and with whom? Do you believe that God is pleased and happy to see you having a good time?

Dear God, Your Word says if I look for you I'll find you. But the world is very big. How am I supposed to know where to look?

CONSIDER THIS . . . Every once in a while, a kid goes missing. Once a little boy was standing with his mother in a clothing store. The lines were long, and the little boy was tired of waiting. *There are more important things to do,* he thought. He slipped his hand from his mom's hand and took off.

He hadn't been gone for very long when the mom realized her little boy was gone! She looked all around her and began calling out his name. He was nowhere to be found. She asked the people around her to help. But he was so small and the store was so big. The little boy had disappeared.

The mom had to think. Where would the little boy have gone? Then she remembered that her son loved pets and had often wanted to visit the nearby pet store. The mom took off, chasing after someone she loved, and found him. He had gone to visit the pets and was waiting for her. She located her boy by remembering where he would want to be found.

When God tells us to look for him, he doesn't expect us to find him like a needle in a haystack. He doesn't expect us to look all over the whole world for him. No, the word he chose for *look* means "to search for in worship and prayer." He has not only asked you to look for him, but he's told you where to find him!

Although Jesus is all around you, and with you, when you sing songs of praise to him, or bring him honor by sharing him with others, or connect your heart with his through prayer, you'll have found him in a strong and powerful way.

He's waiting.

HOW ABOUT YOU?
Where and how can you find God now?

GOD SAYS . . .
If you look for me whole-heartedly, you will find me.
JEREMIAH 29:13

Dear God, Other people around me at school dress kind of immodestly. It's awkward and annoying. What can I do?

CONSIDER THIS . . . Sometimes girls dress inappropriately because they don't know any better. Sometimes what is immodest to you is not to someone else. Different families choose different standards. Many people around the world have a variety of ideas about what is proper to wear and not wear. Some cultures want women to show nothing but their eyes. Some cultures find it okay if women are dressed in very little. Christian people are called to dress decently and appropriately, which means with good taste and modesty. They must show respect for their own bodies, and respect the fact that others around them may not want to look at a lot of their skin.

No matter what the issue, though, girls can be catty and mean about other girls. They gossip about if they're wearing too much, or too little. That's being judgmental.

What *can* you do? You can model a healthy, fashionable, modest style with joy. The Bible says that Christians can influence others by modeling good behavior. So persuade people by the way you live. You can act kindly, so that your inner beauty is in line with your outer beauty. Develop your own fun sense of style. Mix and match cute but appropriate clothing. Find a hairstyle that is uniquely you.

Whenever you're tempted to judge someone or talk about her because of her clothing choices, pray for her instead. Just a quick prayer, in your mind. You'll be surprised by how gossiping about someone hardens your heart toward her, but praying for her softens your heart toward her instead.

GOD SAYS · · ·

I want women to be modest in their appearance. They should wear decent and appropriate clothing. 1 TIMOTHY 2:9

HOW ABOUT YOU?

Are you tempted to gossip about or look down on inappropriately dressed girls? Write out a prayer for one of them (you don't need to use her name if someone shares your book).

Dear God, Why do I have to go to the dentist? I hate the noisy drill, I hate the big bib, and I hate the smell. Help!

May 14

CONSIDER THIS . . . You gotta admit that pretty much no one likes going to the dentist. Don't you feel bad for those dentists, who try so hard to help you keep your teeth in good shape, when no one wants to visit them?

Visits to the doctor, shots, and fluoride treatments are definitely not on anyone's list of fun things to do. But the Lord gave each of us a wonderful, one-of-a-kind body. We need to take care of it. Our bodies are our helpers and friends. Our hands allow us to do work, play sports, cook meals for our families, and hug people. Our feet take us where we want to go. And kick soccer balls! Our stomachs digest dinner, and our ears listen to music. And then there's the mouth!

Mouths help us eat dinner. Can you imagine chewing a steak, or a carrot, or a candy bar with no teeth? It would be nearly impossible. Our mouths help us to speak words of love or to call for help. Our tongues help us to taste good food. (Just don't stick yours out at your brother or sister!)

A lot of times people think it's holy and important to take care of the spirit, or the mind, or the heart, and they forget about the body. But God wants us to take care of our bodies, too. Be sure to do what you need to do to keep your body healthy. Even dentist visits. Take care of your body, because your body takes care of you!

HOW ABOUT YOU?

What part of taking care of your body, and keeping it healthy, bothers you the most? Exercise? Getting shots or taking medicine? Can you see a good reason to keep doing it . . . when you have to?

GOD SAYS . . .

Dear friend, I hope all is well with you and that you are as healthy in body as you are strong in spirit.
3 JOHN 1:2

Dear God, Why does Jesus love children so much?

CONSIDER THIS ... Have you ever been in a home where a toddler lives? The parents take care not to drop pennies or other small objects—they don't want the baby to put such things in her mouth and choke. They put locks on toilets so their young child can't fall in and drown. They lock cupboards where poisons are stored to keep a curious toddler safe. When there are people around us who need special care or looking out for, we naturally tend to look out for them more.

The Bible tells us that God places great importance on taking care of people who need extra help. Maybe it's someone who doesn't have a dad. Maybe it's someone who doesn't have a husband or much money. Maybe it's kids. Jesus himself warns that a terrible death would be better than the judgment that waits for people who lead children astray. He also tells us that the angels that protect children are always in God's presence—a place of instant access. Kids are important. They have important things to teach adults here on earth, too.

Girls like you get used to learning from adults. Jesus says adults can learn from kids, too. The kind of faith that kids have is the faith Jesus is looking for. Just like a toddler trusts that her parent will catch her if she jumps into deep water, so, too, do most kids trust God to catch them wherever life leads. Kids talk openly and honestly with Jesus. They usually aren't ashamed of his name. They run toward Jesus. They are often humble. That's the kind of faith you can model for the adults around you. You can be a good teacher too.

GOD SAYS ...

Anyone who becomes as humble as this little child is the greatest in the Kingdom of Heaven. MATTHEW 18:4

HOW ABOUT YOU?

Who around you needs your protection? Who in your life protects you? Can you be a good example for adult Christians by being humble, honest, open, and trusting of Jesus?

Dear God, There are a lot of scary things going on in the world. Am I safe?

CONSIDER THIS . . . More bad things do seem to be happening in our world right now. Or maybe we just have the technical ability to report it all, quickly, from everywhere. There are changes in governments and lots of people protesting. The economies of many countries are struggling, and people are losing their jobs. Many floods, tornadoes, and other natural disasters are occurring. Earthquakes happen more frequently.

The earth quakes when parts of it hit other parts of it underground. It's almost like bumper cars hitting one another and causing a shake, or someone sticking something under a bottle cap to pop the top off. If you happen to be outside when an earthquake strikes, you'll see the street rippling just like a blanket that someone is shaking up and down. If you're inside, you might feel the building go from side to side. It can be scary!

You don't have to be in an earthquake to be scared, though. Sometimes the wars and conflicts in other parts of the world can frighten us. So can changes in our own homes. Earthquakes, wars, and changes are nothing new, though. God has overseen all of those things for thousands of years, and he still has his eye on them, and on you, today.

Life on earth can be unstable, and unexpected things can happen to us. But God never changes. His love is always present to care for us, to help us through whatever comes along. Now that's news worth sharing!

HOW ABOUT YOU?

Are there any natural disasters that you are fearful of? Which ones? How about man-made disasters? You can talk to God about your fears and trust that he will take care of you, no matter what.

GOD SAYS . . .

"The mountains may move and the hills disappear, but even then my faithful love for you will remain. My covenant of blessing will never be broken," says the LORD, who has mercy on you. ISAIAH 54:10

Dear God, My parents yell at each other and sometimes at me. I really hate it when they yell. I worry about them getting a divorce.

CONSIDER THIS . . . It can make anyone nervous to listen to parents fight—even if they don't raise their voices. After all, your whole world seems to rest on how they act. They're your sense of safety! And when that's in danger, it feels scary.

Really, though, your parents are probably just tired and stressed. It's hard to be an adult. When you're a kid, you think it will be so cool to be an adult—you get to do your own thing and make your own rules. But when you *are* an adult, it's hard to have so many responsibilities. One of the most important responsibilities your parents have is taking care of you. They're probably trying hard. Stress overwhelms adults, and when overwhelmed, even the best parents might yell. It doesn't mean they don't love you, and it doesn't mean they're going to get a divorce.

You can't control your parents, but you can control yourself by not yelling back. Some of the most important jobs you have as their daughter are to love, honor, and obey your parents. The Bible says that if we honor our parents, it will go well with us. It's God's promise!

If your parents' yelling upsets you, respectfully talk with your parents during a calm, relaxed time. Tell them how you feel. Tell them when you notice it most, that it worries you, and how you feel when you're yelled at. Most likely it will change how they act, because parents work hard to make their kids feel safe and loved. But even if it doesn't, keep doing what you know is right. Honor your parents in how *you* talk to them—and to others. No matter what someone else does, you can always choose what is right.

GOD SAYS . . .
"Honor your father and mother." This is the first commandment with a promise. EPHESIANS 6:2

HOW ABOUT YOU?
Do your parents ever talk to each other in a way that worries you? What are two things you can do?

Dear God, What's the point of doing dishes all the time? Why don't we just eat off paper plates?

CONSIDER THIS . . . It's true, chores are no fun. Cleaning up after dinner can be especially painful. Everyone is tired, people have homework to do, and it's usually the time of day when the kitchen is the messiest. Loading the dishwasher can be a pain.

It's okay to use paper plates sometimes. They were made for quick meals. Picnics wouldn't be the same without them, or backyard barbecues. A fast supper when you're on the way out the door is okay too. But who wants to invite a new friend or a family from church over to eat on disposable dishes? And who wants to eat Christmas dinner on paper plates?

Pretty much no one. Beautiful dishes with lovely patterns, rimmed in gold, and gleaming with special foods are what many families use for Easter, or Christmas, or even every day. To feel special. Like our time together as a family is set apart. People don't throw away good china, and they don't store it under the sink. They take good care of it because it's expensive!

In a strange way, the Bible tells us that we Christians are very much like those pretty dishes. God has made us for something special, something wonderful and important. Our words and works are not to be disposable, throwaway, of no account. It takes more work to hand wash beautiful dishes than to throw away paper ones. And it takes some effort to keep your life pure. It's okay, though. It's better to be a pretty plate than a dirty dish.

HOW ABOUT YOU?

Do you realize that you are fine china, set apart by God for special occasions? What can you do to keep yourself pure?

GOD SAYS . . .

If you keep yourself pure, you will be a special utensil for honorable use. Your life will be clean, and you will be ready for the Master to use you for every good work. 2 TIMOTHY 2:21

Dear God, Whenever I get money, I want to spend it all right away. What can I do?

CONSIDER THIS . . . There are so many things in the world we live in—things to do, things to buy, places to go. It's like those restaurants that have 150 items on the menu. It makes for a very hard time deciding on just one thing to order! Too many choices can confuse or overwhelm us.

That's sometimes how it is when you get money. Suddenly you realize how many things you'd like, how many things you could buy. You might also realize that there are things you want that cost more than you have. Or you might have a heart to help people in need with your new wealth. Here's a system that might help you make good money decisions.

First, get three containers. They might be plastic food-storage containers, sandwich bags, or baby-food jars with lids. On one write, "Buy Now!" On the second write, "Buy Later!" On the third write, "God's Heart." From now on, whenever you get money, divide it among those three containers right away. Talk with your parents about how much to spend now, how much to save for something bigger, and how much to give in a way that honors God. Whenever you do that, you will get three different great feelings. First, you'll get the fun of having mad money, money you can spend however you want, right away. Even on junk! Second, you'll have the pleasure of looking forward to buying something you need to save for. You'll also have the satisfaction when you get it. Third, you'll have the joy and pleasure of giving something to God, by giving to the people he loves.

GOD SAYS . . .

The wise store up choice food and olive oil, but fools gulp theirs down.
PROVERBS 21:20 (NIV)

HOW ABOUT YOU?

Do you have a good system to spend, save, and give? If not, when will you make one? What do you think happens in a person's heart when she spends some, saves some, and gives some away?

CONSIDER THIS . . . A group of kids planned to celebrate their graduation from middle school at Disneyland with their entire class. Although one of the girls, Brenda, had a broken leg, she did have crutches. With them, she could get around okay. Her best friend, Amber, said she'd be right with her to help.

Once the group of kids got to the park entrance, though, they were quickly separated in the crowd of thousands of people waiting to see Mickey and Minnie. Amber gave the person at the entrance booth her ticket and then set out to find her injured friend. Amber scanned the crowds to the left, and the crowd right ahead of her. She looked at the gate again, and then scanned the crowd to the right. Finally, looking way in the far corner, Amber spotted her friend Brenda, leaning against a tree. She'd dropped one of her crutches and couldn't move!

After Amber picked up the crutch and brought it to Brenda, the best friends were ready to go, sticking together and having fun as they spent the day at the happiest place on earth.

God says that he, too, scans the crowds. He's looking for his friends—that is, people whose hearts are fully committed to him. Once he finds them, he brings them whatever they need to strengthen them for the minute, day, or week ahead.

This isn't the only way God helps us, of course. The Bible is filled with other examples. But it feels good to be so loved that the Lord of the universe is scanning the crowd for you!

HOW ABOUT YOU?

When was one time that God strengthened you?

GOD SAYS . . .

The eyes of the LORD search the whole earth in order to strengthen those whose hearts are fully committed to him. 2 CHRONICLES 16:9

Dear God, Is that your only name?

CONSIDER THIS . . . Everybody has a given name, but there are also names, or titles, we take on that describe who we are. When you go to training and work hard, you are *Athlete*. When you play music and sing, you become *Musician*. Depending on who you're talking to and what you want to show about yourself, you may describe yourself differently. Each of us has different names and titles; they help define who we are.

Sometimes it's easy to put God in a place in our minds where he is only one thing, just "God." But there is so much more to him than that. He has more than one hundred different names. Each one describes an aspect of who he is. Just as it's exciting to find out new things about our friends, it can be so wonderful when we discover a new side of God that we never knew about before.

One of God's names is *Yahweh Shalom*. This means "the Lord is peace." This name tells us that God actually is our peace. He *is* peace and will *give* peace to us as he gives us himself. Just like when we're sad or lonely we might talk to a friend whom everybody describes as cheerful or funny, we go to Christ to find our peace. When we pray to him, ask him for his peace, and bring our troubles to him, he takes them from us and gives us comfort in their place.

So next time you feel stressed out or upset, talk to him and you'll find the peace he wants to give to you.

GOD SAYS . . .
Gideon built an altar to the LORD there and named it Yahweh-Shalom (which means "the LORD is peace"). The altar remains in Ophrah in the land of the clan of Abiezer to this day.
JUDGES 6:24

HOW ABOUT YOU?
What names or titles do you give yourself or use about yourself? Which ones do you prefer, and why?

Dear God, I think my parents love my brother more than they love me. Should I tell them what I think?

May 22

CONSIDER THIS . . . Remember Joseph? His father, Jacob, loved him most of all, and all of his brothers were jealous of that. It led them to sell Joseph to traders, who then sold him as a slave in Egypt. Amazingly, this kind of jealousy goes back to the very first family ever, with Adam and Eve's sons. The oldest son, Cain, thought that God loved his brother Abel more than him. So Cain killed his brother.

Feeling like you don't receive enough love, or that the people who should love you equally have a favorite, is common in every family. It's probably true that there are some parents who really do care for one child more than the other children, and that's sad. But it's more common that parents might feel closer to a sick child, or a child who is hurting or in need for a short period of time. Then they might turn their focus on the other kids.

Maybe one of your parents has more in common with your brother than with you. That may make it easier for them to get along, but it does not mean that parent loves you less.

One thing is true. No matter what parents do, and no matter what Cain thought, God does not play favorites. He loves his children equally. His children may not understand that by looking at his actions, but it's true. We know it because he tells us so. The quickest way to clear the problem between you and your parents is to let them know what you're feeling and why, and then give them the chance to speak for themselves on the matter.

The one who always loves you will be right there in the midst of your conversation.

HOW ABOUT YOU?

Do you think your parents love you less than one of your siblings?

GOD SAYS . . .

God has no favorites.
COLOSSIANS 3:25

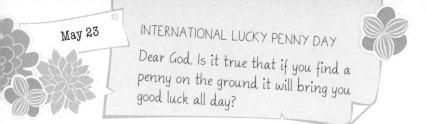

Dear God, Is it true that if you find a penny on the ground it will bring you good luck all day?

CONSIDER THIS . . . It really is fun to be walking down the street and find a dime or a quarter, or to see a dollar bill that has blown into a fence and get to pocket it. (Assuming it doesn't belong to anyone else!) But there's something magical and fun about finding a penny. Maybe it's the copper color, or maybe it's the myth that follows these coins. Are pennies really lucky?

Luck is the idea that something can happen to you that is not in your control, or really in anyone's control, except for the mysterious powers of superstition. People who believe in luck start doing things they think might bring them good luck, like dropping a penny in a well. They stop doing things they think might bring them bad luck, like being near black cats.

Luck, though, doesn't really exist. Things happen because people or the Lord influence them to happen. Or they just happen by chance.

We desire to have something bring good luck, because a lot of times things seem out of our control. We want things to happen, but we know we don't have the power to make them happen. But when you think about it, how could picking up a penny bring good luck? Who would have the power to make something good happen?

Well, God, of course. But God doesn't operate on luck. Instead, he wants us to trust him, to have faith in him. When we trust him, we're really showing him that we know he has both the power to make things happen and the goodness to make the right things happen.

So go ahead. Pick up that penny. It's pretty! Be sure to read the words printed on it: "In God We Trust." That's where the power lies.

GOD SAYS . . .
[Jesus said,] "Trust in God, and trust also in me." JOHN 14:1

HOW ABOUT YOU?
Do you ever catch yourself trusting in good or bad luck? Keep a penny near your bedside or on your dresser to remind you who to trust instead!

CONSIDER THIS . . . Names are really important. They represent the person or thing that carries the name. One of the ways God showed that he was giving Adam authority and power was by allowing him to name all the animals. Naming the animals was a very important task to complete.

God is the "most" of everything good—he is the most powerful, most kind, most wise. His name represents him too. The Bible tells us that *Jesus*, the name of God's Son, is the name above all names (Philippians 2:9). Why? Because Jesus, like his heavenly Father, is the one above all others. There is power in the name of God. Like anything else with power, we don't want to misuse his name. We want to honor God when talking about him. He deserves all of our respect. Like anyone else's name, God's name represents him.

How can you misuse God's name? Anytime you use the name of God or Jesus without talking respectfully to or about him, you're misusing his name. Saying, "Oh my God," when you're amazed by something is not calling upon God. It's misusing his name to show your amazement. Most people who say, "Oh my God," don't really understand what they're doing. They've just always heard the phrase, and they're using the words out of habit. We shouldn't judge those people or think unkindly toward them, but we can set a good example. And if you're close to a person who does use those words, you might gently explain to her why you've chosen not to. You can certainly say words like *amazing, incredible,* or *wow* with just as much effect. When you use another word, you won't be thoughtlessly misusing the name of the one you love.

HOW ABOUT YOU?

Do you ever say "Oh my God"? What other phrase can you use instead?

GOD SAYS . . .

You must not misuse the name of the LORD your God. The LORD will not let you go unpunished if you misuse his name. EXODUS 20:7

Dear God, There is this boy I like, but I'm too shy to tell him. I'm afraid he will laugh at me. What should I do?

CONSIDER THIS ... You're getting to the age now where boys are a little more interesting. Just as you might look at a room full of girls and choose only a few who interest you as good friends, you will feel the same about boys. Some will irritate you, some will be barely noticed, some will be good friends, some might seem even more special. That's okay.

As you grow, though, you'll meet many boys. You'll probably like quite a few of them. Some you may like for only a day or two—before they do something obnoxious and you don't like them anymore! Some you may like for a month or a year. As you move into different classes or schools, or even discover more about yourself, you will probably change your mind about the boy you like too.

Because you're just finding out what you do and don't like, it's best not to talk about it with too many people. It's always good to talk with your mom, and it's okay to talk with a close friend or two—if they can be trusted not to pass on the information! If you go ahead and tell the boy, though, or others, you might be sorry. He might laugh, as you said, or tell others.

At your age it's normal to be interested in boys but not to date or make any big statements about it. Think inside about what you enjoy about this boy—his sense of humor, his kindness, his friendly smile—but it's probably best to keep the thoughts among you, your parents, and a close friend. That way, when you like someone else, you're free to privately consider a change of mind too.

GOD SAYS ...
Be sensible and keep your mouth shut.
PROVERBS 10:19

HOW ABOUT YOU?
Do you think God is interested in hearing about why you like a certain boy? What can you tell him about a boy you may like today?

FAIRY TALE DAY

May 26

Dear God, It's hard to do good to someone who is doing rude things to me. Can you help me figure out how?

CONSIDER THIS . . . One of the best fairy tales of all time is the story of Cinderella. She has such a rough life! First, her mom dies. Then Cinderella's dad, whom she loves, marries a woman who pretends to be nice in front of Cinderella's dad but is totally mean to Cinderella when no one else is looking. The stepsisters, taking a cue from their mother, are mean to Cinderella too. And for a little while, it seems to be paying off. They get the best clothes, go to the best parties, and don't have to do any chores. Cinderella, on the other hand, gets her name from her work: she has to clean out the cinders from the fireplaces. And scrub the floors, and make the beds, and, and, and . . .

But it doesn't stay that way, does it? In the Disney movie, other people around Cinderella, and even the animals, see that she is mistreated. They reach out to help her. The fact that she has remained pure and kind during all of her problems works for her. When Prince Charming finally finds her and slips on that perfect slipper, she hasn't turned into a bitter old bean. Instead, she's still lovely and sweet. Sweet enough to marry a prince—and charm her kingdom.

When we return evil for evil, we become very much like the people who are hurting us. God doesn't want that for us. Most of us don't want to turn into tormenting bullies, either. Instead, keep your gentle, thoughtful character, and trust God to bless you for remaining caring and true.

Maybe you'll even get some beautiful new shoes!

HOW ABOUT YOU?

Who in your life is treating you poorly? Can you, instead of treating the person badly in return, trust that God will bless you for it?

GOD SAYS . . .

Don't repay evil for evil. Don't retaliate with insults when people insult you. Instead, pay them back with a blessing. That is what God has called you to do, and he will bless you for it.

1 PETER 3:9

Dear God, What should I do with all the worried thoughts racing around in my head?

CONSIDER THIS . . . Some days it's easy to fall asleep; I collapse into bed eager for the rest my pillow offers. Other days it's harder to fall asleep. Is it the same for you?

When I'm lying in bed worrying about things, I often look down and find my hands clenched into fists. What do you think of when you see fists? I think of fighting. I think of holding on to something very tightly and not letting go. In either case, it's not a peaceful, easy feeling.

There are lots of things that happen in life that can make us angry or frightened. Those are the nights when we just can't stop thinking about a mistake we've made, or about the schoolwork we didn't finish. Maybe a friend is mad at you. Or maybe there was a practice lockdown at school, and you're worried that next time it might not be practice.

The good news is, Jesus understands. People were sometimes angry with him, too. People always expected more healing and teaching than he chose to do during his years on earth. At the end of his life he was betrayed, let down, and abandoned. There were lots of other things that might have worried him, if he'd let them. But he didn't. Instead, he opened his hands in complete surrender to his Father in heaven.

Are your hands closed tightly around something, someone, or some situation? If so, open them up. You can't hold on to anything with an open hand. Let God take your worries.

No one is strong enough to handle every fear, frustration, and concern on her own. But you have a Friend who is waiting to help. If you open your fist and let him pluck your worries out, you'll sleep tight tonight.

GOD SAYS . . .

Don't worry about anything; instead, pray about everything. Tell God what you need, and thank him for all he has done. Then you will experience God's peace, which exceeds anything we can understand. PHILIPPIANS 4:6-7

HOW ABOUT YOU?

What's worrying you? Will you fall asleep tonight with your palms open, knowing that Jesus will take care of your needs if you ask him?

Dear God, What should I do if I get angry at a friend or she is mad at me? Are friends supposed to be angry with one another?

May 28

CONSIDER THIS . . . The word *hypocrite* comes from a Greek word that means "actor." When the Greeks put on plays, the actors would hold masks in front of their faces. Even if they were sad inside, they'd hold up a happy mask. They did this to try to make the people around them think that they were happy. It might have worked for a little while. It wasn't honest, though. Inside, they were sad.

Being mad at someone is scary because you don't know how they are going to react to your anger. Will they stop liking you? Stop being your friend? Will they be angry back? That's why we often pretend we're not angry when, really, we are. We put up that happy mask because we don't want to risk losing a friend. But inside we're still mad. We're holding on to that anger because we never worked through it. Eventually, it will poison the friendship. Poisoned friendships usually die—just the thing you were hoping to avoid!

When you're angry with a friend, first let your emotions cool down so you don't say something you'll regret later. Practice saying out loud what you'd like to tell your friend. Listen to your own voice and decide if it sounds like something you'd be okay hearing. Pray about it, and then talk with your friend. Chances are she won't even know that she's hurt you. Give her a chance to make things right. You'll want that same chance the next time you hurt her. Be ready to accept when you're wrong too. If she doesn't like you when you take the mask off—if you do it in love and with gentleness—she wasn't a real friend anyway.

HOW ABOUT YOU?

Whom are you afraid to show your anger toward? What response do you fear? What will you do next time you're mad at that person?

GOD SAYS . . .

"Don't sin by letting anger control you." Don't let the sun go down while you are still angry, for anger gives a foothold to the devil. EPHESIANS 4:26-27

Dear God, We don't have a lot of money, and I'm worried about my parents losing their jobs. How can I help?

CONSIDER THIS . . . Wondering about where the money is going to come from is nothing new. The Lord himself said he had nowhere to lay his head (Luke 9:58). Most people around the world struggle from time to time to pay their bills.

If you're a kid, though, it's hard to see your family dealing with money troubles. You know your parents are stressed out, but it feels like there is nothing you can do. Right? Wrong! Although you may not be able to earn money for your family, there are things you can do to help. Here are a few ideas:

1. Be content. In the Bible, Paul says he has learned to be content when he has a lot, and when he has a little (Philippians 4:11-12). See if you can ask for one or two new things that you really need . . . but no more.

2. Share. Can you swap things with friends? It's a great way to get new books, new accessories, and even new clothes.

3. Pray. This seems like it's not doing much. In fact, Christians often say things like, "Well, there's nothing more I can do, so I guess I'll pray." But prayer is what the Lord asks us to do, and he never asks us to do anything meaningless.

Think of ten things you are thankful for. Think of how big God is. And then pray and ask him for what you need.

GOD SAYS . . .

[Jesus said,] "That is why I tell you not to worry about everyday life—whether you have enough food and drink, or enough clothes to wear. Isn't life more than food, and your body more than clothing?" MATTHEW 6:25

HOW ABOUT YOU?

Do you ever worry that your family might not have enough money? Read the verse to the left, close your eyes, and then do just what it says.

Dear God, Sometimes I get so scared about stuff that I feel my heart thumping in my chest, and I can't stop thinking about what I'm worried about. Am I going to die?

CONSIDER THIS . . . Well, you are going to die—sometime! But most of the time, your heart thumping in your chest isn't going to kill you. But it's not good for you either. So you're smart to figure out what to do next.

When we get afraid of anything, our bodies pour a hormone called adrenaline into our blood. It's there to help us "fight" anything that is trying to harm us. Or to take "flight" and run away. But we're not usually afraid of real people or animals coming to get us. A lot of times the things we're afraid of are in our heads.

Have you ever been to a rodeo, or seen one on television? It's a sport that grew out of a time when there were cattle running all over, and the cowboys needed to lasso and rope the cattle to bring them back into the peaceful orderliness of a barn or a herd. At a rodeo, the cowgirl (or cowboy) rides her horse around the arena, swinging her rope around. The rope has a large loop on the end. Once she slips the loop over the head of the cow, she brings it under control.

This is what we're to do with our wildly racing worries and thoughts. They can run around our brains like worked-up cattle in an arena. We need to take our lassos, our willpower, and bring them back under control. Instead of letting our thoughts race, we need to bring them back into line about what we know about Christ. Will he let us fall? No. Has he forgotten us? No. Is he able to care for all of our needs? Yes!

You may not be a cowgirl, but you can get really good at roping in those runaway thoughts.

HOW ABOUT YOU?

What kinds of thoughts do you think you might need to corral?

GOD SAYS . . .

We take captive every thought to make it obedient to Christ.
2 CORINTHIANS 10:5 (NIV)

Dear God, I feel really weird about getting my period. How old are girls when they normally get it? Help!

CONSIDER THIS . . . As you grow older, it's normal to think about the changes that will happen. Your body will change, beginning its path toward being a woman. Your emotions will change. Everything will feel weird and uncontrollable. Sometimes thinking about these things makes us happy—we're growing up! Yay! Sometimes thinking about these things is scary. We're growing up. Uh-oh!

Each girl gets her period just as her body is ready for it, usually between the ages of ten and fourteen. When you begin to reach puberty, your body begins to change. Your breasts begin to bud; your baby fat melts off a bit; your skin becomes oily and breaks out. Soon you begin your period. Getting your period is a way your body reaches toward womanhood. It doesn't mean that you are a woman just yet. No one expects you to suddenly start acting like a woman once you get your period. It just means that you're continuing to grow up in the way God intended for you. This can be an exciting time as you see your future begin to take shape before you.

Things won't seem so worrisome if you're prepared. Talk with your mom about what you can expect. Get some supplies and keep some in your room, some in your locker, and some in a zippered pouch in your backpack. That way you won't be taken off guard. Some girls have light cramps once a month for a few months before their first period. They are aware that something is coming. Some girls are surprised when it just appears one day. Either is perfectly normal.

Look forward to growing up at just the right time. Being a girl is fun, but so is being a young lady.

GOD SAYS . . .
For everything there is a season, a time for every activity under heaven. ECCLESIASTES 3:1

HOW ABOUT YOU?
What questions do you have about puberty? Whom can you talk with about this? When?

Dear God, How will I know when it's time to change something important, like friends, or a school, or a sport, or a boy I like?

CONSIDER THIS . . . Each year, about the first day of June, the June bugs appear in certain parts of the world. They are shaped kind of like eggs, but smaller. They are leaf green because . . . they live near and eat leaves! They sound a little like a cross between an angry fly and a small toy that has been wound up one time too many. When you see June bugs buzzing around your garden and your yard, you know that summer is just around the corner.

Just like the June bugs that hint at summer being near, we have clues in most other areas of life. We see and hear things that make our "antennae" stand on end. Perhaps we begin to see that a friend chooses to hang out with others more than with us, or she doesn't respond to texts and calls very quickly. Maybe you're tired of her bossiness. Perhaps a sport that you've always loved is demanding more and more time and money—and you'd like to explore other things that you're interested in too. Maybe your school isn't able to meet your needs anymore, or there are bullies, or your parent gets a new job that will require your family to move.

If you've ever ridden a bicycle and had to switch gears to go faster or slow down, you'll know that it's best to go one gear at a time—from first to second to third to fourth—rather than go from four to one and strip the gears. Little by little we ease into a new speed . . . or a new phase in life. When God sends you signs to notice, see, and hear, he's letting you switch gears one at a time until it's time to make that change.

HOW ABOUT YOU?

Do you sense that there are any changes coming in your friendships, or your family, or your life? How can you switch gears one at a time?

GOD SAYS . . .

Now learn a lesson from the fig tree. When its branches bud and its leaves begin to sprout, you know that summer is near.
MATTHEW 24:32

Dear God, Why do bad things sometimes happen to Christians?

CONSIDER THIS . . . One day when Abby, who's a Christian, came home from school, her mom sat her down on the couch next to her. She took Abby's hands in hers and told her, "I've got cancer." Meanwhile, across town, Josie, whose family are not Christians, came home from school and her mother told her, "I've got cancer." How do you think each girl responded?

The Bible tells us that God causes rain to fall upon good people and bad. That means that bad things will happen to those who believe in him and those who do not. The difference is in how we respond to the things that happen to us. Once we believe in God, our greatest jobs are to love him and to be a light so others can find him too. One of the ways we do that is by showing our hope and our trust in him when bad things happen. If nothing bad ever happened to us, how would we be able to prove our faith to people who don't know him? If we still trust, if we hope even while we cry and pray, they will see something they can't find just anywhere. They will see that faith is true and strong and that we truly believe we have a helper who loves and cares for us at all times.

Trust God. He says he can cause all things to work together for good, according to his purpose for you (Romans 8:28). He didn't spare himself pain—the crucifixion of his Son—when it was necessary, did he? This doesn't mean you won't be sad or angry or concerned. Of course you will! But you can also show anyone watching that God is faithful in good times and bad.

GOD SAYS . . .
[Jesus said,] "You will be my witnesses, telling people about me everywhere—in Jerusalem, throughout Judea, in Samaria, and to the ends of the earth." ACTS 1:8

HOW ABOUT YOU?
When is it hard for you to trust God? Who in your life is watching you, seeing what your faith really means when it is tested?

Dear God, Why do we have to confess our sins?

CONSIDER THIS . . . Have you ever been bitten by a mosquito? The bite starts out small. After sucking in some of your blood, she leaves a bit of her saliva behind in the small wound. That saliva irritates your body, and it causes swelling. Now it's an itchy bump! Once you have that itchy bump, you know how it can bother you. You can't ignore it or focus on anything else. You want to scratch it over and over, until someone gets you some pink lotion to put on it. After that, you usually feel sweet, itch-free relief until your body breaks down the saliva and carries it away.

Your body doesn't like that bite. It knows something has been introduced into your skin that doesn't belong there. That's not healthy for you. It bugs you—literally!

Your spirit works in the same way. When you sin, it's like introducing a bit of badness, an irritation, into your spirit. Even though you might try to forget about it for a while, your spirit knows it's there. And the Holy Spirit knows it's there. He makes it "itch" or bug you until you do something to get rid of it. Scripture tells us that the way to rid ourselves of sin is to confess it to God. When we confess, or tell about, our sin to other people, it's kind of like applying bug relief on a painful bite. It takes away the sting of the sin. It doesn't mean we won't get bitten—or sin again—but we have some help to make sure it's not as likely.

Go ahead—confess your wrongdoing to God, tell a friend, and tell sin to stop bugging you!

HOW ABOUT YOU?

Do you have a sin you need to confess? Just think of how good it will feel when it's not itching you anymore!

GOD SAYS . . .

People who conceal their sins will not prosper, but if they confess and turn from them, they will receive mercy. PROVERBS 28:13

Dear God, My grandma bought a dress for me, and she's asking me if I like it. I don't. What do I do?

CONSIDER THIS ... Congratulations on both being honest and wanting to do the right thing! When someone gives another person a gift, it's usually for the following reasons:

1. To share a little bit of herself in the selection.
2. To honor the person for whom the gift is intended by choosing something she would like.
3. To offer it as a celebratory item (like for a birthday) or to show love.

You have three choices in your response. One, you could lie to your grandma and tell her you like it so you don't hurt her feelings. But then she'll wonder what's up when you never wear it, and you'll feel awkward for lying to her about it. Two, you could tell her you don't like it. Something tells me this would cause some awkwardness, too. Three, you could answer her carefully, thankfully, *and* honestly. It will honor both of your feelings.

You might consider telling your grandma that you are so thankful that she thinks of you and that you know not everyone has a grandma who buys them gifts. Explain that because fashions change quickly, and so does your body, this particular dress doesn't work. You might suggest spending a few hours shopping together—building your relationship—which will allow you to exchange this dress for something that will work. This allows you to be honest while respecting your grandma's intent in gift giving. It may be awkward at first, but thankful, gentle honesty always builds a relationship after those first few scary moments. Lies, even ones you think are little and said with good intentions, tear relationships down.

GOD SAYS ...

An honest answer is like a kiss of friendship.
PROVERBS 24:26

HOW ABOUT YOU?

Have you ever said you liked something when you didn't, just so you wouldn't hurt someone else's feelings? How did that work out?

Dear God, If we're Christians, why is it important for us to read the Old Testament, which all happened before Jesus was even born?

June 5

CONSIDER THIS . . . Some of the first things that people say when a baby is born, right after, "Oh, how adorable!" are "He looks just like his mother" or "He has his grandpa's chin." All people are put into families, and we all have histories. As we grow older, we might see that we have more in common with our relatives. Adopted children may not look like their parents, but they certainly take on family traits. They may laugh like their mother or debate like their dad. Knowing where we come from gives us a place in the world. It helps us feel like we fit in, and it gives us an idea of what values are important to our family.

Christianity is a faith that grew from Judaism. Jesus, after all, was Jewish. God came first to the Jewish people and called them his own. God gave the first five books of the Bible, called the Septuagint or Pentateuch, to Moses, who shared them with the Jewish people. Then, when Jesus came to earth, he said he came not to do away with the Jewish law but to fulfill it. We, as Christians, want to know exactly what he came to fulfill, right?

When you read through the Old Testament, all of which was inspired by God, read it like you're reading through a family scrapbook. You'll learn lots about the members of your Christian family that you might not have known before. You'll see where you came from, and you'll get a glimpse into where you're going. You'll know lots more about your family and the heavenly Father who leads it. All of the books of the Bible, both the Old Testament and the New Testament, work together to support and explain our history.

HOW ABOUT YOU?

Do you look like any of your family members, or share habits, likes, and dislikes with them? How does that help you to "fit in"?

GOD SAYS . . .

These tablets were God's work; the words on them were written by God himself. EXODUS 32:16

Dear God, How did the world start?

CONSIDER THIS . . . Have you ever skipped through a book? Some people like to flip to the back of the book and read the ending first—just to make sure everything works out okay in the end. You can certainly learn stuff by reading that way. But it won't all make sense. You won't truly understand why people make certain decisions or act certain ways, nor will you care about them as much. When people refer back to what happened earlier in the story to help make sense of what was going on, you won't understand what they're talking about.

What would happen if you had to assemble your new computer, but you started halfway through the instructions? The computer might not work right. At the very least, you might not get all of the benefits that were shared early on in the setup instructions!

Genesis means "the beginning." In this book of the Bible, God tells us all about how and why he created the world. He shows us some people who are important to him and tells us why. He tells the stories well—they are fun to read, if you give them a chance. But mainly he wants you to know more about him and you and the world around you. He wants to show you how it all works, what doesn't work, and what can help.

Genesis isn't only the book of beginnings. It's the book of relationships. God wants to have a relationship with you. It may be tempting to read only the New Testament books in the Bible, but God has a lot to tell you in the Old Testament, too. Turn back, way back, to the beginning of the Bible and start to read. Pay attention. He's writing to you!

GOD SAYS . . .

In the beginning God created the heavens and the earth. GENESIS 1:1

HOW ABOUT YOU?

What is your favorite story in the book of Genesis? Why?

Dear God, Does *Exodus* mean "exit"? They sound alike.

CONSIDER THIS . . . It does mean exit! Think of those big green or red signs in movie theaters. They stay lit even when the movie is on to show you the way out in case there's an emergency. The book of Exodus tells us the story of God's people, who were having an emergency. They were slaves in Egypt under a terrible master. But Exodus is not only about the exit from slavery in Egypt to freedom in the Promised Land. It's also about the exit from our slavery to sin to freedom in Christ. That's an emergency!

Have you read the story of Moses or seen one of the great movies made about his life? God raised him up to show his people the way to freedom. And God had planned for Moses, and for Jesus, long before his people even knew they needed a Savior.

It's kind of like this: say you're going on a field trip, and you've forgotten your lunch—but don't realize it until you're on the bus. Now what will you do? It's a very long day. You tell the teacher, and she only smiles and nods. But when the bus pulls up in front of the museum where you are to spend the day, there's your mom, waiting with your lunch. Before you even realized you'd forgotten your lunch, your mom saw it on the countertop and arranged to "save the day."

Before the Israelites cried out to God for a Savior, he had arranged for Moses to come and save the day. Before we knew that we needed to be saved from our sins, the Lord had arranged for Jesus to pay the price by dying on the cross.

That's much more important than a forgotten lunch, isn't it?

HOW ABOUT YOU?

Has someone ever "saved the day" for you? When and how?

GOD SAYS . . .

I am aware of their suffering. So I have come down to rescue them from the power of the Egyptians and lead them out of Egypt into their own fertile and spacious land. EXODUS 3:7-8

Dear God, I don't suppose Leviticus was named after people who wear Levi's, right?

CONSIDER THIS ... No, although I'll bet the man who invented Levi's jeans was named after the Levi in the Bible! In Scripture, Jacob's twelve sons each grew into a "tribe." The tribe that came from the brother named Levi were the priests, or the pastors, for the Israelites. They were in charge of helping people understand how to worship God and how to interact with him.

We may think certain things are good when done one way, whereas someone else may not. You might think that giving your friend a basketball is a loving gift, but if she doesn't like basketball and she's told you she prefers softball, she won't receive it as loving. If you asked for a slice of cake and someone handed you a diet soda instead, you wouldn't feel that it was loving. It's not enough to just express love; we have to take into consideration how the person will receive it. With worship, it's not enough just to do what we think is right; we have to take into consideration how God receives our actions. God told his people just how to worship and sacrifice in the Old Testament book of Leviticus.

The world still suffers under sin, and therefore it is not holy. God is holy, and he desires a relationship with us. He still shows his people how to worship and how to draw close to him. God made the biggest sacrifice of all—his Son, Jesus—because he wanted to draw us close. Because Scripture tells us that now, in Christ, we are God's chosen people, and that we are all priests, understanding Leviticus is important for each of us.

Much better than a pair of even the best skinny jeans. Right?

GOD SAYS ...

You are a chosen people. You are royal priests, a holy nation, God's very own possession. As a result, you can show others the goodness of God, for he called you out of the darkness into his wonderful light. 1 PETER 2:9

HOW ABOUT YOU?

How can you worship God in the way he desires?

Dear God, I've tried to read Numbers, but it just seemed to keep saying the same thing over and over with lots of counting. What's it about?

CONSIDER THIS . . . The book of Numbers, which is about discipline, is kind of a hard book. Some people refer to it as the book of murmuring, because it's all about God's people grumbling and complaining! The Bible tells us in many places that good parents discipline their children if they love them. It also tells us that parents who don't discipline their children don't really love them. We know that God loves his children, and so by his own words we know that he disciplines them too.

Most kids have had the experience of being disciplined. Maybe you skipped out on doing your chores and were grounded. If your mom told you not to wear a certain item or read a certain book and you did it anyway, you knew that there would be consequences. Good parents prepare their children for the fact that there are consequences for doing things the wrong way after having been told not to. Those consequences aren't to hurt you. They're meant to keep you, and others, from doing the wrong thing the next time.

We all know what it's like to be sassy, grumbling, and complaining to a parent. Eventually, the parent gets fed up! God had provided everything the Israelites needed—someone to lead them out of slavery, food to eat, clothing to wear, and a wonderful place to end up. But still, they complained and disobeyed. So they had a consequence. Most of them didn't get to see the Promised Land they had been heading toward (though their children did). God still loved them, but there were consequences for their actions.

Believe it—those who came after that generation of Israelites listened and learned!

HOW ABOUT YOU?

What have you been disciplined for lately?

GOD SAYS . . .

Think about it: Just as a parent disciplines a child, the LORD your God disciplines you for your own good. DEUTERONOMY 8:5

Dear God, Did you stay mad at the Israelites when they disobeyed?

CONSIDER THIS ... Although most kids get angry at their parents from time to time, and most parents get angry with their kids from time to time, that anger doesn't last forever and ever. The situation is dealt with, talked through, and overcome. And then the good times start up again.

This is how God operates too. He was angry with his people when they disobeyed and grumbled and complained, but his anger did not last forever. The Israelites did make it to the Promised Land just as God had, well, promised! He had made that promise, also called a covenant, to them. Because he is God and always does what is right, he always keeps his promises.

Has there ever been a time when your mom or dad promised to do something and then didn't do it? Parents do not mean to break their promises. Sometimes they promise something that they aren't able to follow through on later because of money issues or lack of time. Sometimes they promise something before they know everything about it. Once they learn the whole story, they realize that fulfilling the promise would not be a good thing. Sometimes, because they are human, they just forget to do what they said, and they feel bad about it later.

Even though our parents are loving but imperfect, God is both loving and perfect. He never forgets and is always able to do what he says he will do. God always keeps his promises, including his promise to lavish his love on those who love him.

He is the perfect parent. His discipline may last for a little while, but his love is everlasting.

GOD SAYS ...

Understand, therefore, that the LORD your God is indeed God. He is the faithful God who keeps his covenant for a thousand generations and lavishes his unfailing love on those who love him and obey his commands. DEUTERONOMY 7:9

HOW ABOUT YOU?

How do your parents show their love to you after you've been disciplined? How does God?

Dear God, A girl I know is always saying mean things about me. I have a few things I'd like to say back. Can I?

CONSIDER THIS . . . Have you ever watched a pig caller? You might have seen one in a movie, on TV, at a 4-H expo, or at a state fair. For sure, you've heard the word that pig callers use most to call their little snout-nosed friends. They open up their mouths, put their hands around their lips, and let out a very loud "Soooooeeey!" For some reason, the pigs just can't seem to ignore that shout, and they especially like it when the crowd around them roars. They turn and run toward the pig caller, and make like they're going to attack him. Pigs don't think. They just act.

For some reason, there are also people in our lives who don't think but just act. These people like to pick fights, and they can't seem to stop themselves from gossiping, bullying, or saying mean things about others. They like it when they're in the middle of a group picking on someone and the crowd roars and laughs.

There's a saying you may have heard before: "Don't get into a fight with a pig. You'll both get dirty, and the pig will just enjoy it." The problem with "getting into it" with this mean girl and saying mean things back to her is that the problem will go on and on and you'll be dragged down to her level. If she's just being rude, walk away and make new friends. If she is bullying you, you definitely don't have to put up with that. You can tell a teacher, a parent, your principal, or a coach. But it's not a good idea to jump into the mud because, well, you'll just get dirty too.

HOW ABOUT YOU?

Is there someone who speaks poorly about you? Is it bullying? If it is, whom can you talk to about it? If it's not bullying, how can you keep away?

GOD SAYS . . .

A washed pig returns to the mud. 2 PETER 2:22

Dear God, Why am I supposed to take such good care of myself?

CONSIDER THIS . . . If you've ever taken a trip to Europe or looked at pictures from the ancient continent, you've probably seen cathedrals. Cathedrals are large, mostly very old, churches. They are carefully made with the best stone, wood, marble, and glass. In fact, some craftsmen spent their entire lives working on the windows in one cathedral. If you enter one of them, it's quiet. People speak in hushed voices. The light filters through and casts gorgeous shadows everywhere. Cathedrals were built to be beautiful, because they represent where God lives and provide a place to worship him.

Can you imagine how anyone would react if someone spat on the floor of a cathedral? Stuck a piece of chewed gum on one of the windows? Crunched up some chips and threw them, and the bag, around? Certainly people would be outraged. The culprit would likely be hustled right out of the cathedral. Everyone would understand: this is not how you treat a piece of art, especially a place built to worship God.

In the Bible, followers of God would visit the Temple to worship him, just like people visit cathedrals today. Scripture tells us that we, God's people, are temples of the Holy Spirit. In fact, we are even more beautiful than those cathedrals because we are made in his image. We are his home—he lives within us. We use our beautiful bodies to work for and worship him.

Take good care of yourself because you deserve to be treated with honor and dignity, and also because your beautiful body is God's home.

GOD SAYS . . .

Don't you realize that your body is the temple of the Holy Spirit, who lives in you and was given to you by God? . . . You must honor God with your body. 1 CORINTHIANS 6:19-20

HOW ABOUT YOU?

Is there some way in which you are treating your temple like a garbage dump? How can you make it beautiful again?

Dear God, Doing wrong hurts, but sometimes getting caught and fixing it hurts even more. If that's the right thing to do, why does it hurt so much?

June 13

CONSIDER THIS . . . Think about a time when you brought home some fruit, maybe a wicker basket of fresh strawberries or a bag of crisp, juicy apples, and looked forward to eating some of it. By the time you got it out of the fridge, however, it was a little too late. Maybe there were some spongy, dark purple spots on the berries. Or a soft brown bruise on the apple, which squished when you touched it. The whole piece of fruit wasn't bad. It was just one little part that wasn't perfect. Although the mushy part didn't seem appetizing, the rest of the fruit looked delicious!

A wise person doesn't throw a piece of fruit away unless the whole piece is spoiled. Instead, she takes a very sharp knife and carves out the part that is bad. If she doesn't, the bad part will spread to the rest of the fruit, making it bad too. Once the spoiled piece is cut out, the remaining part is tasty, nutritious, and good for you!

This is how it works with sin sometimes too. You, of course, are not bad as a whole. But parts of you have been made spongy, soft, and spoiled by sin. A very sharp knife, the conviction of the Holy Spirit, is often applied. And by the changes God asks you to make, that sinful part is removed. Now, being cut by a sharp knife can be painful. Just ask the apple! But when it's over, and the bad parts have been pruned away, you will be healthy once more.

HOW ABOUT YOU?

If you sit quietly and think about it for a minute, where in your life is God pruning?

GOD SAYS . . .

I am the true grapevine, and my Father is the gardener. He cuts off every branch of mine that doesn't produce fruit, and he prunes the branches that do bear fruit so they will produce even more. JOHN 15:1-2

Dear God, What's the point of waiting when I already know that I want to do something?

CONSIDER THIS . . . Today it seems like almost everything fun runs on batteries. Our computers can be plugged in—but if we want to take them anywhere, they need to be on battery power. Phones have batteries, toys have batteries, even remote controls have batteries! There are even little icons that warn us that the battery is low. We need to plug in or lose our data.

Have you ever put the battery in, but then didn't let it charge long enough? It's so frustrating. You might get back to your game, or your e-book, or whatever you were doing for a short time, but there just isn't enough juice to work or play for long. You have to quit before you're ready to. In order to make things go right, play right, and stay right, you have to let the battery fully charge. Yes, that means waiting. But once it's at 100 percent you're ready to do whatever you want to do for a very long time.

Waiting is like that. Think of it as your battery charging. You might need to get stronger, or learn more, or be older. It's hard to wait until you're at 100 percent of whatever you need to be at in order to buy or participate in something. But you don't want to start something you really care about before you're ready to take it all the way, do you? Trust God that at just the right time he will make a way for you to do what you've been waiting for, if it's in his will. Until then, he'll be charging you up and giving you the strength to do it 100 percent.

GOD SAYS . . .
Those who trust in the LORD will find new strength. They will soar high on wings like eagles. They will run and not grow weary. They will walk and not faint. ISAIAH 40:31

HOW ABOUT YOU?
What are you charging your battery for?

Dear God, Why do babies die?
It's so unfair! They didn't even get
a chance to live.

June 15

CONSIDER THIS . . . Babies are so sweet and cute! When a baby is born, we feel that she has her whole life ahead of her. We imagine that the baby will grow to be a toddler and learn to walk. She will go to school and then eventually grow up, get married, and have babies of her own. Someday, after that person has lived a long and rich life, she will die. And while death is never nice, when old people die, we expect it. Because sin exists in our imperfect world, people will die.

We just don't expect young people, or little babies, to die. It seems so unfair when we think about everything they'll never get to do. But maybe we're looking at it from the wrong perspective.

Imagine that you were invited to a friend's piano recital. You'd be able to hear her play, but your mom said you'd have to leave just a little bit before the cake reception because your sister had a birthday party. You might be a bit bummed because you knew your friend would enjoy your company, but after all . . . a birthday party would actually be even fun. You'd get to enjoy a bit of both, and it might not feel like you'd missed everything.

We live here on earth for so few years when compared with eternity, which is forever and ever. Some babies, and people, do have to leave earth a bit "early." We feel sad because we miss their company, but in the great plan of time, they've only missed a tiny bit of time on earth. And who knows? Perhaps they've been called to attend the party earlier than you!

HOW ABOUT YOU?

What do you see going on around you that seems unfair? Can you think of another perspective, one God might have?

GOD SAYS . . .

You saw me before I was born. Every day of my life was recorded in your book. Every moment was laid out before a single day had passed.

PSALM 139:16

Dear God, Why are we supposed to keep ourselves pure?

CONSIDER THIS . . . Some pennies are bright orangey copper. They are brand new, and if one of these pennies were lying in the street or on the floor of your car, you'd see it right away. Some pennies are a little worn. They have a deeper color, and it's harder to read the words on them or see the picture of good old Abe Lincoln, though you can still make out who he is.

Some pennies are just plain gross. They are tarnished, which means that the copper in them has a layer of dull, dark film, almost like dried slime, over the top. It might be almost impossible to see the picture or read the words. If such a penny were lying on the road, you might not even see it out of the corner of your eye.

Surprisingly, the oldest pennies aren't always the ones with the most tarnish. The worst are often the pennies that have been through many hands, been outside the most, or endured the roughest conditions. In other words—they've had the most contact with the world!

The Lord Jesus is pure. When we look at a penny, we don't see Abe Lincoln, but we do see his image. Just like that penny, when people look at us, they see God's image—because we were made in it! But we have to be pure, like that brand-new penny, to fully reflect God's image.

The good news for people, and for pennies, is that once tarnished they can become clean again. Let a penny sit in a cup of lemon juice for a few hours and watch the transformation. Let your heart dwell with Jesus for a few minutes and watch your own amazing change back to purity!

GOD SAYS . . .

We do know that we will be like him, for we will see him as he really is. And all who have this eager expectation will keep themselves pure, just as he is pure.

1 JOHN 3:2-3

HOW ABOUT YOU?

What things do you come in contact with (books, music, fashion, TV shows, etc.) that tarnish you?

Dear God, I am worried that I will lose my friends when my mom starts homeschooling me next year. Any advice?

June 17

CONSIDER THIS . . . Your whole life is changing, isn't it? You'll have a new way of learning, more time with your mom and dad, more time with brothers and sisters, no teachers . . . and now, you think, no friends. But it might not be what it seems. How do you normally make friends? Your friends are probably people you live by or people you go to school with or play on teams with. Perhaps your friends are people you know at church. When you first met them, it was because you had something in common. Doing things together you both liked and spending time together *kept* you friends.

This will be true with your new homeschooling adventure. You can still keep the old friends, even the ones you met at school. Ask your mom to help arrange times when you and your friends can get together, maybe for a sleepover or to go shopping. But also remember that you will have a whole new group of people in your life. There will be other kids you come to know who are homeschooled. Guess what? It'll be like when you first made friends at school—you'll have something in common and you'll do things together that build your friendship.

God knows we need friends. Trust him to help provide you with friends throughout your life. Keep your eyes open to all the kids around you, and keep your mind open to saying, "Hello. What's your name?" to someone new. Remember, to make a friend, you need to be a friend first. Keep an open heart toward the people you meet. Sometimes the person we think we could never be friends with turns out to be the very person God placed in our path to be a best pal.

HOW ABOUT YOU?

What are you worried about with friends? Does Jesus know what you need? Can you trust him to provide for your needs?

GOD SAYS . . .

Your Father knows exactly what you need even before you ask him!

MATTHEW 6:8

Dear God, Do you have a loud voice?

CONSIDER THIS . . . We tend to think of things that are strong and powerful as being loud and big. Large vehicles seem to overpower those tiny little smart cars. Huge winds, like tornadoes, have the power to do a lot of damage, whereas little breezes only make leaves flutter to the ground. Big plows clear more snow than kiddie shovels. And a lot of money can do a lot of good, whereas a little money . . . not so much.

Right?

Maybe not! Sometimes power isn't all about show but about what the object actually does. Take, for example, a tiny watermelon seed. It's flat and black and about the size of your fingernail. No one likes to eat watermelon seeds. In fact, many kids have watermelon-seed-spitting contests! But that tiny seed has a lot of power packed inside. If planted, and watered, it can grow into a watermelon vine that will produce many, many watermelons. Most of them will weigh ten or more pounds each.

God, of course, is all-powerful. Everything that is strength is packed inside of him. But he doesn't need to be loud in order to show his power. In fact, Scripture doesn't say he shouted the world into existence; it says he spoke it into existence. Power isn't known by how loud or big it is, but by what it accomplishes. In order to hear God, you'll have to listen carefully. He doesn't shout in the wind or roar in an earthquake. Instead, he often speaks in a gentle whisper.

Can you hear him?

GOD SAYS . . .

After the earthquake there was a fire, but the LORD was not in the fire. And after the fire there was the sound of a gentle whisper. 1 KINGS 19:12

HOW ABOUT YOU?

When have you heard from God and were completely surprised by it?

Dear God, I understand that you are strong, but I'm kind of afraid because I know that the devil is strong too. Right?

June 19

CONSIDER THIS . . . It's true, Satan is not as strong as God, but he is strong. It's good to know that fact right up front so you don't mess around and assume that your enemy is weak. The good news, though, is that God is stronger than Satan, and he lives within you. The Lord has not left you defenseless, either. He's given you a plan of action for whenever you're tempted. And everyone is tempted. Even Jesus was tempted, although he did not sin (Matthew 4:1-11).

The Bible says the first thing you should do when you're tempted is to humble yourself before God. Being humble means submitting to God. That means obeying him willingly. If you know the right thing to do, or someone you trust tells you the right thing to do, you've just gotta do it! Picture a subject kneeling before her king, saying, "Whatever you want, Majesty." That's what submission, or being humble, looks like.

Next, you have to resist. Resisting temptation doesn't mean you should just kick back and not participate. Resistance is active. You have to do something. Turn off the wrong TV show, change a belly-showing shirt for a modest one, pick a book that doesn't have bad language, say you're sorry when you've done wrong. Actively turn away from the temptation to do, or to keep doing, what is wrong.

You can't just do one or the other of these when fighting temptation. You have to do both. And when you do, the Bible says that the devil will flee. What does *flee* mean? Imagine how you would run away from a large swarm of bees flying directly at you. That's fleeing!

HOW ABOUT YOU?

Can you think of any situations that might call for you to resist the devil and his temptations? How can you do so?

GOD SAYS . . .

Humble yourselves before God. Resist the devil, and he will flee from you. JAMES 4:7

Dear God, Are miracles for real?

CONSIDER THIS . . . We hear the word *miracle* from time to time, or maybe even a lot, in church or with other Christians. But what is a miracle?

Some people describe a miracle as something extraordinary happening in our world that we know noway, nohow could have come about by a person. It had to be God. Miracles break the laws of nature. Miracles are wonders and marvels. They are amazing, they are unusual, they are unexplainable.

Today, June 20 (or sometimes June 21), is referred to as the summer solstice. Some people just call it the first day of summer, but really the word *solstice* means "the sun stopped." Although the sun doesn't stop anymore, it really did one time. The Bible tells us that the Lord was going to deliver a great victory to his people, the Israelites, and he had the sun stand still until the victory was won: "On the day the LORD gave the Israelites victory over the Amorites, Joshua prayed to the LORD in front of all the people of Israel. He said, 'Let the sun stand still over Gibeon, and the moon over the valley of Aijalon.' So the sun stood still and the moon stayed in place until the nation of Israel had defeated its enemies" (Joshua 10:12-13). You had better believe that everyone—those on God's side and those against him—recognized that he was in the battle that day. The victory was definitely a miracle!

We may not see the sun stop anymore, but God is still helping his people win victories, both big and small. The first day of summer is a good time to remember this: God has always been in the miracle business, and he still is today.

Keep your eyes on the Son!

GOD SAYS . . .
The sun stayed in the middle of the sky, and it did not set as on a normal day. JOSHUA 10:13

HOW ABOUT YOU?
Have you ever witnessed or heard of a miracle? What happened?

Dear God, My teacher always picks the same girl to be the leader. But she's such a know-it-all. Do I really have to follow her?

June 21

CONSIDER THIS . . . It's pretty hard to like someone who knows it all—or thinks she does. Usually that person has a very clear idea of the right way things should be said and done: her way! It doesn't leave much room for other people or their ideas. That can make the others, like you, feel upset.

There's another kind of leader. This person understands that she has some strengths and some weaknesses. She doesn't pretend to know it all. She even realizes that she had to learn the things she does know. Sometimes she learned the easy way, and sometimes the hard way. She's not afraid of sharing her mistakes. Because she's honest about herself, and doesn't think she's perfect, she's easy to follow.

Long ago, God set up priests for people to follow. These people were to be leaders—they were to talk to God for and about other people. A priest helped people to understand God and even went before the Lord to ask for things on their behalf. The people trusted the priest to speak for them because he was humble. Scripture says that the high priest knew that he was weak and a sinner too. His humility and honesty made it easy for the people to follow him.

You do have to obey your teacher and follow the person she has appointed to lead, even if you don't like her. But you can prove yourself to be a different kind of leader. A humble one who knows she has to learn too. People will see you do so, and they will naturally follow you. A true leader leads from the head and the heart.

HOW ABOUT YOU?

Do you know anyone who is a know-it-all? Is it easy to learn from or follow him or her? How can you be a different kind of leader?

GOD SAYS . . .

Every high priest is a man chosen to represent other people in their dealings with God. He presents their gifts to God and offers sacrifices for their sins. HEBREWS 5:1

Dear God, Why does life have both good and bad things in it, when only good would be so much better?

CONSIDER THIS . . . Have you ever sat down with an entire bag of M&M's? No, not a little fun-size bag. The king-size bag! The first candy was probably delicious, chocolaty, and sweet. Maybe the tenth or twentieth M&M was pretty good too. But if you'd kept eating, say, one hundred or three hundred M&M's, you would learn something: sweets don't taste sweet, or even good, when you've had too many of them.

The same is true with salty snacks. A grab bag of chips or pretzels is tasty. A family-size bag? No thanks. The salt starts to hurt your tongue, and after a while the formerly tasty snacks just taste bland. Some of the best foods are sweet and salty together:

- a chocolate-dipped potato chip or pretzel
- a caramel with sea salt on top
- trail mix with nuts and candies blended together

Life is like that, too, mixing the salty with the sweet. What seems "bad" might not always be. Perhaps a difficult situation makes you stronger, wiser, or kinder. Some bad things happen because, well, this isn't heaven yet! Also, if we have too many things that go our way, sweetly, eventually we don't appreciate what we have. We can become greedy or impatient to have everything our way. We don't have the ability to wait or share, even. Too many sad things—which cause salty tears—can bring a person down. But if you have a mix of happy and sad, they actually add to each other. The hard times make you stronger, wiser, gentler, and grateful for what you have. Then the happy times seem that much sweeter!

GOD SAYS . . .

[Job said,] "The LORD gave me what I had, and the LORD has taken it away. Praise the name of the LORD!" In all of this, Job did not sin by blaming God. JOB 1:21-22

HOW ABOUT YOU?

How do the "salty" things in your life make the "sweet" things taste even better?

Dear God, How is a person supposed to get what my grandma calls "the faith that saves"?

June 23

CONSIDER THIS . . . Have you ever climbed a mountain, or ridden in an elevator to the top of a tall building? How about flown in an airplane? Once you reached a certain height, the pressure of the air inside your inner ear probably pushed against your eardrum, expanding it like a balloon. The air filling up the space in your ear made it very hard to hear. Your ears can get "stuffy" and your hearing can suffer when you have a cold, too. That's because there is actual "goo" that fills up your inner ear. Eew.

This is how it is, spiritually speaking, for people who haven't heard the Good News. Perhaps their spiritual ears are so stuffed up for one reason or another, maybe by sin or lack of knowledge, that they haven't heard about the Lord. Maybe they didn't want to hear the gospel. Maybe they live in the middle of nowhere and couldn't hear the Good News!

Scripture says that faith comes by hearing, so that means two things:

1. Someone has to share the Good News so others can hear about it. Is that you? Don't be shy. It may seem a bit awkward at first, but remember, it's the GOOD News. And some will find it exciting.

2. Ears need to be cleared to hear. Be prayerful about asking God whose ears have been opened enough to hear the Good News once you share it. He knows who is ready to hear, and he will point you in the right direction.

Listen carefully. That popping noise you hear might just be a friend's ears opening to the Good News about Christ!

HOW ABOUT YOU?

Do you have the faith that saves? Do you have any friends or family members who do not? How can you share the Good News with them?

GOD SAYS . . .

Not everyone welcomes the Good News, for Isaiah the prophet said, "LORD, who has believed our message?" So faith comes from hearing, that is, hearing the Good News about Christ. ROMANS 10:16-17

Dear God, My family has an exchange student living with us this summer. I don't want to share my room with her. What can I do?

CONSIDER THIS . . . It's not easy to take the normal rhythm of your house and suddenly change tunes. Your family is like a little band—everyone knows what instrument he or she plays and plays his or her part. Your family gets used to having a drum, a guitar, a piano, and a flute.

Now a clarinet has moved in. Things feel and sound kind of strange. It's definitely not what you're used to. You always did fine without a clarinet, but now you have to make room in your music for *her* parts. She squeaks and squawks sometimes. You have to find pieces that include parts for a clarinet.

That's kind of what it feels like when someone new, like a foreign exchange student, moves into your home. Suddenly your parents have to make time for her. You change your family schedule to accommodate her needs too.

If you look at it from her point of view, it's really scary. She's changed her whole band. She can feel your vibe—you don't like her so much. It makes her feel vulnerable. The food is weird. She can't understand what people are saying. She doesn't know when to talk and when to be quiet or what to wear. She needs someone to guide her. That someone is you.

For this short time, include her, kindly, in your life. Make her visit as comfortable as you can. Ask God to change your feelings. He can! Someday *you* will be the stranger. Try to treat your exchange student the way you'd want someone to treat you. As a friend.

GOD SAYS . . .
Anything you did for even the least of my people here, you also did for me." MATTHEW 25:40 (NCV)

HOW ABOUT YOU?
Have you ever had an exchange student, an extended family member, or someone not normally a part of your family live with you? How did it go?

Dear God, Someone hurt my feelings a few months ago. I said I forgave her, but whenever we see each other it still hurts. Did I really forgive her?

June 25

CONSIDER THIS . . . Have you ever broken a bone, or sprained an ankle, or twisted your wrist? How about banged your funny bone, which doesn't feel so funny after all? All of those hurt a lot right away. And then after a little while, the pain fades. But the stronger the injury, the longer it takes for the pain to go away. Sometimes a bruise still hurts a little bit as it's disappearing. But one day, for sure, the hurt will be gone.

Our feelings can be hurt the same way. When the situation that causes the pain happens, it hurts a lot right away! You can forgive the person who has done something that hurt you. Forgiveness, after all, is a decision you make and not an emotion you feel. But the pain probably won't disappear as soon as you forgive the person who hurt you. Instead, it will likely go away little by little, as time goes by. That old saying "Time heals all wounds" is not completely true, because some wounds don't heal. But it is true that time heals *most* wounds.

There is someone who heals all wounds, though, and that is Jesus. He tenderly comes alongside you when you've been hurt. It doesn't matter if it's your body or your emotions that were hurt. He's there to help. He bandages you up so that the part that was injured has time to heal. And then he cares for heart wounds, too.

Soon enough the pain will fade, and someday you may even forget it. Jesus will always be there, ready to help, no matter how or where you are hurt.

HOW ABOUT YOU?

Do you have a heart wound? God has promised that he will heal your hurt. Talk to him about it today.

GOD SAYS . . .

He heals the brokenhearted and bandages their wounds. PSALM 147:3

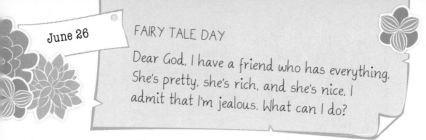

FAIRY TALE DAY

Dear God, I have a friend who has everything. She's pretty, she's rich, and she's nice. I admit that I'm jealous. What can I do?

CONSIDER THIS . . . To envy means to want something that someone else has or to feel like you always have to be the best. People can envy stuff—clothes, a house, or friends. People are often jealous of the way other people look. But being jealous never ends well. Remember the story of Snow White and the seven dwarfs?

A wicked stepmother, the queen, was jealous of her beautiful step-daughter. When the stepmother's mirror told her that Snow White was the most beautiful, the queen ordered that Snow White be killed. A huntsman took pity on the girl, though, and left her in the woods, where she met seven dwarfs who took care of her. But one day, the queen found out that Snow White was still alive. She tried to poison her with an apple, which only led to a handsome prince saving Snow White. Finally, the queen went too far, and in her last effort to kill the girl, she died herself instead!

People think they'll be happy if they get what others have. The truth is that we all have some good things in life and some bad things. Although it may seem like your friend has everything, you can't see her family life, or her fears, or her concerns. You don't know what troubled roads she has had to walk down, or those that lie ahead. You also don't know what beautiful things God has in store for you in the future. The Lord tells us that when we complain, we're really grumbling against him. Why? When we complain, we aren't trusting in his perfect plan for our lives.

Try to focus on what you have, and the good you know God has for you just ahead.

GOD SAYS . . .

Our lives were full of evil and envy, and we hated each other. But—"When God our Savior revealed his kindness and love, he saved us, not because of the righteous things we had done, but because of his mercy." TITUS 3:3-5

HOW ABOUT YOU?

What are some of the wonderful things that the Lord has given to you?

Dear God, I definitely like following you, but it's not always easy. Should I make it seem like it's always fun so other people will want to be Christians too?

CONSIDER THIS . . . Have you ever wanted something really, really badly? Maybe it was a new phone, one that cost a lot of money. Or it could have been a computer, or a game, or a week at an amazing summer camp. It was something that you knew you'd enjoy, but saving all the money you'd need to get it would definitely not be easy to do. When that happens, you have to choose—do you buy (or ask for) the one expensive thing that you want, knowing that if you get it, you'll have no money left for anything else? Or do you save your money and decide to be happy with what you already have?

If it's truly important, most people say yes to buying the expensive item. They're willing to pay the price, to do without other stuff, in order to get the thing that matters most. It's called counting the cost. You literally add up everything you'd have to do without in order to have the thing you most value.

Jesus doesn't fake anyone out or make Christianity seem easier than it is. He tells us right up front that there will be people who hate us, that we have to be holy, that we have to put away things our flesh (our bodies and minds) really want. He tells us to count the cost of everything we'll have to do without in order to have what matters most—him.

When you tell people about God, or share about your own faith, be sure to tell them all of the great things. But don't be afraid to share that it's hard, too. Your friends will need to count the cost, too, so they're not surprised later.

HOW ABOUT YOU?

Do you think people are mostly honest about the great things *and* the difficulties of being a Christian? Why?

GOD SAYS . . .

[Jesus said,] "But don't begin until you count the cost. For who would begin construction of a building without first calculating the cost to see if there is enough money to finish it?" LUKE 14:28

Dear God, Why do we have to do chores all the time? Now that it's summer, we have yard work to do too!

CONSIDER THIS . . . Part of being in a family is sharing responsibilities for what the family needs to get done. Take a soccer team, for example. You need to have several forwards to push the ball toward the opposite goal, several people in defense to guard your goal, and a goalie who guards the net. You need a team to get the victory. One person alone cannot score, defend the field, and guard the goal. A team of one would be overwhelmed and lose the match.

Your family is a team. There are many things that need to be done. Parents need to work, pay bills, keep up the yard, and do housework. They have to arrange for schooling, music lessons, and sports for you. Their most important task is to help you learn about and love Jesus. In order to help your team win, your parents need the rest of the family—kids—to help with those tasks.

Chores aren't fun, so it's okay if you don't jump up and shout hip-hip-hooray! They're not fun for parents, and they're not fun for kids. But not everything that is good for you is fun. Sometimes a challenging task can be rewarding. If you learn to take pleasure in a job well done as well as in fun things, you will live a fulfilled life. Satisfaction with yourself is something that is earned—like a paycheck—and comes from pulling for and helping your team without complaining or arguing.

God tells us that not only will he give us the power to do what pleases him, but he'll even change our hearts.

Pull on your gloves and get weeding with a happy tune in your heart!

GOD SAYS . . .

God is working in you, giving you the desire and the power to do what pleases him. PHILIPPIANS 2:13

HOW ABOUT YOU?

What can you find in chores to be thankful for? Come on, keep thinking until you find something!

Dear God, I need help being a better athlete. What can I do?

CONSIDER THIS . . . Our bodies are incredible. We can't even see most of the work that goes on inside. Our hearts pump about 6,000 times every hour, which adds up to more than 100,000 pumps each day. Our brains are faster and smarter than any computer yet invented. Dozens of other organs are at work. And all of this happens at the same time, keeping us alive!

We may choose to push our bodies a bit to make them faster, stronger, or able to endure more. This is an important part of being an athlete. If you enjoy sports, you probably enjoy working out, too. Even if you don't enjoy sports, it's important to take good care of your body.

The Bible says that our bodies are temples of the Holy Spirit. In the Bible, the Temple was the place where God dwelled. God gave many pages of instruction on what his Temple was to be like. People treated the Temple with care and concern. You need to take great care of your body, too. It's the temple the Holy Spirit lives in now.

It's good to be the best you can be, whether it's in athletics, academics, or character. If you're involved in sports, train your body, practicing the moves you need for whatever sport you are trying to excel in. Ask a coach or a more experienced athlete what you can do to be better. Increase your workouts a little each week to build strength and endurance. Whatever area you are trying to excel in, keep in mind that the time you spend working on your goals will affect only this life. Make sure you leave enough time and energy to be with the Lord each day too! He doesn't even mind if you're sweaty.

HOW ABOUT YOU?
How much time do you spend on spiritual training each day?

GOD SAYS . . .
"Physical training is good, but training for godliness is much better, promising benefits in this life and in the life to come." This is a trustworthy saying, and everyone should accept it. 1 TIMOTHY 4:8-9

Dear God, Do you ever change your mind?

CONSIDER THIS . . . As people, we change our minds all the time. As girls—we change our minds even more than guys. (Just ask a guy about it and see what he thinks!) We change our outfits several times a day. We decide what we want to be when we grow up. And then we change our minds week after week as something more exciting comes along. We may be crushing on one boy one week and then the next week wonder what we ever saw in him. Sometimes we change our minds about what we want to eat at a restaurant, only minutes after we order.

But Scripture tells us that God is not like us. Instead, we see that he is not human and that he would never lie (we know we do!) or change his mind. The Bible says that his ways are higher than our ways (Isaiah 55:9). And because he knows everything, he never has to have a "do over."

This doesn't mean that God doesn't have feelings, though. Genesis 6:6 tells us that when humans turned wicked and all of their thoughts turned evil, God was sorry that he had made them. But notice that the verse doesn't say that he changed his mind about humans. It just says that his heart was broken because of their evil actions.

It's a wonderful thing to realize that the God we love and serve has feelings just like we do. We can trust our joys and our broken hearts to him because he understands. But he never changes his mind about anything or anyone . . . and that includes you!

GOD SAYS . . .

God is not a man, so he does not lie. He is not human, so he does not change his mind. Has he ever spoken and failed to act? Has he ever promised and not carried it through? NUMBERS 23:19

HOW ABOUT YOU?

How does it make you feel to know that the Lord will never turn his great love away from you, no matter what?

CREATIVE ICE CREAM FLAVOR DAY

Dear God, Has any Scripture been written since the Bible was finished?

July 1

CONSIDER THIS . . . Many families love to visit ice cream parlors or shops in the summer. Among the favorites? The places where you can choose your ice cream, then choose which candies you want to mix into the frozen confection. Want vanilla ice cream with crushed chocolate cookies and pieces of fudge? You got it. Does your brother want cake batter ice cream with a handful of gumballs? (It may not sound good to you, but it does to him.) Coming right up! You can have as many add-ins as you want . . . and as you're willing to pay for. It's great to have choices.

There are some things, however, that don't allow for add-ins. You can be married to only one person at a time. If you choose to follow Jesus, you can't worship or admire any other gods. And Scripture, as it was written, is complete. Nothing more can be added in! The Bible not only says that no more words should be added to it, but it says that the Lord may rebuke you if you add to it. This means that religions that came about later and claim they have things to add to the Word of God are, simply, wrong. It also means that we as Christians have to be very careful before we tell someone, "The Bible says. . . ." Make sure it says, and means, what you're about to share.

Add-ins are great for yogurt, for potato salad, and especially for creative ice cream combos. Just make sure you don't add anything to the Truth!

HOW ABOUT YOU?

Have you ever told someone, "The Bible says . . ." but then weren't 100 percent sure that's what it actually says? What can you do to make sure you share only what's in the Bible?

GOD SAYS . . .

Every word of God proves true. He is a shield to all who come to him for protection. Do not add to his words, or he may rebuke you and expose you as a liar. PROVERBS 30:5-6

Dear God, Could you explain what guys think when they see a girl wearing immodest clothes and what they think when they see a girl in modest clothes?

CONSIDER THIS . . . Although God gave us five senses, without a doubt the most powerful one of them all is sight. What we see goes into our brains and becomes a part of our thoughts. That's why it's so important for us to guard our eyes—that is, pay careful attention to what we look at. Although everyone wanting to live a holy life must do this, it's particularly important for boys and men. God has designed them to be very sensitive to what they see, kind of like girls are more sensitive to the emotions they feel. When a guy sees a girl wearing immodest clothes, his attention may be drawn in an unhealthy way to how she looks instead of focusing on the person she is on the inside.

As Christians, we are to encourage one another on to good works. A boy is responsible for where he looks and what he lets his gaze linger on. But a girl is responsible to help him by not wearing clothing that might lead his thoughts in a wrong direction. That doesn't mean you have to be covered from the top of your head to the tip of your toes. But it does mean that you have to be modest—wearing only what you feel comfortable with your dad, your grandpa, a male teacher, and even the Lord seeing.

Doing this also treats yourself with respect. Your value as a person is not in how many eyes you can draw. Your beauty is deeper than that: in your spirit, in your mind, and in your heart. The boys around you may look at girls who are skimpily dressed, but they respect the girls who respect themselves.

It's okay to look nice. Just dress as "good" as you look!

GOD SAYS . . .
I [Job] made an agreement with my eyes not to look with desire at a girl. JOB 31:1 (NCV)

HOW ABOUT YOU?
Are you ever tempted to dress immodestly? Why?

Dear God, Are there really evil spirits?

CONSIDER THIS ... Yes. How do we know for sure? Because Jesus tells us in Matthew 10:1 ("Jesus called his twelve disciples together and gave them authority to cast out evil spirits") and in other places too.

The name *Satan* is a Hebrew word that means "enemy, one who goes against you." Satan is the chief evil spirit, the enemy of God. If you are a Christian, anyone who is God's enemy is your enemy too. Satan hates you because you love God and God loves you. Evil spirits, who obey Satan, are also your enemies. They can tempt you to do wrong, or they may try to take advantage of your weaknesses. They can accuse you or lie to you. They try to make bad things look good and good things look bad. These enemies fight against us and want us to lose and be hurt.

Jesus tells us, though, that he has already won the fight against this world's evil. So even though Satan and his evil spirits (demons) can make a lot of noise, Jesus is already the winner. You are, too, if you are a Christian. A Christian is someone who recognizes that Jesus is God, acknowledges that he died on the cross for her sins, and trusts in Jesus as her Savior. The Holy Spirit lives in you, and because he is God, he is stronger than any evil you face.

Jesus also tells us that nothing can take us away from him or his care. Even though evil spirits exist, you are always protected.

HOW ABOUT YOU?

Are you afraid of evil spirits? If so, whom can you talk to about this? What (who) protects you? Can anything separate you from God's love?

GOD SAYS ...

I [Paul] am convinced that nothing can ever separate us from God's love. Neither death nor life, neither angels nor demons, neither our fears for today nor our worries about tomorrow—not even the powers of hell can separate us from God's love. ROMANS 8:38

Dear God, I don't feel like I hear from you or see anything special that you are showing me. What am I doing wrong?

CONSIDER THIS . . . A family once went to the state fair in the middle of the summer. There were lots of rides, and there was lots of noise. People shouted out at passersby, asking them to buy hats, balloons, jewelry. There were hundreds of smells in the air: corn dogs and deep-fried pickles and scones with strawberry jam. Sounds and sights and tastes and smells were everywhere. By the end of the day, sore feet were everywhere too.

So the family sat on a nearby bench. As they did, the girl looked up into a tree. Tucked way back in the branches—behind an escaped balloon—was a small nest. In that nest was a mother bird and her baby birds. For just a minute the bird caught the girl's eye, and they stared at each other. Then the mother went back to feeding her babies, who snuggled into their nest. Although there had been lots of excitement during the day, the touching moment between the baby birds and their mother was the one the girl loved most.

Often in our daily lives, the bright sights, strong smells, loud noise, and constant activity keep our minds and bodies hopping. There is so much to take in that we miss the things that might come to us if we set aside a quiet moment. God sometimes gets our attention in a big way. But mostly, he comes to us and shares his Word, his heart, and his direction when we take time to sit down and be quiet. Even Jesus himself chose to withdraw to quiet places, often, to meet with his Father.

Lay the distractions aside for just a minute and close your eyes. What do you hear? Sense? See?

GOD SAYS . . .
The news about [Jesus] spread all the more, so that crowds of people came to hear him and to be healed of their sicknesses. But Jesus often withdrew to lonely places and prayed.
LUKE 5:15-16 (NIV)

HOW ABOUT YOU?
How often do you sit in a quiet place for a little while and listen or look for what God is eager to share with you?

Dear God, Do I need to do my devotions or read the Bible in the morning? I'm always really rushed and kind of tired in the morning.

CONSIDER THIS . . . Morning can definitely be a busy time of day for most people. Adults are rushing to get ready for work, and kids are scrambling to get ready for school. Breakfast happens—sometimes. Lunches need to be packed. Permission statements need to be signed. Homework needs to be gathered and stuffed in backpacks. Clean clothes? Clean shoes? Socks that match?

But then again, the time after school can be hard too. The day has been long and you're tired. All you want to do is veg in front of the TV for a while. As soon as you get your snack, and your energy back up, it's time for homework.

And then, there are sports. And dinner. And chores. By the end of the day, if you're like most people, you fall into bed exhausted, ready to start it all over again, until you realize, *Hey! I spent, like, zero time with God today!*

It's not that you have to do your devos in the morning. It's just that it's easy to let a whole day slide by and leave God waiting by the door. It's easy to keep putting if off until later. But later often never comes.

Pick a time, maybe early before you get up for the day, or maybe right after dinner, or perhaps late at night when everyone else is asleep. Make that your do-not-miss time with God. Set an alarm on your phone to remind you. Turn off the phone, the computer, and the music once the time arrives. If a friend asked you to save time to spend with her, you would, wouldn't you?

HOW ABOUT YOU?

Does God usually get some quality time or your leftover time? When can you make sure you take time to spend with him?

GOD SAYS . . .

I rise early, before the sun is up; I cry out for help and put my hope in your words. I stay awake through the night, thinking about your promise. PSALM 119:147-148

Dear God, I'm homeschooled, but I want to go to a public school because I've never gone to one before. But my parents don't want me to.

CONSIDER THIS . . . You might not believe this, but there are some kids in public and Christian schools who want to be homeschooled. Some homeschooled kids want to go to Christian or public schools. Some kids in public schools want to go to Christian schools. When the going gets tough, the other choices look sweet!

There are a lot of considerations a family makes when they choose schooling for their kids. Parents consider the strengths of the schools where they live, how much money they have, their job situations, and what kind of schools work best for them and their children. They think about how their children learn and what their children will be learning. Many times there are reasons for the choices your parents make that they haven't told you about.

Could you ask your parents to explain exactly why they chose to home-school you? Be sure to ask for, and not demand, an explanation. This explanation is not for them to defend their decision, but to help you feel better about it. Then you can tell them what you feel you are missing—more friends, a locker, or whatever it is you wish you had by going to public school. Perhaps by brainstorming, your family can figure out how to solve your problem.

There is no perfect schooling option—each one has some strong points and some weak points. But after prayer and discussion, you ultimately have to accept that your parents have selected with great love what they believe is best for both you and your family. Choose to be satisfied with their decision. Then settle back and enjoy the parts of schooling that make it special for you, your family, and your friends.

GOD SAYS . . .

I have learned to be satisfied with the things I have and with everything that happens. PHILIPPIANS 4:11 (NCV)

HOW ABOUT YOU?

Do you wish you were schooled in a different way? What do you feel you are missing? How could you get that in your current schooling situation?

Dear God, I'm having a really hard time with some stuff. Do you see me, and if you do, why are you letting this happen?

July 7

CONSIDER THIS . . . A favorite summer activity is swimming in a river, or in a lake. Sometimes lakes and rivers have sandy bottoms, which makes them fun to walk on. But sometimes the bottoms of the lakes are rocky. Those rocks hurt when you step on them! But they are good for one thing—they are beautiful to behold.

Have you ever tried using a rock polisher? You open the little container and put the sharp-edged rocks in. After that, a little polish powder is added, and then the machine is turned on. Rock polishers are also called rock tumblers because the rocks go round and round, bumping into each other, rubbing up against sharp edges, for hours.

Don't turn the machine off early, though. If you wait the full cycle, which can be a very long time, you won't have rocks at the end. You'll have soft, smooth, pretty jewels. Pretty enough to be made into rings and bracelets and necklaces.

Life is like that sometimes. It has sharp edges—and so do some of the people we bump up against. Stuff happens, and some of it hurts. But ultimately, because God is all-powerful and in control, he's the one allowing the tumbling. He's not allowing those things to happen to harm you, even though they might hurt. It's because he knows that after just the right amount of time, that tumbling will turn you into a gleaming jewel.

HOW ABOUT YOU?

What difficulties do you have in your life right now? Can you ask God to show you how to make it through?

GOD SAYS . . .

When troubles come your way, consider it an opportunity for great joy. . . . When your faith is tested, your endurance has a chance to grow. . . . When your endurance is fully developed, you will be perfect and complete, needing nothing. JAMES 1:2-4

Dear God, My new neighbors are very nice, but they eat weird things. Now they've invited us over for dinner. What if they ask me to eat goat?

CONSIDER THIS . . . Most countries around the world have their own language. We each have our own unique tastes, too! In fact, one of the best parts about visiting another country, or even another state, is trying out their food. It might not seem exciting to eat, say, crawfish, if you visit Louisiana. But Louisianans love them, and you might, too, if you give them a try. Louisianans might not like your state's best offering, say, pickled fish or mustard dogs. But you'd hope that they'd try it if they came to visit.

Long ago God gave his people some food rules. He told them what they could eat and what they couldn't eat based on what was "clean." These rules became a part of their faith, but they also led to better physical health. When Jesus came, he did away with those food rules. God told Peter that it was okay to eat what everyone around him was eating. By doing so, Peter became friendlier to his neighbors and was better able to share his faith.

Your neighbors have offered an invitation to you to eat with them. Unless you have an allergy, or are a vegetarian, it might be the kindest thing you could do to eat what they offer. It's a way of showing respect for them.

You might eat goat, but that's not the worst thing in the world. Most countries think eating peanut butter is disgusting, but we Americans love it. And did you know that the government says it's okay for a few bug legs to appear in your peanut butter? Even the Bible says eating insects is okay . . . and they are much less tasty than goat!

GOD SAYS . . .

The insects you are permitted to eat include all kinds of locusts, bald locusts, crickets, and grasshoppers. LEVITICUS 11:22

HOW ABOUT YOU?

Are you willing to give up a little comfort to reach out a hand of friendship to someone who is different from you?

Dear God, Is it okay if grandparents spoil their grandchildren, or will it cause problems?

July 9

CONSIDER THIS . . . Being a parent is hard work. Parents love their kids, but they must enforce rules. It's your mom and dad's job to raise you to be healthy and godly, not always to make you happy. I'm sure you've figured that out by now. It also costs a lot of money to raise children—one study estimated it costs almost $500,000 to raise a child. And if your family has more than one kid, your parents are spending even more money to raise you. Wow! That means parents must work hard, and a lot of the money has to go for "needs" and not "wants."

The responsibilities of grandparents are different from the responsibilities of parents. The Bible says that older men and women are to set a good example for younger men and women (Titus 2:1-7). Your grandparents should support your parents in what they do—help when they can, share wisdom, and give love. They also have more time—and often money—to spend on you! Many times they will have a listening ear and a ready hug because they don't have to discipline you. They may have money to spend on fun things like a vacation or a ball game or an unexpected outfit. They can do and say things to let you know just how special you are, with no expectations in return! It's pleasant for them to see the children of their own beloved grown children.

As long as your grandparents respect and support the rules and patterns set down by your parents, you're not being spoiled—you're being loved! Be sure to be thankful, not expecting these extras, but enjoying them as they are freely given.

HOW ABOUT YOU?

What are three nice things your grandparents do for you? Have you written your grandparents a thank-you note (not just talked to them by phone or on e-mail) lately? When will you do so?

GOD SAYS . . .

Grandchildren are the crowning glory of the aged.
PROVERBS 17:6

July 10

Dear God, My cousin and I argue all the time and usually have one really big fight every year. How will we ever get along?

CONSIDER THIS . . . You have asked a wise question. You already know something is wrong, and you know that the way you act toward each other isn't the way God wants you to act. The Bible says people will know we are Christians by the way we love one another. Loving others is a very important part of being a Christian, maybe the most important after following Christ. So here's a little prescription for peace with your cousin. You can't make her follow it, but you can follow it yourself. I'll bet if you change the way you act, she'll change the way she acts too. Love is hard to resist.

1. Tell your cousin you are sorry if you've done anything to hurt her feelings.
2. Ask her if there is anything you can do to make your relationship smoother.
3. Be kind to her, putting her interests above your own.

Loving someone who acts like she's your enemy will not be easy. In fact, it will be hard. You've been fighting a long time, and our pride does not want us to put others before ourselves. If we call ourselves Christians, though, we must choose to act as Christ did. Unselfishly. You can do it, girl.

GOD SAYS . . .
When you do things, do not let selfishness or pride be your guide. Instead, be humble and give more honor to others than to yourselves. . . . In your lives you must think and act like Christ Jesus. PHILIPPIANS 2:3, 5 (NCV)

HOW ABOUT YOU?

Is there someone you fight with a lot? What can you do just once to put that person's needs above your own?

Dear God, My family is having troubles again. I'm feeling pretty angry about it all. Whom should I be mad at?

July 11

CONSIDER THIS . . . Maybe . . . no one? It's really tough when one hard thing comes your way, and it's even more difficult when challenges come one right after another. Believe it or not, troubles have a point.

Consider the people who make airplanes. Airplanes take years to develop. When engineers are trying to decide what kind of metal to use on the airplanes, they make them undergo "stress tests." These tests, which place pressure and stress on the metal, show the engineers if the metal is strong enough for the job it has to do. Will it break up at 20,000 feet in the air? If so, you definitely don't want to fly on a plane made out of that. Will it withstand a bird flying into it? If lightning strikes, will the metal shuffle that electricity off where it won't do damage?

When a weakness shows up, the engineers go back and figure out a way to make the metal stronger. They add or subtract materials until the plane is just right. When it's finally built, ready to soar, it is strong and doesn't crumble no matter what comes against it.

Every time you undergo a test, God says you are to be thankful. Now, that might seem strange at first, but he's not asking you to be happy that hard things are going on. Instead, he's helping you undergo a "stress test" so that any weaknesses in your faith can be located. Once fixed, those weaknesses disappear, and you're stronger and better able to endure than ever.

He's a tender engineer. He's not here to hurt you. He's here to make you perfect and complete.

HOW ABOUT YOU?
How might the troubles you face right now actually be making you strong?

GOD SAYS . . .
When troubles come your way, consider it an opportunity for great joy.
JAMES 1:2

Dear God, Some of my friends swear, and sometimes I feel tempted to swear. Can I?

CONSIDER THIS . . . One thing that helps when you see others doing things is to remember this: we live by standards, not by comparisons. What does that mean? It means you do or don't do something not because others are doing it (or not doing it) but because it fits in (or doesn't fit in) with the way you have decided to live your life. If you're trying to live a life according to what God says is good, swearing would be out.

Our language helps identify us with others. If we are Americans in Spain and we hear someone else speaking American English, we instantly feel a bond with that person. We have something in common! We belong together, somehow. When your friends swear, you might want to do it, too, to fit in with them. When others hear you swearing, though, they might assume you are just like the kids who swear. Kids and adults will associate you with that group's behavior whether you want them to or not.

The Bible tells us not to use bad language, only words that would be helpful and encouraging to others. If you were to swear, it would tell your friends that you think it's okay. If you don't think it's okay, you would be helping them to do wrong.

Pray and ask the Lord to help you overcome your desire to swear. You can find other ways to identify with your friends. Maybe you all sit at a certain lunch table. You share music. You text each other, and you remind one another about homework. These are ways that you can be similar and still be helpful to one another. When they choose bad language, remain silent. Your silence will be even more powerful than their bad language.

GOD SAYS . . .
The temptations in your life are no different from what others experience. And God is faithful. He will not allow the temptation to be more than you can stand. When you are tempted, he will show you a way out.
1 CORINTHIANS 10:13

HOW ABOUT YOU?
Do you feel tempted to make poor choices to fit in with your friends? What can you do to fight the temptation?

Dear God, If I'm a Christian, will I ever lose my chance to go to heaven?

July 13

CONSIDER THIS . . . Have you ever had a friend give something to you, then decide that she wanted it back and ask for you to return it? How did that make you feel? Or say that she gave something to you, and then later told you she was only letting you borrow it and now she wanted it back. When someone gives you a gift, she means for you to keep it unless she tells you up front that it is a loan and it has to be returned. God is a good friend; he does not ask you to return the gifts he's given you.

This helps you to live in freedom and happiness within your relationship to the Lord. Think about a time when you were waiting in line to go on a ride at an amusement park. You're standing there in a long line, with your friends and family. A roller-coaster car pulls up and the park attendant starts allowing people through to get into the ride. If you're toward the front of the line, you're certain that you're going to get on with those you came with. So you're not nervous, just excited. You can wait patiently and think of the fun you'll have.

If, however, you're toward the back of the line, you might start getting antsy. Will you make it on? Will you be separated from those you love and have to ride alone? It doesn't feel peaceful, and you can't enjoy the wait.

Knowing that your faith is intact and that you will go to be with Jesus if you're a Christian helps you enjoy the waiting time without being worried about being separated from him eternally. Nothing is more powerful than God. Nothing can take you from his hand.

HOW ABOUT YOU?

Are you secure in your faith in Christ?

GOD SAYS . . .

I give them eternal life, and they will never perish. No one can snatch them away from me, for my Father has given them to me, and he is more powerful than anyone else. No one can snatch them from the Father's hand. JOHN 10:28-29

Dear God, You're the creator of the universe. I'm one of seven billion people on earth. Are we really friends? I'm not even that popular in school. How can you know who I am?

CONSIDER THIS . . . There's no doubt that people were made to work together—the happiest people, who live the longest, are those with close family and friends. Our friends know us best. They know what we like and what we don't like. If they're close friends, we might even tell them our embarrassing secrets, like that we're afraid of the dark, or are scared of dogs, or have a crush on a boy that no one else knows about. If sad things happen, we rush to tell our closest friends because we know they care. They might come over and sit with us, or take us someplace to take our minds off whatever is bothering us. If someone trash-talks us, true friends will stick up for us. They're faithful and loyal, no matter what!

Amazingly, Jesus is our friend, a good friend. He's the best friend we could ever have!

It's true that God is the creator and sustainer of everything, and that he is all-knowing and all-powerful. But he knows who you are. The Bible says that he even knows the number of hairs on your head (Matthew 10:30). There are places where Scripture says that we are to serve him, and we do. But Jesus himself tells us that we are not his slaves. A master doesn't confide in his slaves; they aren't close—there is no love relationship. Jesus tells us exactly what he thinks of us. Now, we are his friends.

GOD SAYS . . .

I no longer call you slaves, because a master doesn't confide in his slaves. Now you are my friends, since I have told you everything the Father told me. JOHN 15:15

HOW ABOUT YOU?

Do you ever think of Jesus as you would a friend—someone to confide in, draw close to when you're sad, share joy with? What can you share with him today?

Dear God, My friend's brother started smoking, and now my friend is smoking too. She wants me to try it, and if I say no, she won't be my friend anymore.

CONSIDER THIS . . . It's very hard to sit by and watch your friend go down a wrong path, especially someone you've been friends with for a long time. You sound a little fearful, too, that you're going to have to choose—between keeping your friend while doing something you know is wrong (smoking) and losing your friend when you refuse to smoke.

Your friend has taken on a very unhealthy habit. She gave in to pressure from her brother to smoke. Who knows what kind of pressure she might give in to next? And she's already told you that you have to do something you don't want to do to keep her friendship. That's not a very good friend. Sometimes, when people do things they know are wrong, they try to get others to do those things with them. That way, they tell themselves, it's not so bad. After all—you're doing it too!

The Bible tells us that to honor the Lord we must obey the law of the land (1 Peter 2:13-14). The law of this land says it's illegal for kids to smoke. In order to protect us, the Bible also tells us that we are to stay away from people who keep on doing wrong things. It doesn't tell us to stay away from them only when they're doing wrong; it just says to stay away from them. Why? Because everyone is able to be tempted. Sooner or later your good habits might be set aside. Although you may need to tell your friend she'll have to choose between smoking and you, you don't have to give up on her. Faithfully praying for her is a way to express your love and concern even when you can't be together.

HOW ABOUT YOU?

Has anyone pressured you to do something you know is wrong? What should you do?

GOD SAYS . . .

Bad company corrupts good character.
1 CORINTHIANS 15:33

Dear God, My parents are getting a divorce. I'm so upset. What can I do to feel better?

CONSIDER THIS . . . Divorce is one of the hardest things a kid may ever have to deal with, but you don't have to go through it alone. Sit in a quiet place and pour your heart out to God. Tell him how sad you are about the whole situation, that you feel hurt and angry, and whatever else you're feeling. God is not uncomfortable hearing about your feelings. He wants you to be honest with him. Pray and ask the Lord to help you make it through the hard days.

The great news is that you *can* handle it with God's help. God has many names; some of them will help you remember what he will do for you in this (and any other) tough situation. He is called Comforter and Counselor. His comfort and counsel will help to heal your broken heart. He is a Friend, remember. He is a strong Rock who will never leave you. He is a mighty help in time of trouble.

Talk with your mom and dad about your fear that once they are divorced you won't be able to keep in touch with each family. Ask them to set up times to make sure you get to see all of your grandparents and cousins, if that's what worries you. Brainstorm some special things you can do with each of them—hiking only with Dad, for example, or having dinner together the first Thursday of every month. Maybe you and your mom can do your clothes shopping or have a beauty night. If you set up special routines with each person you want to stay close to, it will help you set aside time for each other.

GOD SAYS . . .
The LORD is a shelter for the oppressed, a refuge in times of trouble. Those who know your name trust in you, for you, O LORD, do not abandon those who search for you.
PSALM 9:9-10

HOW ABOUT YOU?
What routines can you set up so you can spend more time together with each of your parents, even if they aren't divorced?

Dear God, If you knew Adam and Eve would eat the fruit, why did you put the tree of the knowledge of good and evil in the Garden?

July 17

CONSIDER THIS . . . God is the creator of everything. He made all the trees, plants, animals, planets, stars, angels, and human beings. Most of his creation has no personal relationship with him—that is, it can't interact with him. God can create trees, and he can enjoy their beauty, but trees don't love God back. Only angels and human beings are able to love God back.

Do you remember how you felt about your favorite stuffed animal or doll? You loved it, and you cared for it. But even the most tender stuffed animal can't love you back. People can love us, though. That is why, as much as we loved our dolls, we didn't love them as much as our best friends, parents, or siblings.

When God created humans, he wanted beings that could love him back and choose to worship and obey him. In order for us to do that, he had to give us a choice. We could choose to love and obey him or not. By putting the tree in the Garden, God gave people the opportunity to choose. If there were no way to sin, we could never make that free choice. As we know, Adam and Eve chose to disobey when they ate the fruit, but there were other times when they obeyed. Adam and Eve had the same choice we have every day—to obey God or not. Sometimes we choose to obey, sometimes we choose not to.

Love isn't really love unless the person has a choice to love or not. God wants our love, so he allows people to make choices for or against him every day. Adam and Eve had the choice to obey and follow God or to sin. You have that choice too!

HOW ABOUT YOU?

How do you choose to show God your love in your every-day life?

GOD SAYS . . .

Jesus replied, "'You must love the LORD your God with all your heart, all your soul, and all your mind.' This is the first and greatest commandment."
MATTHEW 22:37-38

Dear God, What if my parents died? I think it would be awful, and I wouldn't be able to stand it afterward.

CONSIDER THIS . . . For any kid, pretty much the worst thing they can think of happening to them is for one or both of their parents to die. We not only love our parents more than anyone else in the world, but we depend on them. *If they were taken away,* we think, *all would be lost.* Sometimes, if we let that fear get hold of us, it can take over our thoughts and steal our happiness—even when nothing's happened!

It sounds like the story of a girl who had a very real fear of drowning. She was so afraid of drowning that she never went near the water. Once, though, on a family vacation, she saw what fun the others were having, so she ventured into the ocean. After a few minutes, a series of large waves rolled in, and one of them knocked her down. She waved her hands in the air, desperate to get someone's attention before she sank for good. Finally, she was able to hear someone call out to her, "Stand up!" The waves had knocked her down, but she was so fear-filled that she hadn't realized she was on her knees. When she stood up, she saw she was okay and well above the water.

God knows that we all have fears and that some of them come true. But most of them do not. If you live in fear of what might happen, you could let every wave that knocked you to your knees seem like it was the end. Trust the Lord. If something happens to your parents, or when any hard thing happens, he promises to be right with you. He'll help you stand again, no matter what knocks you down.

GOD SAYS . . .

I will protect the orphans who remain among you. Your widows, too, can depend on me for help.
JEREMIAH 49:11

HOW ABOUT YOU?

What do you fear? Can you trust God to protect you, and will you depend on his promise to help?

Dear God, Why does everyone have to be so prejudiced?

CONSIDER THIS . . . The word *prejudiced* means judging someone else without knowing very much about him or her. Maybe almost nothing at all! Normally when we talk about others being prejudiced, we mean they have decided they are better than other people. Usually they feel they are superior to people of other skin colors, people who have less money than they do, people who are younger than they are, or even people who aren't good looking.

Sometimes people are scared to get to know people who are different from them. They are afraid that if they talk to someone different from them, they will be rejected or feel left out of that person's group because they may not have anything in common. They are also afraid of what other people may think. For example, they may be afraid that if they are friends with someone younger, people will think they are babyish. But most of the time when people are prejudiced, they just like to raise themselves up by stepping on others.

The Bible says that we are all equal, and that God himself does not focus on what people look like on the outside, only at what's in their hearts. The Bible never favors richer people over poorer people—it's usually just the opposite! The Bible says that if we judge each other, we will be judged in the same way. Instead, we are to treat each other as brothers and sisters.

As Christians, we can show the world a better way by refusing to pre-judge people based on their outsides. Love others for who they are on the inside, just like God does!

HOW ABOUT YOU?

Whom are you prejudiced against? (Be honest. It's just between you and God.) How can you get to know that person, or that group of people, better?

GOD SAYS . . .

There is no longer Jew or Gentile, slave or free, male and female. For you are all one in Christ Jesus. GALATIANS 3:28

Dear God, Sometimes I feel like I have so many pressures on me that my brain is going to explode. Could that really happen?

CONSIDER THIS . . . Some days it feels as though we are overwhelmed by all of the opportunities in our society—we have lots of technology to use, fun activities to do, interesting books and magazines to read, and good music to listen to. Most girls participate in a sport or go to an event at church during the week. Some girls are involved in theater or in band. And then, of course, there's always homework and chores to complete and family and friends to spend time with.

It really can seem like a lot of pressure, especially if you want to do everything well.

There's nothing wrong with stepping back from some of your activities if they feel like they are too much or there are too many. Sometimes we put too much pressure on ourselves because we want to do everything perfectly. It's okay to do some things imperfectly and just for fun. Sometimes, the things we think are going to cause us to explode are actually the new activities that we try: a new sport, class, or instrument. If we stick with it past that awkward beginning time, we might find it to be something we love and are talented at.

Society, other people, and even we ourselves can load things on us that add stress. But remember—a diamond is formed by taking a lump of coal and adding just the right amount of pressure on all sides. No pressure? No diamond! See if you can figure out which activities might make you want to cave and which might be forming the jewel of a lifetime inside of you. God will help you make these decisions, along with your parents, so your brain won't explode!

GOD SAYS . . .
We are pressed on every side by troubles, but we are not crushed. We are perplexed, but not driven to despair. 2 CORINTHIANS 4:8

HOW ABOUT YOU?
Do you have activities or stress in your life that feel like they are too much to handle? Who can you talk with about this?

NATIONAL JUNK FOOD DAY

July 21

Dear God, Does it really matter what I eat?

CONSIDER THIS . . . Have you ever heard the potato chip commercial that dares, "Bet you can't eat just one"? Most of us think we can eat just one . . . chip, or small handful of chocolates, or tiny bowl of caramel corn. But oftentimes, we go on to eat more than one, or two, or ten! All of that junk food is delicious, but if we eat too much, it makes us feel kind of gross. Our stomachs may hurt or feel queasy, or we may feel tired (especially after the initial sugar rush) and sluggish.

There's a phrase that computer programmers use: garbage in, garbage out. In other words, when you're designing a game or a word processing program, you have to put good computer code in if you want to get a fun game in return. If you don't, you're just going to get a lot of confusing mistakes. This is true, too, for what you put into your body. Junk in—junk out! If you want shiny hair and healthy skin, if strong bones and pretty teeth are important to you, you need to eat well. It's okay to eat a few treats and some junk food. You have twenty-one meals each week. Pay attention to putting healthy things in for twenty of them, and it won't matter what you eat for the twenty-first.

As you get older, your parents will make fewer and fewer decisions for you; you'll get to make more and more on your own. That's really fun . . . but it also comes with responsibility. You're definitely old enough to make some of your own decisions now. That goes for wise food choices too.

Bet you don't eat the whole bag!

HOW ABOUT YOU?

Do you choose to eat things that are good for your body, or junk? What healthier foods can you start eating?

GOD SAYS . . .

Do you like honey? Don't eat too much, or it will make you sick!
PROVERBS 25:16

Dear God, It really bothers me when I see people treating animals poorly. Is there anything a girl my age can do?

CONSIDER THIS . . . People who have pets, and even those who don't, know that animals have feelings. We can see that they can be happy or sad. Some pets pout when you don't play with them, or they tuck their tails between their legs when they're in trouble. When they sense that you are sad, pets will often curl up next to you until you feel better.

Animals in the wild, and in the zoo, have feelings too. Although animals are not the same as people because they haven't been made in the image of God, they are still important to him. When animals were made in the Garden of Eden, the Lord gave people the responsibility to rule over them. Ruling well means caring for them. Most animals are helpless against humans, so it's our job to speak up for them.

If seeing the elephants caged in zoos bothers you, you can e-mail your local zoo and ask how they are cared for. Maybe an explanation will help you see that the zookeepers really are taking good care of the animals. Maybe if the zookeepers know how much people care, they'll do an even better job. If there is a pet shelter nearby, you might donate some of your time or allowance to it. You might consider doing a school project about endangered animals. There is a lot that you can do to make sure that those who can't speak for themselves get justice. When you do, you are being like Jesus. God cares for the animals too.

GOD SAYS . . .
Speak up for those who cannot speak for themselves; ensure justice for those being crushed. Yes, speak up for the poor and helpless, and see that they get justice.
PROVERBS 31:8-9

HOW ABOUT YOU?
What can you do to help animals in need?

Dear God, I can feel that you are changing me in some ways that are good, but why does it always seem to be uncomfortable?

July 23

CONSIDER THIS . . . Did you realize that kids' toys are good for teaching important lessons? Take, for example, one of those blue-and-red blocks with cutout shapes. The idea is to fit the square shapes through the square holes, or the star-shaped ones through the star-shaped holes. You can't fit the star-shaped block through a round hole. It just won't work!

Play-Doh is another good example. There are molds that, when you fit the Play-Doh into them and crank a handle, will form a certain shape. If you put the dough into a cat-shaped mold, it will look like a cat—though blue or green or red—when it's squeezed out.

Clay is very much like Play-Doh, and God tells us that he is a potter and we are his clay. In the Bible the Lord tells Jeremiah, "Go down to the potter's shop, and I will speak to you there." Jeremiah writes, "So I did as he told me and found the potter working at his wheel. But the jar he was making did not turn out as he had hoped, so he crushed it into a lump of clay again and started over. Then the LORD gave me this message: 'O Israel, can I not do to you as this potter has done to his clay? As the clay is in the potter's hand, so are you in my hand'" (Jeremiah 18:2-6).

God says he knew us in advance, and he wanted us to become like his Son. That means that we have to be pushed and pulled, and sometimes crushed, to be reformed. This doesn't always feel good—for Play-Doh or for people! But keep in mind that the shaping only lasts for a little while, but you, God's Jesus-shaped work of art, will last for eternity.

HOW ABOUT YOU?

Did you realize that God wants to fit you into the image of Jesus? How is he shaping you now?

GOD SAYS . . .

God knew his people in advance, and he chose them to become like his Son.
ROMANS 8:29

Dear God, There is a lot of stuff going on in the world, but my problems aren't really earth shattering. Are you ever too busy to listen to me?

CONSIDER THIS ... Now that almost everyone has a cell phone, it seems easy to get in touch with anyone you want, whenever you want. You can call your friend if you want to hear her voice. Or you can text if you want to send a quick note. If you call someone and she doesn't pick up, you might wonder, *Where is she?* If you leave a message and it's not returned, you might feel like you're being ignored. If you text back and forth with someone for a while, and suddenly she doesn't answer, it can feel like she's gotten angry. Or distracted. Or maybe she found someone more interesting or important than you to talk to!

Sometimes you may think that God is too busy to answer your call. But God is different. He is always present, everywhere. He's never out of range and has been close by for thousands of years before cell phones. Although God is very busy, he is never too busy to listen to the cries, whispers, prayers, and celebrations of all of his children. He had David write a psalm to tell us that he will answer and that he bends down to listen to us when we pray. You don't need to keep him in your contacts, because even if you forget how to get ahold of him (prayer! worship! Scripture!), he never forgets how to get ahold of you.

Go on. Tell him anything you like, anytime you like. He's listening.

GOD SAYS ...

[David wrote,] "I am praying to you because I know you will answer, O God. Bend down and listen as I pray." PSALM 17:6

HOW ABOUT YOU?

Do you realize that God is listening to you all day, every day? He never feels that your concerns are unimportant, and he's not too busy to listen. What can you talk to him about today?

Dear God, Why does the Bible say girls are supposed to have long hair but boys can't?

July 25

CONSIDER THIS . . . Many of the books in the New Testament are letters that were sent to local churches. Christianity was a new faith, and like many new believers, people in those churches didn't understand exactly what it meant to follow Christ. So they wrote to or spoke with church leaders to understand. It's kind of the same thing as you asking a Sunday school teacher or a youth group leader a question. You want to do what is right, so you ask!

The city of Corinth wasn't known for being a clean, moral place. There was a lot of nasty stuff going on. When some Corinthians became Christians, they wanted to make sure that people knew that they were now different from the people they had been—they had been made new! They were also different from the immodest and immoral people around them. One way to do this was to make sure that they looked and acted respectable. In that culture, a woman with short hair, or a man with long hair, was seen as rebellious and immoral. Paul wanted to help the new believers make sure that they weren't seen that way anymore.

In our society, a woman with short hair or a man with long hair isn't seen as rebellious to faith or immoral. But there are other ways of dressing, or of adorning your body, that might be. God still wants us to be good representatives of him. We should be people who look different, clean, holy, and set apart. He also wants men and boys to look masculine, and women and girls to appear feminine, because that's how he made them. Hair, of course, can be cut or grown out, and fashions can change. But doing what's right never goes out of style!

HOW ABOUT YOU?

What are some fashions that you think show rebelliousness in our culture?

GOD SAYS . . .

Isn't it obvious that it's disgraceful for a man to have long hair? And isn't long hair a woman's pride and joy?
1 CORINTHIANS 11:14-15

FAIRY TALE DAY

Dear God, There are a lot of bullies at my school. But they never get caught. Will bullying ever go away?

CONSIDER THIS . . . Sadly, bullying is not a new problem, and even though there are better and stronger laws against it today, it's not likely to go completely away. Remember the story of the ugly duckling?

A whole nest of eggs hatched. One of the eggs was larger than the others, but the little hatchling didn't know that. He looked different than the other ducks in his nest, and when he came out, the ducklings made fun of him. Finally, he went to live alone where no one could make fun of him. But he was lonely. One day, when he was older, he decided to risk it all and joined a flock of swans that he found by the river. He was so surprised! He looked into the water and saw his reflection—he looked just like those swans, and they accepted him as one of their own.

Although you don't have to look like everyone that you feel you belong with, you will find people who will love you for being yourself. You'll like them, too. For now, you might just find one or two "swans" in your school or church group, and that's okay. You can speak to an adult about bullying, and ignore what can't be fixed. As you grow older, though, and grow into your beautiful self inside and out, you'll learn more about your likes and dislikes, and it will be even easier to find a bunch of other swans who get your humor, get your heart, and, well, get you! At just the right time, God, who always accepts you, may even let those bullies see how wonderful you are.

GOD SAYS . . .
Humble yourselves under the mighty power of God, and at the right time he will lift you up in honor. Give all your worries and cares to God, for he cares about you. 1 PETER 5:6-7

HOW ABOUT YOU?
Does anyone make you feel different, weird, or strange? Will you trust that, in the right time, God will reveal you as a beautiful swan?

Dear God, If my parents are divorced, does that mean that I will get divorced when I get married?

July 27

CONSIDER THIS . . . Divorce is hard. In the book of Malachi, God says that he hates divorce. I'll bet that if you ask anyone who has ever been involved in a divorce—man, woman, or child—they would say that they hate divorce too. All people marry with the intention of staying together.

Because our world isn't heaven, it is full of both health and sickness, purity and sin, giving and selfishness. We all struggle to make right decisions. Some of the choices people make hurt their spouses so much that the hurt people rightfully ask for a divorce. Other people make wrong decisions to divorce. Some people are divorced when they don't want to be. Most of the time it's a complicated situation.

Most parents want their kids to grow up to be wiser, stronger, godlier, and happier than they themselves are. Because of this, your parents will not want you to undergo the pain of a divorce, even if they are divorced themselves. Reassure your parents of your love, and then ask them, "What can I do to avoid a divorce?" Although it might be painful for them to hear this question, your mom and dad will be glad that you eventually want to make the strongest marriage choice possible. They will share their experiences in this area with you so that you can make the best decision. Just because your parents divorced doesn't mean you will. You can learn from their experiences. You can keep your eyes on the Lord. You can get Christian counsel. God can take something that was painful for your parents and your family and use it to protect you and prepare you for your future. He can give you skills and insight that perhaps your parents didn't have.

HOW ABOUT YOU?

No matter if your parents are divorced or not, ask them this question: what kinds of things can I do to have a healthy marriage when I grow up?

GOD SAYS . . .

We know that God causes everything to work together for the good of those who love God and are called according to his purpose for them. ROMANS 8:28

Dear God, A kid who sits next to me is really smart in math. I'm not. Sometimes I want to copy his answers. What harm would that do?

CONSIDER THIS . . . There's a funny story about a boy who wanted to eat the beautiful gelatin salad that his sister had made and put into the refrigerator. She had made two salads, and she'd warned him not to eat either of them, but he thought differently. The boy thought, *Surely she could do without one of them.*

He quietly opened up the fridge late at night and saw both of those salads, jiggling in their containers, pink and red and sure to be sweet. He decided to take several large scoops of one of them, and then just one more, before heading off to bed.

In the morning, he woke up with a terribly sick stomach. It seems that the gelatin salads were part of a science experiment, and one of them had been made with dirty pond water!

Taking something that doesn't belong to you seems like a good idea for a moment, whether it's a math answer or a plate of dessert. Later, though, it brings sickness. Taking a math answer won't help you learn math any better, so people may not know that you need help, which means you fall further and further behind. It also robs from someone else, and that isn't good for your spirit or your heart. The first piece of dessert, or the first few stolen answers, pave the way for you to take more, later, that don't belong to you. That's not the road you want to travel.

Make a promise to yourself that you will not steal. Write a symbol like a star or a cross on your hand to remind you of it when you're tempted. Then ask your teacher for help. You'll feel amazing when you truly do understand and can ace those tests on your own.

GOD SAYS . . .
Stolen bread tastes sweet, but it turns to gravel in the mouth. PROVERBS 20:17

HOW ABOUT YOU?
Are you ever tempted to steal? What can you do to keep from being tempted?

Dear God, My mom says I'm beautiful, but does anyone else think that too?

July 29

CONSIDER THIS . . . Sometimes when people are trying to get your attention, they talk loudly, raise their voices, or shout in your direction. It might make you turn your head, but if they keep it up you end up turning away or even covering your ears. Ouch! On the other hand, when someone starts to whisper, our natural response is to lean toward her to hear every word she says.

Prettiness is sometimes like that. People who wear a lot of expensive fashions, bright make-up, or hair designed to make a statement rather than bring out natural loveliness do draw our attention for a while. But eventually even our eyes get tired of the "noise." That's not how it is with gentle beauty, though. It's more like a group of jellyfish in a tide pool, bobbing and swaying together like synchronized swimmers. Or the time-lapse film of a flower opening from bud to bloom or a masterpiece on a museum wall. None of these things need noise to draw and hold our attention, and they do so much better than a pretty, but squawking, blue jay.

There's nothing wrong with wanting to look cute, but your *beauty* should come from the quiet, natural spirit of who you truly are. That's what God says is of great value to him, and he created beauty! When you are loving, patient, helpful, friendly, caring, strong, and wise, then people will be drawn to you without your even trying. God, who loves you even more than anyone else does, finds that to be of great worth.

Remember, firecrackers catch our attention once or twice a year, but a melted orange-pink-purple sunset quietly holds our attention almost every night.

HOW ABOUT YOU?

What do you think the beauty of a gentle and quiet spirit looks like for girls your age? Be reassured that God finds your quiet beauty to be of great worth.

GOD SAYS . . .

You should clothe yourselves instead with the beauty that comes from within, the unfading beauty of a gentle and quiet spirit, which is so precious to God. 1 PETER 3:4

Dear God, There's a girl in my class who pesters me to lend a hand with her English papers. Should I keep helping her out?

CONSIDER THIS . . . There's a crazy fact about two things that seem to be unrelated: ants and flower buds—in particular, the flower buds of peonies. When peonies start out, they are hard little buds on the plant. Think of a baby's fist, which is tightly closed. On the outside of those buds is a thick layer of sweet wax.

And then along come . . . ants! Now, we often think of ants as pests, and truthfully, sometimes they are (especially when they invade our picnics). But in this case, they're helpers. The ants nibble all of the wax covering off of those buds, and then the buds can open into full flowers and shine. No ants? Then there will be small blooms later on. Many ants? You'll enjoy bright flowers. The deal works for both the ant, who gets a sweet meal, and the plant, which gets to bloom and open into the sun.

You might be surprised that some of the people you think are pests can actually help you too. As long as she's not asking too often, you might find that as you edit her papers your own writing skills get stronger. Could she help you out with something too? Maybe she's good in science or art, places you need to grow. Or in a sport.

There's a famous quote by John Donne: "No man is an island entire of itself." Each of us needs help from time to time. Therefore we each need to offer help from time to time. When you do, do it in an encouraging way. That way, when it's your turn to ask for help, people will be glad to lend a hand to you, too.

GOD SAYS . . .
Encourage each other and build each other up, just as you are already doing. 1 THESSALONIANS 5:11

HOW ABOUT YOU?
Do you have anyone in your life who helps you to be your best as you help that person to be the best?

Dear God, What is speaking in tongues? Am I supposed to do that?

July 31

CONSIDER THIS . . . Imagine that you are a gardener and you want to grow a lovely, large garden with many healthy plants. You have a big toolbox and many people to assist you with your garden. You open your toolbox and begin to hand out tools. To some you may give shovels to till the soil and to dig holes. To others you might hand rakes, seeds, a hose, or some plant food. Each person is given the tool that the gardener wants him or her to use as they all work together to help grow a beautiful garden. No tool is most important—the garden needs all of them. The gardener selects just the right gift, or tool, for each helper.

In the same way God gives spiritual gifts to Christians. First Corinthians 12 tells us that the gifts are chosen by him and are to be used to help other Christians. The spiritual gifts include things like wisdom, discernment, and the ability to speak in tongues.

Speaking in tongues is both a special prayer language used to communicate with God (1 Corinthians 14:14) and a language that people who speak languages from other parts of the world can understand (Acts 2). The Bible has rules for speaking in tongues. For instance, 1 Corinthians 14:27 says, "No more than two or three should speak in tongues. They must speak one at a time, and someone must interpret what they say."

Are you supposed to speak in tongues? Only if God has given you that gift. If not, then you are supposed to use the gifts he gave you. He loves you and chose you to be an important part of his garden!

HOW ABOUT YOU?
Which spiritual gifts has the Lord given to you?

GOD SAYS . . .
God has given each of you a gift from his great variety of spiritual gifts. Use them well to serve one another.
1 PETER 4:10

Dear God, Why do people say the Lord's Prayer all the time instead of just whatever comes to their minds?

CONSIDER THIS . . . When Jesus came to earth, he not only came as Savior, but he also came as a teacher. His followers knew that he was teaching them different things about God and how to relate to him. One thing Jesus did was help them learn how to pray.

Many Christians say the Lord's Prayer in their church services or even on their own, which is perfectly okay. The real purpose of the prayer seems to be for the Lord to show us what things are important to God to hear each day. That means that God feels those things are important for us to review each day. What are they?

- Remember that God is in heaven, our real home, and that he is holy.
- Hope that God's Kingdom, where all is set right, comes soon, and desire that people here on earth would do things God's way, just as the people and angels in heaven do.
- Look for God to provide the food we need only for today—not for tomorrow—so we'll be back to chat again soon.
- Request that God forgive us this day's sins, because we likely sin every day. In so doing, we remember that we need to forgive others, too.
- Ask God for help in avoiding temptation, and for protection from the evil one (the devil).

This isn't a "magic formula," and all Christians can and should talk about anything they'd like to with God. But it's important to remember the things that God felt we should talk about each day, too, and include them in our prayers.

GOD SAYS . . .

When you pray, don't babble on and on as people of other religions do. They think their prayers are answered merely by repeating their words again and again. Don't be like them, for your Father knows exactly what you need even before you ask him! MATTHEW 6:7-8

HOW ABOUT YOU?

Do you speak with God freely, or do you only say the Lord's Prayer? How can you change things up when you pray?

Dear God, Who made you?

CONSIDER THIS . . . Some people get hung up on the question, Which came first, the chicken or the egg? For people who believe in the story of Creation in the Bible, that's an easy question to answer. Of course the chicken came first! God himself made the first of every animal.

A much harder question, which is a brain buster, is, Who made God? If God made everything else, who was here to make him? The question isn't a brain buster because the answer isn't available—the answer does exist. It's just that it's hard to imagine how God came to be.

God says that he already existed in the beginning of all things. The Bible calls Jesus the Word, and it says that he existed in the beginning with God and as God. (If you want to learn more about that, go a few months back to that question on the Trinity from March 21.) God created everything. Nothing at all was created by anyone other than him. This means, of course, that God was not created. He has always existed. And always will exist.

This is hard for us to understand on one hand, because we know that all other things were created at a definite time and place. We can't wrap our minds around God always being around since before the beginning of the world. And yet, we don't worry so much about the part that says we will live eternally after dying, right? The rules seem to be different in God's plan. Everything except God is created, and some things—those with a soul (like us)—will live forever.

HOW ABOUT YOU?

If you can accept that eternal life goes on forever after death and outside of time, can you accept that eternity, for God, started outside of time too?

GOD SAYS . . .

In the beginning the Word already existed. The Word was with God, and the Word was God. He existed in the beginning with God. God created everything through him, and nothing was created except through him. JOHN 1:1-3

Dear God, I would like my neighbors to know you. What should I do first?

CONSIDER THIS . . . It's really cool when you realize that God has placed certain people in your neighborhood. It's no accident that they live there and that you do too!

In Luke 10:30-37, Jesus tells us the story of the Good Samaritan. In the story, the Samaritan comes across a man lying in a road, hurt. The Samaritan might be late for his appointment, lose business, or not make it home on time if he stops to help. But he doesn't put his interests first. Instead, he takes the time to care for a stranger. The Samaritan helps the hurt man, takes care of his needs, and makes sure he is safe and well looked after. He doesn't get anything in return—maybe not even a thank-you! He doesn't ask for anything in return. He shows unconditional love, which means loving someone without expecting anything at all—not even love or a thank-you.

That's how God loves us, and it's radical and different. When you start loving people without expecting anything in return, people stop and notice. Why? It hardly ever happens. Then they want to know *why* you do what you do. Your friends and neighbors might come out and ask you, "Why did you help me with my homework?" or ". . . get my toddler's ball?" or ". . . let me take your turn?" You'll be showing them the same kind of love that Jesus shows you.

Even if they don't come right out and ask you why, they'll see that you're different. The word *Christian* means to be like Christ. As Christ shows unconditional love for you, you show it to your neighbor. Heads and hearts will turn.

GOD SAYS . . .

"Now which of these three would you say was a neighbor to the man who was attacked by bandits?" Jesus asked. The man replied, "The one who showed him mercy." Then Jesus said, "Yes, now go and do the same."
LUKE 10:36-37

HOW ABOUT YOU?

What are three things you can do to show love to others?

Dear God, I have a hard time making friends. Can you give me some advice?

CONSIDER THIS . . . Making friends is hard work—for everyone. You may feel like you're the only one having a tough time making friends, but you're not. The more popular kids may not look like they have trouble, but everyone feels shy about making new friends. Thankfully, God gave us a kind of instruction sheet for building friendships. He tells us in Proverbs that the seeds of good deeds become a tree of life, and follows that up by the fact that a wise person wins friends.

In order to grow those friendships, you need to plant good-deed seeds! These seeds might be inviting someone to your house to hang out. If you like what your potential friend did with her hair, you might give her a genuine compliment. Or maybe you could invite her to work with you on a school project. If she's having trouble with her schoolwork, you could help her by going over facts or working through math problems with her. If her family doesn't have much money, you could share something you have with her.

Planting good-deed seeds is the first step, but you need to remember one thing. Not all seeds that are planted will grow into plants. Your good-deed seeds may not grow into friendship. A lot depends on the soil (your culture: school, church, the area you live in), temperature (is she warm to your friendship?), oxygen (is she open to new friends?), and water (do you have a lot in common?). Sometimes only 10 percent of seeds planted actually grow into plants. But the friendships that do sprout are certain to be the most rewarding.

If you go about making friends wisely, the Lord says you'll have a beautiful bouquet of friends to hang out with someday.

HOW ABOUT YOU?

Is there someone you'd like to be friends with? What good-deed seed can you plant?

GOD SAYS . . .

The seeds of good deeds become a tree of life; a wise person wins friends.
PROVERBS 11:30

Dear God, I have a really good friend who says she's a Christian, but she never acts like one. How can I make her love Jesus like I do?

CONSIDER THIS . . . It's often been said that God is a gentleman. He doesn't force anyone to be his friend, his follower, or his servant. He invites us to do that, but we have to make the next move and accept his invitation. If you read through the Bible, you'll see that God makes an invitation and then waits for us to make the next move. "Come close to God, and God will come close to you" (James 4:8). "Keep on seeking, and you will find. Keep on knocking, and the door will be opened to you" (Matthew 7:7). We have to make a move to be his followers. Your friend is no different.

As wonderful as you are, you can't "make" her be a Christian. If she's already a Christian, she has to choose to spend time with God. There is something you *can* do, though. What's that? You can set a great example.

Do you remember playing the game Follow the Leader when you were younger? Someone was chosen as leader, and everyone who lined up after her had to do just what she did. If she raised her right hand, everyone else raised their right hands too. If she was a great leader and did entertaining things, like squawking like a chicken or a somersault, the game could go on for a long while because she was fun to follow. Maybe your friend is a new Christian and hasn't had many good examples to learn from. Let her watch you and see your shining light. Maybe she'll see you enjoying your faith and want to try too.

GOD SAYS . . .

Follow my example, as I follow the example of Christ.
1 CORINTHIANS 11:1 (NCV)

HOW ABOUT YOU?

Do you have Christian friends for whom you'd like to set a good example? What are some practical ways you can do that?

Dear God, People keep saying that David had a heart after your own. How do I get a heart like that?

August 6

CONSIDER THIS . . . Today, when someone has something wrong with her body, there are many kinds of doctors she can visit and many kinds of tests that can be run to figure out what is causing the problem. If, for example, you are concerned that something is wrong with your heart, you might visit a cardiologist—a heart doctor! The heart doctor will run some tests on you; she might even take a scan of your heart. The scan will show her if your heart is working properly. If it isn't, you can take medicine to fix the problem or even get a heart transplant to make it better. That fresh heart will work as good as new!

Because we're born in sin, we each have something wrong with our hearts. Our physical hearts are fine, but our "spiritual" hearts need some help. Scripture says that not one person, not even one, seeks for God on her own (Romans 3:10-11). In order to get a new heart, one that looks for God, we have to have a "heart" transplant. God himself gives us one.

When you ask God to give you a new heart, he takes your own heart, which is sick with sin and sluggish, and gives you one in perfect working order. Although this new "heart" doesn't pump blood, it does recognize God for who he is. The more time you spend spiritually exercising that heart, the stronger it becomes. Then the heart returns to God wholeheartedly. This is the kind of heart that David had; he looked to honor and praise God in every place, in every way, and he loved him with all of his heart. Wholeheartedly.

HOW ABOUT YOU?
Has God given you a new heart? How can you exercise it enough to make sure it's returned to him, wholeheartedly?

GOD SAYS . . .
I will give them hearts that recognize me as the LORD. They will be my people, and I will be their God, for they will return to me wholeheartedly.
JEREMIAH 24:7

Dear God, I know I can talk to people, but it is hard to talk to you when I feel like you don't talk back. How do I get to know you?

CONSIDER THIS . . . People are easy to understand . . . kind of. After all, a person gave us life, and people raise us, befriend us, help us, and sometimes anger us. We talk to people we get along with, find out what they like, ask questions about them, and help out when we can. We cry on their shoulders. We look at their work, the things that they create that they are proud of. We eat the special meals they make for us and invite them to our homes to eat too. We invite them to parties and go to the ones they throw. We give them gifts, and we receive the gifts that they give to us, too.

But God, well, it's another whole story to get to know him.

Or is it?

Is there anything in the list above that we can't do with and for God? We get so used to thinking of him as "other"—and to be sure, he is—that we don't realize that he can relate to us in ways we are used to too. Maybe we get so used to looking for God in the "typical" places—in the Bible, at church, or at a Christian concert—that we're not seeing him in everyday life too. He's there, and he knows you're looking for him. Think of a time when you played hide-and-seek with a little kid. Did you hide in the hardest place possible, a spot where that little kid could never find you? Or did you hide somewhere easy, like behind a pole, where he could spot you for sure? You wanted to be found, and you enjoyed the delighted squeal when he found you.

God's waiting for you to find him, and he's not hiding!

GOD SAYS . . .

The LORD sees every heart and knows every plan and thought. If you seek him, you will find him.
1 CHRONICLES 28:9

HOW ABOUT YOU?

Do you seek God every day in the same way, or do you look for him in different places? Where can you look to find God today?

Dear God, Sometimes I feel like I don't exactly fit anywhere. Is that normal?

August 8

CONSIDER THIS . . . Last year a family went for a long vacation to London, England. It was absolutely gorgeous, and the British people were both kind and funny. A lot of things looked just like they did at home. The family ate breakfast in the morning and dinner at night, and they got coffee at Starbucks. But some things were different. For example, people got from place to place on something called the Tube. *Steak and kidney pie* and *bubble and squeak* appeared on menus. And people asked them to "have a look" rather than "take a look" when they were shopping.

That's kind of what life on planet earth is like for Christians. It's a beautiful place to be with lots of wonderful people. But somehow, deep inside, we know it's not a perfect fit. There's more somewhere else for us. We know it! And even though we enjoy ourselves, we know that one day we'll be going home. Our real home is heaven, and Jesus, who loves us deeply, has prepared a perfect place for us there. That should make you feel glad. You get to go from good to even better!

Christians are kind of living on the horizon, that special place where the sky seems to touch the earth. We have our feet on the ground, but our minds and our hearts, the things that help us decide what matters most, are mainly in the skies, looking toward heaven. God is always with us. He lives with us here on the earth, as the Holy Spirit, and he prepared a place for us there in heaven.

That just leaves us to wonder—does heaven have Starbucks too?

HOW ABOUT YOU?

Do you have anywhere that you feel perfectly comfortable? Imagine taking that feeling with you wherever you go— only ten times better. That's heaven. What else do you think heaven will be like?

GOD SAYS . . .

If they had longed for the country they came from, they could have gone back. But they were looking for a better place, a heavenly homeland. HEBREWS 11:15-16

Dear God, My parents discipline me way more than they discipline my sisters. I always get in trouble first too. I think it's unfair, but what can I do?

CONSIDER THIS ... It hurts when you feel someone's picking on you, doesn't it? And sometimes when our hearts ache, we allow a hard little knot to grow inside them, thinking that will stop us from being hurt again. This is just what the devil wants us to do in a situation like yours.

But maybe things aren't exactly what they seem to be. Perhaps your mom and dad know you're a responsible young lady and expect more from you. Maybe you're older, so your name comes out first. It might be that your parents call on your sisters as much as you, but it doesn't seem that way when it's you in the hot seat! Maybe you *are* disobeying more. Or perhaps they're just tired and trying to solve the problem quickly, and sometimes unfairly, because they, too, are only human.

No matter what the cause, the Bible tells us if we are angry, we're to work things out as soon as possible. This is really hard, because the *last* person you feel like talking to is the person who hurt your feelings. Wait until everyone's tempers cool down—maybe an hour or two. Then ask your mom and/or dad if you could talk with them alone. Explain that when they shout at you or always call you first when there's a problem, it makes you feel less loved or like you're always to blame. Then listen to their perspective on the situation too. Ask if there's something you can do together to solve the problem. Then hug one another tightly and feel that knot in your heart melt away.

GOD SAYS ...

And "don't sin by letting anger control you." Don't let the sun go down while you are still angry, for anger gives a foothold to the devil. EPHESIANS 4:26-27

HOW ABOUT YOU?

Are you angry with anyone? What should you do? When will you do it?

Dear God, I've seen some kids my age smoking. Why do so many people smoke?

August 10

CONSIDER THIS . . . When people start smoking, it feels good. They think they fit in with the cool kids. But guess what? The good feeling doesn't last too long. Pretty soon smoking doesn't feel good either.

When you breathe, air goes into your lungs, and then your lungs send the air all through your body. When you smoke, it's like you are painting tar over those lungs. It gets harder to breathe. You cough up ugly brown stuff. Your skin gets wrinkled sooner, and your nails crinkle. You smell bad. That's not good.

Most people don't expect to become addicted when they start smoking. Being addicted means you have the desire to keep doing something, even though you know you should stop. Most adults who smoke want to stop, but they have a hard time doing so. Many people expect to be able to quit smoking whenever they want. But most people can't. Many people who smoke die from lung diseases or early heart attacks. Almost all adults who smoke would tell you to run away from cigarettes, and that they'd do the same if they had a second chance.

The Bible tells us that our bodies belong to God. First Corinthians 6:19-20 says, "Don't you realize that your body is the temple of the Holy Spirit, who lives in you and was given to you by God? You do not belong to yourself, for God bought you with a high price. So you must honor God with your body." Smoking hurts our bodies, and hurting our bodies is not honoring to God.

Remember to honor God by treating your body right. If someone offers you a cigarette, say, "No thanks." Then walk away.

HOW ABOUT YOU?

Has anyone ever offered you a cigarette? What will you answer when they do? Be prepared in advance!

GOD SAYS . . .

There is a path before each person that seems right, but it ends in death. PROVERBS 16:25

Dear God, Sometimes I think I'm an okay person. But then I'll do bad on a test and feel like I'm not okay after all. How can I change that?

CONSIDER THIS . . . Lots of people go to a state fair in the summertime. There are rides and animals and food and . . . a fun house? Have you ever been in a fun house? There are floors that shake as you walk across them, and some have spinning discs that send you in the wrong direction if you don't get off of them in time. Just try to dash around that blast of air coming from the wall . . . or avoid all of those fun-house mirrors.

Ah yes, those mirrors. When you stand in front of one of them, it makes you seem much, much taller and thinner than you are in real life. If you move a bit forward and stand in front of another one, you'll be shorter and rounder. Some of them make your face seem big and your feet seem long. What's one thing that isn't in a fun house? A mirror that shows you just as you are.

When you rely on what other people think of you to get an idea or an image of who you are, it will never be a true picture. People will look at you differently depending on their own problems, worries, jealousies, or concerns. Even we don't have a clear picture of ourselves because our thoughts are clouded with fears and troubles. But God has a clear picture of you, and he loves you just the way you are. God also promises that when you get to heaven, you will see everything, including yourself, just as you are.

No tricks!

GOD SAYS . . .
Now we see things imperfectly, like puzzling reflections in a mirror, but then we will see everything with perfect clarity. 1 CORINTHIANS 13:12

HOW ABOUT YOU?
Do you think you see yourself clearly? What parts do you imagine are bigger than they really are?

CONSIDER THIS . . . Our God is an endlessly creative God. He designed all the plants, all the animals, even all of the natural laws. For example, he designed the way the moon's cycles work and direct the ocean tides. Everything God created displays his individuality, shows his tender care, and is designed with his purposes in mind.

Men and women are both created in God's image. They are equally valuable to him. But, like everything else God created, they each have slightly different purposes. Men's bodies are formed to father children. Women's bodies are formed to mother children. While mothers and fathers are both important, they are not the same. Both men and women are relational, but women typically enjoy and need relationships more. While both women and men are competitive, men are typically more so. These strengths allow men and women to better perform the tasks God has set aside for them to do.

Today, some people try to make boys and girls out to be the same. They think that if boys and girls are given the same opportunities and told the same things, they will come out the same. This is not true. Even when boys and girls are given the same opportunities, they often freely choose to be involved with different things and approach life differently. God did not make boys and girls the same, and being able to act as we were designed to act is true freedom and equality.

Be honored to be a girl. In the same way, honor boys, too, in the ways that they are different from you. Someday you may find that one of those boys grows up to be a man who perfectly complements the woman you are, and together, you'll form one family as husband and wife.

HOW ABOUT YOU?

What differences do you see between boys and girls? How is your dad different from your mom?

GOD SAYS . . .

God created human beings in his own image. In the image of God he created them; male and female he created them. GENESIS 1:27

LEFT-HANDERS DAY

Dear God, So, I'm left-handed, and different. Why?

CONSIDER THIS . . . Although you may feel different, you're definitely special. Did you know that only 10 percent of the world's population is left-handed? Being left-handed means that you write, eat, and work with your left hand when most people work with their right hand.

Being different in any way can be kind of tough because it seems as though societies are built for what the majority is like. A long time ago left-handers were made to write with their right hands, even though it didn't feel natural to them. Society was trying to make them just like everyone else. The good thing is that today, people have more freedom to be themselves, including the freedom to be left-handed.

Whenever you are different from those around you, you're forced to be creative, to think outside the box, and to adapt to more things. This makes your brain quicker and more nimble. More than half of the most recent presidents of the United States have been left-handers. Because left-handers have to adapt to a world made for right-handed people, they often end up being ambidextrous, meaning they can do tasks well with both hands. You may see left-handers who can cut with scissors using either hand or bat lefty and righty in softball. Most right-handers, however, can only function well with their right hand. Don't believe me? Ask a right-hander to write her name using her left hand and you'll see!

No matter what makes you unique, be proud that you're different and that you've learned to adapt in a world that doesn't work exactly like you do. God has made you different, and beautiful, and you have skills that the majority don't have!

GOD SAYS . . .
Among Benjamin's elite troops, 700 were left-handed, and each of them could sling a rock and hit a target within a hairsbreadth without missing. JUDGES 20:16

HOW ABOUT YOU?
Even if you're not left-handed, can you see a way that you're unlike a lot of the people around you? How can that be a bonus?

Dear God, Why do you test us?

CONSIDER THIS . . . There's something about testing that makes us nervous. We're finding out what we know—and what we don't know.

If we use test results to tell us if we're good or bad people, we're going to be in *big* trouble for life. Tests come every day, and most of them have nothing to do with school. *Will I say something I will regret later? Should I give the money back?* What tests show us is where we are weak and where we are strong. The strong areas are no sweat. You don't worry about 1 + 1 anymore, do you? In fact, you could probably teach a preschooler some easy math. Multiplying decimals, however, is probably a different story. You're still learning. Someday you'll master it. Until then, it's best to know where the holes are and get help to understand.

God allows tests to come to all of us. Sometimes we pass with no problem. (I gave the money back!) Sometimes we fail. (I bad-mouthed that girl I'm angry with.) When we're tested, we see where we're weak. When shoe companies make shoes, they fit them on a "fake foot" and make them mechanically walk for miles and miles to make sure the soles won't wear out, and then fix any weak spots. Aren't you glad they do that?

In the same way, God tests you and then takes the time (if you're willing) to strengthen your weak parts. He wants to use you, but he makes sure you're ready first. In everything we do, our goal is to be more like Jesus. That means letting God point out the weak parts and getting help to make our "soles" strong enough to walk everywhere he wants us to go!

HOW ABOUT YOU?

What character tests do you face? What and who can help you get strong enough to pass those tests as easily as 1 + 1?

GOD SAYS . . .

These trials will show that your faith is genuine. It is being tested as fire tests and purifies gold—though your faith is far more precious than mere gold.
1 PETER 1:7

Dear God, My mom seems like she's mad at me more than she's happy with me. How do I even know that she loves me?

CONSIDER THIS ... Sometimes the people that we should show the most love to get shown the least. Maybe that's because when we come home we kind of relax and stop worrying about the things we say and do. Could your mom be really busy? Is she stressed? Could you be adding to the situation somehow? Usually, when there's a conflict, there are two people who contribute to the concern. But a mom is the parent, and she's the one who should take responsibility to fix things.

The Bible shows us how much mothers love their children in the book of 1 Kings. There were two women who each had a baby. One of the babies died, and in the middle of the night, the mother of the dead baby switched her child for the one that was still living. When both women went before Solomon to claim the child, he gave them a test. The woman who was the real mother was willing to do anything to give her child life—even giving up the baby.

For some reason, it sometimes seems like parents are more willing to make the big sacrifices than to pay attention to the little things along the way. Sometimes all of us focus on the little annoyances and irritations of the day instead of the big blessings we've been given. Talk to your mom and tell her you miss being close, that you feel that she's mad at you, and ask how you could grow close again. Mothers want their children to be close to them and to live happily.

GOD SAYS ...
The woman who was the real mother of the living child, and who loved him very much, cried out, "Oh no, my lord! Give her the child—please do not kill him!" 1 KINGS 3:26

HOW ABOUT YOU?
Is anything stopping you from being even closer to your mom? How can you help to fix that?

Dear God, I keep praying to you about my problems, but then almost as soon as I'm done praying I start worrying about them again. Is this normal?

August 16

CONSIDER THIS . . . Have you ever watched a movie about someone who was stranded on a desert island? In order to get some help, those stranded often roll up a little scrap of paper with "SOS" or "HELP ME" written on it. They share their location, roll the paper up, stuff it into a bottle, and cork it. Then they throw it into the sea. However, the ocean almost always works against them. It very often brings the bottle right back to shore, carried in on the waves that roll back to the island. No help can come if the bottle never makes it off the island.

Or consider this: would you, or anyone that you know of, write and mail letters addressed to yourself? You'd place your thoughts about a problem you're having, and maybe your request for advice, on a piece of paper and then seal it in an envelope. You'd address it to yourself. You have to admit that it wouldn't be helpful to send it back to yourself.

Giving our problems to God and then taking them right back by worrying is very much like mailing ourselves a letter asking for help. Or throwing an SOS bottle into the sea to come back again. God is pleased to help us with all of our worries and cares. But when we hand them to him in prayer and take them right back again, we're telling him that we can solve them better/quicker than he can. So then, why send the SOS at all? God cares for everything you're concerned about. Mail the letter to him, in prayer. And don't take it back! Watch for him to work. He will!

HOW ABOUT YOU?

What are some things you worry about that you hand off to God only to take right back again?

GOD SAYS . . .

Give all your worries and cares to God, for he cares about you. 1 PETER 5:7

Dear God, Why is it so important that I confess my sins daily?

CONSIDER THIS . . . Almost no one likes going to the dentist, but we all have to do it. Now, the dentist and hygienist are probably nice. You sit on pretty comfy chairs, and sometimes there's even a TV or stereo headphones to make you more comfortable. When you're done, you get a free toothbrush. So what's to be worried about?

Cavities!

When teeth aren't cared for as well as they should be, they start to get an infection on or in them. This infection starts as tiny white spots. If you catch the infection early, you can get rid of the spots, and the infection clears up and that part of the tooth grows back. If you don't catch it in time, it turns into a cavity—a hole of disease in your tooth. Once it's a cavity, all you can do is drill out the infection and fill it with artificial material. There's no way for the tooth to grow back again.

This is true with sin. Although all sin can be forgiven, if you can catch it right away, you can usually stop things before they do too much damage. But sin is like an infection to our souls. If we don't repent and confess (clean up the mess) it can cause more and more damage, to ourselves and to others.

It's no fun to go to the dentist, but it's much less fun to have lots of drilling because you didn't care for your teeth. It's no fun to confess your sins and repent of them, but it's much less fun to deal with the damage that sets in when you don't let God cure it right away.

Meet God, morning and night. No, not to brush and floss. To confess!

GOD SAYS . . .

People who conceal their sins will not prosper, but if they confess and turn from them, they will receive mercy. PROVERBS 28:13

HOW ABOUT YOU?

How often do you confess your sins to the Lord?

Dear God, What is the most important part of being a Christian?

August 18

CONSIDER THIS . . . Have you ever heard of a friendship baking party? The hostess decides what is to be baked—maybe chocolate cakes for everyone—and then asks each person attending to bring an ingredient. One girl might be assigned flour and another girl chocolate; one might bring butter and another the eggs. If everyone brings what she's supposed to bring, each person goes home with a delightful treat to share and eat.

The thing about baking, though, is that there are some ingredients that are really important, and some that won't be terribly missed. For instance, if someone doesn't bring vanilla, it might make the cake taste a little less delightful, but the cake will still be, well, a cake. If no one brings flour, though, there will be no cake at all. Only a greasy chocolate river.

When making a cake, you can do without a lot, but not without flour!

Christianity is like that too. There are many things that Christians enjoy doing and that, when we do them, please God. When we're kind to others, or give and share, or praise and worship, all of those things deepen our relationship with the Lord. There's one ingredient, though, that we cannot leave out. That ingredient is faith.

The Lord himself tells us that it is impossible to please him without faith. Our faith tells him that we love and depend on him from first breath through eternity. That we trust him. That we want to be close.

It's perfectly okay to do many good things for the Lord and for others. Just don't forget that one important ingredient. Faith.

Hey . . . cake anyone?

HOW ABOUT YOU?

How is your relationship with God? Are you trying to be good, look good, and do good, but not add the "main ingredient" of faith?

GOD SAYS . . .

It is impossible to please God without faith. Anyone who wants to come to him must believe that God exists and that he rewards those who sincerely seek him.

HEBREWS 11:6

Dear God, The world is so big that I am not always sure I'm going to find my way in it once I grow up. Will you help?

CONSIDER THIS . . . Today, if you get into the car with your mom and she doesn't know where she is going, she can turn on the GPS navigation system. The driver (or her helper) types the destination that you'd like to go to. Satellites high up in space check out the starting location from your phone (cool!) or GPS unit, and then the GPS gives you directions on exactly where you need to go. Sometimes a nice voice even comes on and says, "Turn left in 100 feet at Broadway." By using this application, and the sky-high satellites, you're easily guided to the place you want to go. Make a mistake? No problem. The GPS will recalculate from wherever you are and give you a revised set of directions. You never have to be lost again.

Hundreds of years ago, way before the kind of cool technology we have today, people had to navigate by using stars. They'd look up in the sky, find the North Star or other stars, and know whether they needed to walk or ride or sail left or right and by how much.

High tech or low tech, direction from God has always been provided to all people. If you're a Christian, you have your own holy "GPS" living right inside you. The Holy Spirit will guide you better than any red, blinking satellite or white, twinkling star. Today, tomorrow, next year, or anytime thereafter, if you ask God to help you find the way, he'll help you. And if you make a mistake, he'll help you recalculate. With him, you will never be lost.

GOD SAYS . . .

When the Spirit of truth comes, he will guide you into all truth. He will not speak on his own but will tell you what he has heard. He will tell you about the future. JOHN 16:13

HOW ABOUT YOU?

When do you feel lost? Do you ask for directions?

Dear God, I feel like my family is weird and everyone else's family is normal. Why can't I stop comparing my family to everyone else's?

August 20

CONSIDER THIS . . . Most of the time we feel just fine about our clothes or our gear—until we go to the mall and see what's in the store windows or watch TV and see some commercials. Suddenly the clothes look a little out of touch. And the gear looks a bit, um . . . ragged. What was fine before isn't fine anymore. Why not? Because we begin to compare.

To compare means to measure one thing against something else. When we measure, one ends up being better, bigger, and cooler than the other. They almost never come out equal. That's how it is when you begin to compare your family with other families. Because you know annoying little things about your family, like your dad sneezing in a totally embarrassing way or your mom tweezing her eyebrows while she's driving, your family might start to look weird compared to other families. Other people's older sisters may seem nicer, or their little brothers may seem cuter. But guess what? They're probably thinking the same thing about your family!

The secret to being happy is contentment, or being satisfied with what you have. It doesn't mean that you can't ever buy a new outfit or paint your room that cool frosty lavender you've wanted to try. But it does mean that you choose to be happy with what you have, not always comparing what you have with what someone else has, whether it's their clothes or their family. The Bible says that God sets people in families, meaning he chooses for them. Be content with what God, in his great love, has chosen for you.

HOW ABOUT YOU?
What fun things does your family do together? What are you thankful about in your family?

GOD SAYS . . .
Father to the fatherless, defender of widows—this is God, whose dwelling is holy. God places the lonely in families. PSALM 68:5-6

Dear God, I'm only a kid, really. What can I do to tell others about you? I'm afraid if I speak up, people will laugh at me.

CONSIDER THIS . . . Most kids, at one time or another, play a sport. Around the world the most popular sport for all kids is soccer. Before heading onto the field, most soccer players put on shin guards, to protect their legs, and soccer shoes. Those shoes have little teeth-like cleats on the bottoms. The cleats help your shoes to clamp onto the ground so you don't slip or fall in wet or muddy grass or turf.

Once you run onto the field, you have to make a lot of decisions about what to do, but you're not on your own. You've been to many practices, so you know what you're doing. And your coach is almost always standing by the sideline calling out instructions to you. When you get tired, you can stand on the sideline, drink some water, and then get sent out to the field again.

Just like on your team, you have an important role to play in the Kingdom of God. It doesn't matter how young you are. There are people you can reach with the Good News that no adult can reach. (Maybe those girls on your team!) Your childlike faith will be an encouragement to older people watching you. And the innocent questions and concerns you have will remind everyone of what matters most.

The Lord, your coach, has sent you into the game. He says he'll protect you, and he can do it much better than shin guards and cleats. He'll remind you of what to say. It's game time, so don't be afraid.

Jump in!

GOD SAYS . . .
The LORD replied, "Don't say, 'I'm too young,' for you must go wherever I send you and say whatever I tell you." JEREMIAH 1:7

HOW ABOUT YOU?
Where and when are you afraid to speak up for your faith?

Dear God, I really don't like shots. The needle scares me! Why do I have to get so many?

August 22

CONSIDER THIS . . . Have you ever been in a doctor's office when a little baby is getting shots? Usually a lot of crying accompanies the painful jabs. It doesn't seem like a nice thing to do to a baby, but giving a baby shots is a good thing. It wasn't very long ago when almost half of all babies who were born died of illnesses. And just before your grandmother was born, many kids died from illnesses that we wouldn't even think about being too dangerous today, like strep throat. Now that we have stronger medicines, we can save lives by giving shots.

You probably don't remember the shots you received as a baby, but the shots you're getting now are also a good thing. They help your body to build its defenses against diseases you've never had and, hopefully, will never get. The shot is painful. But getting the disease that it prevents is much more painful, lasts a lot longer, and might even require—gasp!—many more shots to treat it!

The book of Proverbs tells us that we are wise to prepare for what's ahead. People of all ages have to do things they don't want to do. Saving money isn't as fun as spending it, but it's important to have some set aside if a problem arises. Going to bed early the night before a test isn't exciting, but it's important to be well rested before an exam. Shots are definitely not something anyone looks forward to. But a little pain and preparation now save a lot of pain and problems later on.

Sometimes worrying about the shot in advance hurts more than the real thing, actually. Stick out your arm and close your eyes or look away. There. That wasn't so bad, was it?

HOW ABOUT YOU?

What hard, painful, or uncomfortable things can you do now to save yourself from bigger problems down the road?

GOD SAYS . . .

A prudent person foresees danger and takes precautions. The simpleton goes blindly on and suffers the consequences.
PROVERBS 22:3

NATIONAL GARAGE SALE DAY

Dear God, Our church sponsors some missionaries in Mexico. I'd like to help, but I don't have a job. What can I do?

CONSIDER THIS . . . Nearly everyone has been to a garage sale, where people set out tables and sell the stuff they no longer need or want. A garage sale doesn't even have to happen in a garage! They're also called yard sales and rummage sales, because the buyers rummage through the stuff to find treasures. British people call them jumble sales because the clothes for sale can get all jumbled up. Sometimes they're even referred to as junk sales!

Remember, though: one girl's junk is another girl's treasure.

You can hold a garage sale to clean up your house and raise a little extra money for a good cause. Raising money for missions by selling things you no longer need or want is an amazing way for a girl to raise money. If you don't know of any missionaries to help, churches and people also hold sales to raise money for good causes.

Ask your parents if you can hold a sale, and have fun together sorting through the things your family no longer wants. Pick a day and advertise free online. Make some signs for your neighborhood, too. Be sure to tell people that the money is going to a good cause—they'll often spend more to support you. After the sale is over, consider donating whatever doesn't sell to the Salvation Army, which also continues the Lord's work.

You can't always give hand-me-downs to people in need, because they may not wear the same size you do. You can't deliver food to missionaries in a far-off place. But you can give out of what you have, that which you don't need anymore, and even that which you do! As you send away the money you've earned, be sure to pray for the people who will get it.

GOD SAYS . . .

All the believers were united in heart and mind. And they felt that what they owned was not their own, so they shared everything they had. ACTS 4:32

HOW ABOUT YOU?

What cause would you like to raise money for?

Dear God, Do animals really go to heaven?

CONSIDER THIS . . . The Bible doesn't specifically say if animals go to heaven or not. It would be easier for those of us who love animals if it did! But there are several things the Bible does tell us about both animals and heaven:

1. God cares for his animals. He created them and took special care in designing each animal with its own special features, strengths, and beauty. Genesis 1:21-22 says that God not only created birds and everything in the sea, but he also blessed them.

2. God watches his animals. Matthew 10:29 tells us that not even a sparrow falls to the ground without God knowing about it. Amazing!

3. In heaven there will be no unhappiness. Revelation 21:4 says, "[God] will wipe every tear from their eyes, and there will be no more death or sorrow or crying or pain. All these things are gone forever." Whether pets are there in heaven or not, we will still be happy. We may not be able to understand how that can be, but we can trust that God is true to his Word.

Although we don't know if there will be animals in heaven, we can do our best to take care of animals here on earth. If you have a pet, you can make sure that it is fed and that it is loved. If you don't have a pet, you can still care for God's creation. Maybe you could volunteer at an animal shelter or make a bird feeder for the birds in your backyard.

We don't know if dogs really go to heaven, but we can definitely love and take care of the animals here on earth!

HOW ABOUT YOU?

Do you help care for animals? If you have pets, do you show them love and give them time? If you don't have any pets, how can you take care of the animals God created?

GOD SAYS . . .

You care for people and animals alike, O LORD. How precious is your unfailing love.

PSALM 36:6-7

Dear God, A lot of things bother me. Part of me knows it's wrong to be annoyed, but the other part says, so what? What do you think?

CONSIDER THIS . . . Have you ever been in a house where the smoke alarms went off? Those alarms are designed to be really, really loud. After all, if you're asleep when the house catches on fire, you want something to wake you up right away so you can get yourself and your family to safety.

Some alarms, though, go off for almost no reason. It might be that their batteries are getting low—*beep, beep, beep!* Maybe something spilled in the oven and a little wisp of smoke sneaked out. *Ayooga! Ayooga!* When those alarms go off with just the tiniest amount of smoke, it doesn't help. It hurts. Everyone gathers around and waves fans and pillows to clear the area out. Windows are opened. Dogs hide under the bed. An alarm system that's meant to go off in a real danger has become a little oversensitive.

This is how our anger alert system works. *Annoyed, irritated,* and *frustrated* are all words for being angry—not a lot, just a little. All of those are normal emotions. The problem is, when your sensor is set too low, you can end up making too many noises that aggravate yourself and everyone around you for little or no reason. See if you can ignore it if someone or something rubs you the wrong way, offers a different opinion, or just gets under your skin a little bit, like a bug bite. They're likely to do that for you, too. God tells us that love isn't easily irritated. He also shares that he is love (1 John 4:8).

If God's perfect, and not easily irritated, maybe we can let a few things go too!

GOD SAYS . . .
Love is patient and kind. Love is not jealous or boastful or proud or rude. It does not demand its own way. It is not irritable. 1 CORINTHIANS 13:4-5

HOW ABOUT YOU?
Are you easily irritated (more than two times per day)? How can you work on becoming less annoyed?

CONSIDER THIS . . . Do you remember the story about Beauty and the beast? There was a young girl named Beauty, whose beloved was about to go on a journey. Beauty's older sisters asked him to bring back expensive clothes and jewelry, but Beauty wanted only one thing: a rose. You see, roses didn't grow by her home.

Beauty's father brought back a rose, but he had plucked it from the garden of a mean and ugly beast. The beast made her father promise to send Beauty back to him to make things right. Over time, the beast fell in love with Beauty. Although she was kind to him, she didn't find him very, well, attractive! Beasts are not known to be cute! He was very kind to her, though, treated her well, helped her out, and was gentle and funny.

Beauty got homesick and returned to her family, promising to come back to the beast for a visit. Her return was delayed, though, and when she got back he was dying. She knelt over him, realizing how much she loved him for what he was inside: kind, gentle, smart, and giving. She enjoyed being with him. He treated her kindly. She shed a tear, and when that tear fell on the beast, he turned into a handsome prince.

The Lord tells us that people who appear cute and good looking on the outside might be rotten or mean on the inside. And those who don't appear to be so appealing on the outside might be amazing people inside. Good looks change over time, but good character generally sticks around.

No promises that your tears will turn a beast into a prince, though!

HOW ABOUT YOU?

What kind of person do you want to hang out with?

GOD SAYS . . .

The LORD said to Samuel, "Don't judge by his appearance or height, for I have rejected him. The LORD doesn't see things the way you see them. People judge by outward appearance, but the LORD looks at the heart." 1 SAMUEL 16:7

Dear God, It's time for new school clothes, which I love to buy! Do you have anything to say about clothes, besides the fact that they should be modest?

CONSIDER THIS ... One of the reasons we buy new clothes is to prepare us for a new school year. We like to show up looking our best, wearing clothes that represent us and maybe the group we hang out with. A new school year is the start of a new grade, new challenges, new joys, and new tests, and not just the kind with a pencil and paper. In order to be prepared, make sure that you dress yourself in the armor of God, too.

Wait—armor? Really?

Armor, during the time when the Bible was written, was used to protect soldiers from the harmful things that would definitely be flung their way. The apostle Paul used the idea of a soldier wearing protective gear to show us how we could protect our spiritual lives too. As you're buying your new school clothes for this year, consider what you'll need to be getting dressed in each morning to guard your heart and soul, too.

The first item of defense Paul talks about is the belt of truth. What does a belt do? It holds up your pants and pulls your entire outfit together. Some belts, like those in martial arts, identify you as having a certain level of achievement. Just by looking at you, people can tell what you stand for—and what you've stood for.

All of us will be tested, and each new school year will bring new friends, new lessons, and new ideas. You can test everything that comes your way by the truth. If you do, your ideas, as well as your pants, will always hold up!

GOD SAYS ...

Put on every piece of God's armor so you will be able to resist the enemy in the time of evil. Then after the battle you will still be standing firm. Stand your ground, putting on the belt of truth. EPHESIANS 6:13-14

HOW ABOUT YOU?

Have you ever come across an idea that taught something different than your Christian beliefs taught? What did you do?

Dear God, So, when I wear the armor of God, I'm not actually wearing armor, like the knights in history books?

CONSIDER THIS . . . Scripture does say that we are to wear body armor. But it doesn't have to be made of metal.

Through the years, armor has been made from many different materials. During the time when the Bible was written, people might have worn armor made out of animal skins to camouflage themselves, or even leather to protect them from arrows and stones. Then there was armor made of metal to protect knights and jousters. But I'll bet you know someone who wears armor right now—Under Armour! These shirts and pants fit really close to the skin. During the summer months, they draw the sweat away from your body while you're playing sports, to keep you cool. During the winter, they add a layer to trap and keep the heat your body makes so you can run faster and longer without getting chilled.

Under Armour is soft, and it blends in under your clothing to protect you. This is what the body armor of God's righteousness, which he gives to us, does too. God's armor may not be made of material like Under Armour or metal, but you wear it all the time. It helps you to stay pure, to think good thoughts, to do the right thing, and to make good decisions—time after time, season after season. It's copying God's integrity—doing what you say you'll do. It's adopting his virtue—that is, being good. If you live a righteous life, you'll be able to run faster and longer, enjoying the things you love most and having your teammates in the race for Christ look up to you and cheer you on.

And hey—if you want to wear a ball gown over your armor of God, go right ahead!

HOW ABOUT YOU?

Are there times when you're tempted to do the wrong thing, or not follow through on what you promised you'd do? How might that allow things to hurt you in the long run?

GOD SAYS . . .

Stand your ground, putting on the belt of truth and the body armor of God's righteousness. EPHESIANS 6:14

Dear God, I'm not much into ball gowns, but I'm totally into shoes. How can they help me?

CONSIDER THIS . . . Buying new shoes is fantastic fun. The trick, of course, is to find some that not only look good but feel good too. This can be hard when you're still growing. Feet don't always grow at the same rate as the rest of your body.

If you buy shoes that are too tight, you're in pain most of the day, hobbling about, which is probably not the look you're after. Untied or too loose shoes? Don't trip and fall! Shoes, like clothes, change styles year after year, and most of us want to wear shoes that both we and our friends admire.

You also have to keep in mind what you'll be wearing the shoes for. Little kitten heels might be good for church or a school dance, but they definitely would not be good on a basketball court. On the other hand, you don't want to wear a dress-up outfit with your track shoes. You need to choose shoes that fit well, look good, and are suited for the purpose you want to wear them.

In the list of God's armor, Scripture tells us that we need to choose our "life" shoes too. These "shoes" are the ones you'll slip on nearly every day, the ones you'll wear without thinking about it. God's shoes give you the peace that comes from knowing that Christ came, died, and rose for you. And not just for you, but for the whole world.

Unlike your favorite pair of shoes, the message of Good News never gets too small. It never goes out of style, and it's perfect for every situation. Now, the question is, can you share it with your friends?

GOD SAYS . . .

For shoes, put on the peace that comes from the Good News so that you will be fully prepared. EPHESIANS 6:15

HOW ABOUT YOU?

What is your favorite pair of shoes? Why do you love them so much?

Dear God, One of my favorite parts of getting dressed is putting on my bling: necklaces, earrings, bracelets, rings. Does the Bible talk about accessories?

August 30

CONSIDER THIS . . . One summer day, a married couple was tending to their business at the convenience shop they owned, just living their everyday, ordinary life. They swept the floors, stocked the shelves, and took care of the occasional customer. Suddenly, a masked man rushed in with a gun, held them up, and demanded their cash. To protect his wife from the robber, the husband shoved aside his wife and refused to hand over the money. The frustrated robber fired his gun directly at the store owner before running away. Was the store owner killed? No! Why not? His big, gold medallion necklace had deflected the bullet, saving his life.

Shields are not offensive weapons, made to harm others, but they are defensive weapons, made to protect those who use them. Scripture tells us that our faith is a shield that will keep the arrows (and bullets?) of the devil from striking us, just like the store owner's gold medallion necklace protected him. When you hold up your shield of faith, the things meant to harm you drop to the floor, having done little damage, if any at all.

Now, there are no promises that your lovely rings and blings are going to protect you from a speeding bullet, but the Bible promises that your shield of faith will protect you from the things that come at you in everyday, ordinary life.

Best part of this true story? The gold medallion the man was wearing was inscribed with "God Is One."

HOW ABOUT YOU?

People (and Satan) aren't shooting literal fiery arrows at you, but they do send painful little barbs your way. What do those look like in your life?

GOD SAYS . . .

In addition to all of these, hold up the shield of faith to stop the fiery arrows of the devil. EPHESIANS 6:16

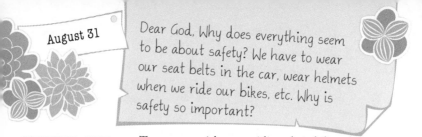

August 31

Dear God, Why does everything seem to be about safety? We have to wear our seat belts in the car, wear helmets when we ride our bikes, etc. Why is safety so important?

CONSIDER THIS . . . Two young girls were riding their bikes along a neighborhood street on the way to a third friend's house, to hang out together. They navigated the sidewalks and streets, the stoplights and stop signs, until all of a sudden a car came careening around the corner. Unable to brake soon enough, the car hit both girls, who fell to the ground.

An ambulance was called, and the twisted metal of their bikes was thrown away. At the hospital, both girls were admitted and treated. The doctor caring for them told their parents that the girls were lucky to be alive. "Their helmets saved them," she said. "Without the protection those helmets gave them, the girls would surely have died." The brain is the master control of the whole body; when it's dead, the body, which may have no other injuries, cannot live.

Safety measures aren't usually meant to protect us from the things we know will happen. They're meant to protect us from the unexpected and the unusual. If you knew when your car would be hit, you would wear your seat belt then, but not at other times, right? Unfortunately, you can't predict when the unexpected will happen, so you need to wear your seat belt whenever you're riding in the car.

Scripture tells us that salvation is our helmet. We don't know when we will die, but we do know that we will. The salvation that Jesus offers is, like the bike helmet, the difference between (eternal) life and (eternal) death. It's not always popular to wear a helmet, and honestly, it's not always popular to say that Jesus is the only way to heaven. But trusting in both will save your life.

GOD SAYS . . .

Put on salvation as your helmet. EPHESIANS 6:17

HOW ABOUT YOU?

Have you ever been in an accident of any kind? Did it happen slowly, or suddenly? What helped or saved you?

Dear God, Why does the Bible say we should carry a sword? Aren't they made to hurt other people? Besides, I thought swords were for guys.

September 1

CONSIDER THIS . . . Many languages other than English have what are called "masculine" words and "feminine" words. "Masculine" is related to men and boys, and "feminine" is related to women and girls. For instance, in Spanish, *señor* is used for "man" and *señora*, with the feminine *a* at the end, is used for "woman." Believe it or not, the word for "sword" used in Ephesians is a feminine word. That weapon is a woman! Although women are called to be feminine, we are also called to be strong and powerful. Deborah in the Bible was both a wife and a warrior!

Swords are used to defend ourselves, but they are also weapons that can help us to move forward against our enemies. When enemies see a sword and someone who knows how to use it, they back off. Our sword, the Word of God, is the sharpest weapon against our enemies.

When someone is coming at you with arguments that are against your Christian beliefs, if your sword is sharp and with you, you have a weapon to use to fight back. When someone is attacking a friend, if your sword is sharp and with you, you have a weapon to protect her with. When you see the world around you going in a direction you know it's not supposed to, if your sword is sharp and with you, you can take some ground back from the enemy.

It's important that you know how to use your weapon, so spend time reading the Bible and make sure you're getting good teaching at church, youth group, or Sunday school. Then you'll be stylin'. Wear those beautiful shoes, flaunt those accessories, but don't forget to pack your sword. You can be both a girly girl *and* a warrior in this world!

HOW ABOUT YOU?

What's the one weapon that's 100 percent appropriate for you to take with you no matter where you go? How can you make sure it's with you at all times?

GOD SAYS . . .

Take the sword of the Spirit, which is the word of God. EPHESIANS 6:17

Dear God, Why didn't you make my hair shiny or curly?

CONSIDER THIS . . . Everyone has one part of their beauty routine that they care the most about, and for most girls, it's hair, hair, hair! No one talks about a bad shoe day, for example. Only a bad hair day.

God knows that women care about their hair. In the Bible a woman's hair is compared to a royal tapestry, a beautiful, costly wall hanging made of soft and silken threads (Song of Songs 7:5, NIV). When Mary poured expensive perfume on Jesus' feet and then wiped them with her long hair, it was seen as a gift of very personal devotion. A woman's hair is described as her glory, and we're warned not to depend on it too much to feel beautiful.

The thing is—the Bible never says what color hair is the prettiest, or if really shiny hair is prettier than hair that is not as shiny. Maybe curly hair is what you find most beautiful (bring on the curling iron), or maybe your hair is curly, but you want it straight. Each girl's hair is unique to her.

When those royal tapestries are woven together, each one has a different set of colored threads, or textured threads, and they are sewn using many special techniques. The seamstress picks out just the right threads that will work together to make that picture beautiful.

Blonde hair might not look good on you. Shiny hair might not be as nice for you as beaded cornrows. Curly hair might work best with your friend's face shape, but straight brings out the beauty in yours. Experiment and have fun. But don't forget to be thankful for what you've been given, no matter the style, color, shape, and design!

GOD SAYS . . .

Let the peace that comes from Christ rule in your hearts. For as members of one body you are called to live in peace. And always be thankful.
COLOSSIANS 3:15

HOW ABOUT YOU?

What is one thing about your hair that you love and are thankful for? Tell God, right now! He gave that lovely thing to you!

Dear God, I'm always criticizing myself about what I wear, how I look, the way I act with my friends, what I say. Why?

September 3

CONSIDER THIS . . . Are any of these sentences things you would say to your best friend?

> "That was stupid. You should know better by now."
> "I knew you'd look really dumb in that outfit."
> "Every time you talk, people think you sound stupid."
> "Your hair is so flat and boring. No wonder none of the boys have crushes on you."

You would *never* say something like that to a friend—probably not even to an enemy! But those are the kinds of things we tell ourselves, inside, when we mess up or feel bad.

Self-talk is exactly what it sounds like. It is the words we say to ourselves. Sometimes we know we are talking to ourselves. Sometimes we have been doing it so long that we don't even recognize we are still doing it. The things you say to yourself will absolutely, positively change how you feel about *you*. If you tell yourself that you're dumb or stupid or ugly, it will make you feel more that way. If you cut yourself some slack—otherwise known as grace—you will feel better about yourself. When you feel better about yourself, you have some strength to keep trying, growing, and changing. If you feel bad, though, it makes you want to run and hide.

The next time you catch yourself saying something mean about yourself, stop. Ask yourself, *Would I say this to my best friend? What would I say instead?* Be honest. You need to treat yourself with love, respect, and grace. Just like you treat others.

HOW ABOUT YOU?

When do you say mean things about yourself— even just inside your head? What can you say instead?

GOD SAYS . . .

Always be humble and gentle. Be patient with each other, making allowance for each other's faults because of your love. . . . Let the Spirit renew your thoughts and attitudes. EPHESIANS 4:2, 23

Dear God, Sometimes I look at poor kids who have no hope because most of the world is richer than they are. Do they have any chance?

CONSIDER THIS . . . Once a family moved into a house that had been neglected for a while. They decided to remodel, and after the inside was done, they took a turn with the yard. What a wreck! Nearly every square foot had to be dug up and started over. They pulled every straggling plant, big and little, and put it into the yard-waste container.

Or so they thought!

The entire area was replanted with brand-new flowers, shrubs, and trees. But after a few months, the family noticed that, way in the back of the yard, a small group of daisies was growing. They hadn't included any daisies in their new landscape . . . but some old ones had been ripped out and thrown away. The blooming flowers were coming up right next to where the yard-waste bin was parked. Someone had tried to throw those flowers away but had missed their shot. Instead of dying, the persistent, stubborn little plants bloomed anyway without any tender loving care at all. In fact, because they had to be tough enough to survive, the daisies spread faster than some of the weaker, new flowers. The daisies brought their dogged delightfulness to an overlooked part of the yard.

There are many circumstances that are unfair in life, but it's not good to get into the habit of thinking that life is only about circumstances. Circumstances matter, situations matter, and what we do matters. But in the end, it's the Lord who can help the poor people become rich, if that is part of his plan. Poor people can become rich, and rich people can lose everything. In the end, a good and mighty God is in charge of it all. We can trust his plan for both the rich and the poor.

GOD SAYS . . .
It's not important who does the planting, or who does the watering. What's important is that God makes the seed grow. 1 CORINTHIANS 3:7

HOW ABOUT YOU?
What do you see that looks hopeless? Can God provide hope?

Dear God, The Bible says I can do anything. Really? Anything?

September 5

CONSIDER THIS . . . When you were a little baby, after about a year, you were ready to learn to walk. So your mom or dad or grandparents or a sibling held onto your fingers and helped you toddle across the floor. Soon enough they let go and said, "Come on, walk toward me! You can do it." And guess what? You could!

I'm pretty sure they didn't tell you to run a marathon, though!

A few years later, you probably learned how to ride a bike. You might have had a few wipeouts, but when the person teaching you how to ride finally let go of the bike and let you pedal on your own, he or she might have said, "Don't worry! You can do it!"

I'm pretty sure the person didn't tell you to drive a motorcycle, though. 'Cause you couldn't have!

Scripture does tell us that we can do everything through Christ, who gives us strength. But "everything" doesn't mean anything at all, no matter what. If that were true, people would be making geese lay golden eggs, solving the world hunger problem, and finding a cure for cancer. What it does mean is that you can do everything that God has called you to do, asked you to do, and told you to do.

So if God nudges you to share your faith with a friend, he'll give you strength. If he asks your family to move, he'll help you to find friends. And if he wants you to be a world-famous scientist, he'll help you get into the right college. You can't claim that promise in order to do things he doesn't want you to do, though.

But do you really want to do something if he doesn't want it for you?

HOW ABOUT YOU?
What things has God asked you to do in the past? Were you able to do them?

GOD SAYS . . .
I can do everything through Christ, who gives me strength.
PHILIPPIANS 4:13

Dear God, I heard a few older kids in my school talking about drugs. I don't understand why people do drugs. Why do they do something that can hurt them?

CONSIDER THIS . . . People start taking drugs for a lot of reasons. Sometimes they are pressured by their friends to try drugs to fit in or be cool. People don't want to lose their friends, so they go ahead and try drugs. Often people who use drugs have problems at home or at school, and they think drugs will make them feel better. They hope that the drugs will help them forget about their problems, at least for a little while. Sometimes people feel bad about themselves, so they start taking drugs because they think it will make them seem older or more interesting.

This world is filled with both good and bad. Until we die, we will have sadness, trouble, anger, and disappointment. We choose how to deal with those emotions. We can try to smother them with drugs, but that doesn't solve the problems. It only adds more. Jesus says that in this world we will have trouble, but that we should be brave because he has defeated the world (John 16:33). Because we belong to him, we don't have to depend on drugs for help. He will be our help.

The Bible says people are slaves to whatever controls them. If people have to take drugs to fit in, to forget about their problems, or to feel good about themselves, then drugs control them. They are slaves to drugs and need help to get free. If you know someone who is taking drugs, talk with your parents about it so they can give you advice about what to do next. And never take drugs yourself. A Christian should serve only Jesus Christ.

GOD SAYS . . .
You are a slave to whatever controls you. 2 PETER 2:19

HOW ABOUT YOU?
What will you do if someone tempts you to try drugs? What will you do if you know someone who takes drugs?

> Dear God. There is a forest behind my house that has many animals. A company is going to cut down a lot of the trees and build houses. Is that right?
>
> September 7

CONSIDER THIS . . . When we walk through a forest, the many shades of green fall down around us, and the air is cool and sweet. We hear many voices we don't normally hear—chirping, croaking, clicking. God made many creatures and plants, and he asked us to reign over them all.

Part of taking care of his creation means we are careful managers. We don't mow down all of the trees. Instead, we cut the ones we need to use, we replant, and we save some for the forest. We can carefully plan where houses will be built so as not to use up *all* available land.

But when God made everything, he made an order. In his order, people are more important than plants and animals. People are made in his image. He told people to reign over plants and animals. This means we should make decisions that recognize both sides of the issue, because everything God made, including plants and animals, he declared to be very good.

Maybe there's a girl like you whose family can't afford a home right now, but she will be able to have her own room in the houses they are building behind you. She might even turn out to be a good friend! Then you can walk through the rest of the forest together. In being concerned about plants and animals as well as people, you're a good manager of God's creation.

HOW ABOUT YOU?

How can you be a good manager of both plants and animals, and the people around you?

GOD SAYS . . .

Reign over the fish in the sea, the birds in the sky, and all the animals that scurry along the ground.
GENESIS 1:28

Dear God, Do I always have to do what my parents want me to do?

CONSIDER THIS ... Remember the story of Queen Esther? She married a king named Xerxes. The law of the land said that everyone, even the king's wife, must honor him and do as he asked. When it came time for the king to choose another wife, he chose Esther. Esther was beautiful and kind and godly. But even though Esther was queen, she knew that she must respect the rules of those in authority over her. That would be the king, who was also her husband.

Because of the schemes of an evil man, all of the Jewish people in Xerxes's kingdom were to be killed. Her cousin Mordecai begged Esther, who was also Jewish, to go to the king and save them. Because Esther had shown honor and respect to her husband and his rules, he was willing to listen to her request. She asked for what she wanted and saved the Jewish people of the kingdom from death.

What can we learn from Esther's story? Dishonor authority and get sent away to be killed? Respect your parents and become a queen? No way! But if you show respect for those in authority over you and honor them when the time is right, you can respectfully present your point of view!

You can try this three-step plan when faced with unpleasant but appropriate requests from your parents: (1) Agree to obey. (2) Ask to present your point of view. (3) Respectfully give your point of view and then obey.

It can be hard to follow rules sometimes. Esther knew this. But there is a payoff sometimes that you can't see right away. Obey your parents now and trust that the Lord will bring that payoff at just the right time.

GOD SAYS ...
Children, obey your parents because you belong to the Lord, for this is the right thing to do. EPHESIANS 6:1

HOW ABOUT YOU?
What situation can you use the three-step plan on?

Dear God, There are some girls at school who act like they're grown-ups. Do people always try to act older than they are?

September 9

CONSIDER THIS ... Some people definitely try to act older than they are. Or richer than they are, or more experienced than they are. Some people, who are sometimes called poseurs, pretend to have gone on vacations to places they haven't been or to own cool gear and technology that they don't have. One girl even pretended that she could speak French—until someone answered her back, in French, and she had no idea what the person was saying!

Most people who are "faking it" are really insecure. They think that people will like them better if they are the person they pretend to be, not the person they really are. Unfortunately, somewhere along the way, they might actually forget who they really are.

Jesus tells us to represent ourselves exactly as we are—let our yes mean yes, and our no mean no (Matthew 5:37, NCV). That means no fudging on the truth! This helps us to be pure. What is pure? Think of holding up a glass of clean water. You can almost see right through it. Now stir in a spoonful of sand or lemon juice. You can see right away what doesn't belong there—what it is that is making the water impure. If that water was concealed in a dark mug, you might not know that something wasn't right. Eventually, when you took a sip, you would, though!

Being pure means telling the truth all the time—especially about yourself. Then when people want to be friends with you, it'll be the real you they like. Just like clean water, when people get to know you, what they see is what they should get!

HOW ABOUT YOU?

Do you ever fake anything about yourself? Why?

GOD SAYS ...

I want you to understand what really matters, so that you may live pure and blameless lives until the day of Christ's return. PHILIPPIANS 1:10

Dear God, When my teachers say that evolution is true and God is made up, I feel so discouraged. What can I do?

CONSIDER THIS . . . Most people are proud of their independence. We're proud of the way we can do things on our own. When people are too proud of themselves, however, that pride is like poison to the soul.

Too much independence makes us think that we are in charge. We think we can make our own decisions without obeying or following anyone else. It means we don't have to answer to anyone. The only way *that* can be true is if there is no God. If we believe in God, we know he is bigger than we are. He is in charge. If someone wants to pretend to be in charge, she has to believe there is no God. Then she needs some other way to explain the beginning of the earth and the beginning of life. This is where the theory of evolution comes in. It's an explanation based on some true things around us and allows people not to believe God made the world. Some people believe God made the world and then it changed, or evolved. That is a different kind of evolution from the theory that says God was not involved at all.

The book of Romans says that people know God because they can see his work all around them. Keep peace in your heart during these discouraging moments, knowing that your eyes are opened to the truth and that God will protect you during these times. Work hard to have a respectable life. Then when you have the chance to speak the truth about Creation or evolution—and you will—people will listen to your thoughts even though they may disagree.

GOD SAYS . . .
Ever since the world was created, people have seen the earth and sky. Through everything God made, they can clearly see his invisible qualities—his eternal power and divine nature. So they have no excuse for not knowing God. ROMANS 1:20

HOW ABOUT YOU?
Whom can you ask to help you prepare a short answer about your beliefs?

Dear God, Will terrorists get me?

CONSIDER THIS . . . We live in a world that seems to be filled with dangers. Every time we travel on an airplane we're reminded that there are terrorists that want to hurt us. There are sicknesses that seem out of control. Your parents warn you about strangers, and even not-so-strangers, who can hurt you if you're not careful. And then there are car crashes, strong storms, and bad news about money, or moving, or school.

Help!

But when you sit down, take a deep breath, and think about it, you may realize that the world is no more dangerous now than it has ever been. There have always been bad people who want to hurt others, and people in times past had even more sicknesses than there are today. One hundred years ago, there weren't car crashes, but there were buggy accidents—and people have always had too little money for the things they want. Bad news is nothing new.

The truth is, the thing that you fear the most is the thing you believe has the most power. And God wants us to fear him. That doesn't mean he wants us to worry that he will harm us; he won't. He just wants us to rest assured that he is big enough to protect us from everything, and to help us through the few anxious times that all of us will experience while we live on the earth.

Remember when you were a little kid and you'd threaten a bully with, "My dad is bigger than your dad"? This is still true! Your heavenly Father is bigger than anything that your enemies can throw at you. Knowing God, and fearing him in the right way, will free you from worrying about anything else that might harm you.

HOW ABOUT YOU?

What are some of your deepest fears? Can you talk with God about them tonight, and ask him to help you become fearless and confident because you know your "Dad" is bigger and stronger than any of them?

GOD SAYS . . .

They do not fear bad news; they confidently trust the LORD to care for them. They are confident and fearless and can face their foes triumphantly. PSALM 112:7-8

September 12

NATIONAL NO NEWS IS GOOD NEWS DAY
Dear God, When I tell people about you, what should I say?

CONSIDER THIS . . . Sometimes, when life gets tough, people say, "No news is good news." Maybe you've tried out for a team or for a play, and only those who would be cut would get called. No phone ringing . . . no news is good news! The doctor says he'll call right away if something is wrong. No phone call . . . no news is good news!

There are plenty of times, though, when no news is bad news. What if those who won a big prize would be called? Ring, phone, ring! Or if everyone who made the team was to be called? You'd be watching all afternoon for your phone to light up with an incoming call. When people expect to hear something good, something that will help them and bring them life or health or happiness, they want to hear about it.

As a Christian, you have heard and understood the very best news of all—the gospel! The fact that Jesus is God, paid the penalty for our sins, and made salvation available to all who confess and believe is not only good news, it's great news! You don't have to share all the news at once, though. When something unfair happens, you can tell your friends that God is just—he makes things fair for everyone in the end. When they have a friend who dumps them, share that God's so faithful and his love so strong that he will never leave or let go of us. When you have bad news, it's hard to share it even when you have to. When you have good news, though . . . let it out!

GOD SAYS . . .
I have not kept the good news of your justice hidden in my heart; I have talked about your faithfulness and saving power. I have told everyone in the great assembly of your unfailing love and faithfulness. PSALM 40:10

HOW ABOUT YOU?
Do you think that what you have to share about God is slightly embarrassing or good news? How can you share the Good News—the gospel—today?

Dear God, How can I stop being bossy to others?

September 13

CONSIDER THIS . . . You're a wise girl to see this in yourself or to have listened when someone else told you that you were bossy. That's half of the battle. Now, if you can understand why you boss others around, and then change your actions, you'll be all the way there.

People boss others when they want their own way. Sometimes this happens because a girl feels like she always needs to be in control. She feels scared that she will be left out or ignored if she isn't in control. By controlling others, she thinks, she'll keep them close to her. But the opposite usually happens. When people get smothered from the bossing, they run away.

Sometimes girls boss people around because they feel that their way is best. They don't see that there are lots of different ways to do or say things. When you let others choose what to do or what to say, you are giving them honor. You're telling them that you value their ideas, their thoughts, and their words. If you're always in charge, you're really telling them that they must always honor you. I know that's not what you mean! When you let others choose to be with you, rather than your always controlling it, it's really better. Why? Because you're allowing them to show you love, to pick you rather than be forced to be with you.

Next time you're tempted to tell others what to do, keep quiet. It will be hard, and it will take practice. Allow others to do things their way till they ask you if you have an idea. Then you can share! Allow others to plan things and include you. When they do—and they will if you give it time—you'll feel real love.

HOW ABOUT YOU?

Are you always the boss in your group of friends? Do others get to share and do their ideas? How can you let others have a chance?

GOD SAYS . . .

Don't just pretend to love others. Really love them. . . . Love each other with genuine affection, and take delight in honoring each other.
ROMANS 12:9-10

Dear God, Sometimes I don't know what to do. When that happens, how should I act?

CONSIDER THIS . . . Imagine this. . . . You're lying awake in bed at night, and you hear a noise. It's not a normal house noise. What do you do? Do you jump out of bed right away? Nope. You lie very still and see if you can figure out where the sound is coming from. Ever see a bunny rabbit or a squirrel in the wild? Once they see you, and they know you see them, they freeze. They're hoping you'll go away, or turn another direction, and then they can safely escape. Until we know what's going on and what to do, all critters, and people, normally keep still.

This is like a fun game called Statue Maker. A group of people get together outside and one person swings each of the others around and around. When the "swinger" lets go of the hands of the person she's twirling, that person must fall to the ground in a pose. When everyone is posed, the "statue maker" must go around and guess what each "statue" is. If you move before it's your turn, you lose. It's the hardest thing in the world to hold perfectly still, waiting, no matter what is going on around you.

That's how it is in real life sometimes too. We want to move! But sometimes, like the bunny or the squirrel, we're not sure what's going on around us. We need to get more information before scampering forward.

The next time you don't know what to do, stay still, doing nothing except asking God to lead the way. It's okay to wait for him to lead you, and when you do, you know you'll be moving in the right direction.

GOD SAYS . . .
Be still in the presence of the LORD, and wait patiently for him to act. PSALM 37:7

HOW ABOUT YOU?
Are there times when you don't know what to do or say? Do you believe that if you wait, quietly, God will act or tell you to act?

Dear God, What should I do if my friends try to act cool and I don't get it, and then they make fun of me?

CONSIDER THIS . . . Keeping up with what is cool can be really hard. Words and songs and clothes that are cool one day are not so cool the next week. You can spend a lot of time trying to be cool. Trying to be cool might make you feel good some of the time. But sometimes it will make you feel like you're running in a race that you will never, ever win. It's important to fit in, to belong with a group of others. There's no doubt about it. But the real question to ask yourself is, Whom do I want to fit in and belong with?

A real friend doesn't care if you're cool according to what other kids think. She thinks you're cool because she knows all about you and thinks you're terrific. A real friend sticks up for you even when it's hard.

It's important to take a quiet moment and consider why you want to be friends with these girls. Do you feel cooler when you're with them? No one enjoys being made fun of and teased, and most people don't want to make fun of and tease others. It may seem like you'll have more power if you're their friend, but they are showing you the nasty ways they're using that power. A real friend will stick by you no matter what trouble comes your way. She doesn't care if other people think you're cool or if they think you're not. If you fit in and belong with girls like that, you'll find that having the power that comes with being cool won't matter at all.

HOW ABOUT YOU?

Why do you sometimes want others to think you're cool? Are you willing to hang out with kids who make you uncomfortable in order to be cool?

GOD SAYS . . .

A friend is always loyal, and a brother is born to help in time of need.
PROVERBS 17:17

Dear God, Could one of my parents lose his or her job?

CONSIDER THIS . . . Yes, your parents could lose their jobs. In this world, almost everyone will lose a job at one time or another. If someone loses a job and wasn't expecting to, it's very painful. It feels like rejection. It can make a person very sad, and that's hard to watch. Especially if it's your mom or dad.

Losing a job can also seem scary because you wonder what you will do next. Will your parent get another job? Will it be one that he or she likes? Will there be enough money to live on?

One great truth to hold on to is that God is like a safety net. Have you been to a circus? The trapeze artists get out there and swing, twirl, and jump. They often catch one another as they go from swing to swing. From time to time, though, the acrobats fall. Instead of reaching the swing, they miss their grip. As they fall, it probably feels like they're going to go *splat!* But they know that, ahead of time, someone has strung up safety nets. They will fall, but they won't go *splat*. It will feel scary, but they'll be safe. They can shake themselves off, recover a bit, and try again.

Our lives are like that too. We go to work or school and are swinging and twirling and jumping. Occasionally we miss our grip or something out of our control goes wrong. When that happens, a buddy might catch us. But if not, God is our safety net. He will allow us to fall but not go *splat*. He catches us, cares for us, and provides for our needs. Even if it seems like it takes a long time, he helps find a new job where your mom or dad can shine.

GOD SAYS . . .
This same God who takes care of me will supply all your needs from his glorious riches, which have been given to us in Christ Jesus. PHILIPPIANS 4:19

HOW ABOUT YOU?
How is God like a safety net in *your* life?

Dear God, My mom won't let me do things she let my sister do when she was my age. How can I tell my mom that I've grown up?

CONSIDER THIS . . . When we're five we can get a library card. When we're sixteen we can drive. We start to expect that everything should happen to us at a certain age. But really, most things happen because of a combination of how old we are *and* how responsible we are. This is also true (though it doesn't feel good to hear it): some things aren't safe for kids, and parents protect their children by forbidding them to do those things.

Maybe your parents let your sister do something at an early age and it didn't work out well, so they're making a better plan for you. Maybe they're not aware of something you want to do or something you feel you deserve to do. Maybe you've been a wee bit irresponsible in some way, and they're waiting just a little longer to trust you with other things. Those are hard things to think about, but you have to look at them honestly before you can solve your problem.

If there's something special you want to be allowed to do, ask your mom. Explain that you are willing to prove you're trustworthy. If it's something she feels isn't right for you, respect and live with that decision. If it's a matter of your being faithful and trustworthy, ask how you can prove that. She may ask you to stop sassing or to do your schoolwork without being asked or to clean your room. All of these things help her understand that you're a more grown-up girl. Keep on this path of being faithful with the little things. You'll be surprised at the big things people will trust you with once you've proven yourself!

HOW ABOUT YOU?

How do you respond when your parents tell you no? Ask your parents how you could be more faithful in managing the responsibilities you already have.

GOD SAYS . . .

A person who is put in charge as a manager must be faithful.
1 CORINTHIANS 4:2

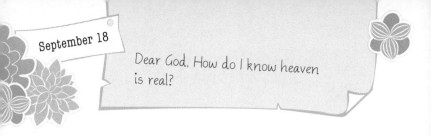

Dear God, How do I know heaven is real?

CONSIDER THIS . . . The Bible talks about heaven more than five hundred times. If God says something once, it's important. If he mentions something five hundred times, he really wants you to pay attention! Jesus himself says he is preparing a place for us to go when our lives on this earth are over.

Imagine if you were having a houseguest, someone you really loved. You'd prepare the nicest guest room you had. Maybe you'd put some fresh flowers in it or a couple of candy bars for late-night snacks. You'd use the best towels—not the ones you use to wash the car. You might even put fresh sheets on the bed and fluff the pillows. The windows would be opened to let in a refreshing breeze. Just like we prepare a wonderful place for the person we're expecting, the Bible tells us that God is expecting you and preparing a wonderful place for you.

Don't be afraid to move forward into heaven when this life is over. If you have received Christ as your Savior, heaven awaits you. The Bible says that God is the source of all good things (James 1:17). Considering that, can you imagine all the good things he's preparing for us in heaven?

GOD SAYS . . .
When everything is ready, I will come and get you, so that you will always be with me where I am. JOHN 14:3

HOW ABOUT YOU?
Do you know for certain that you are going to heaven? If you don't know if you've received Christ as your Lord and Savior, ask the person who gave you this book to talk with you about it.

Dear God, I always study hard for my tests, so why don't I get As?

CONSIDER THIS . . . We have all known someone who seems to never have to study and is always out having fun while we're studying, working, rewriting, and pinching our cheeks to stay awake so we can keep studying!

It may seem unfair that you have to work so hard, but remember that sooner or later, everyone finds something that doesn't come easily to her. Then she may have to buckle down and study . . . if she has learned how to!

Now, some kids do study hard for their As. They earn them! There is nothing wrong with that, and they—and you—can feel good when they get the higher grades. But you'll also find in life that hard work doesn't always bring rewards—the lead in the play, great grades, awards—right away. During all that time you spend studying or learning to stick with jobs that don't come easily, you are quietly building the skills you'll need to be successful in life. And people *do* notice that! You may not earn As, but your hard work will be noticed. You are training yourself to tackle and beat tasks no matter how hard they may be. You are learning about perseverance when you work hard, not knowing if the effort you put into your task will pay off right away. No matter what you're working on, work knowing that the one who sees all of your work will reward your effort some way, sometime.

Keep on learning. You are becoming wise and smart and building good habits. The way of life you develop by studying and doing what is right—no matter what grades you get—will repay you for a lifetime.

HOW ABOUT YOU?

Have there been times when your work has gone unrewarded? What are your two best study skills?

GOD SAYS . . .

Let's not get tired of doing what is good. At just the right time we will reap a harvest of blessing if we don't give up. GALATIANS 6:9

Dear God, When I was little I used to suck my thumb whenever I felt afraid. I'm too old for that now. What can I do instead when I'm scared?

CONSIDER THIS . . . Lick lollipops? Chomp chewing gum? Just kidding!

Almost everyone has seen a *Peanuts* TV special. Snoopy is always on his doghouse, sometimes typing his book. Charlie Brown is trying to get some respect, and avoid falling flat on his back while kicking a football. Lucy is a bossy psychiatrist who charges five cents for her advice. And Linus van Pelt, Charlie Brown's best friend and Sally's crush, always has his security blanket.

In fact, Linus never lets go of that blanket, even during his most famous scene in the Christmas special, where he's telling everyone the real meaning of Christmas, that is, the birth of Jesus Christ!

As smart as Linus is, and as much as he knows about the Bible, he's obviously never figured out that he can leave his blankie behind and find his true sense of security from the one who was born on Christmas, our Savior, Jesus Christ. There's no dog big enough, no lock strong enough, no thumb tasty enough, and no blanket soft enough to keep you safe 24-7. Only God can do that, and the best thing is, he's willing! He tells us in the Bible that we shouldn't worry. He himself will be our security during the scary times.

Linus's blankie may not provide true security, but it makes a great shepherd's outfit. In the same way, thumbs may not keep us safe, but they are good for cooking, writing, and holding hands! Let God be your "security blanket" today.

GOD SAYS . . .

You need not be afraid of sudden disaster or the destruction that comes upon the wicked, for the LORD is your security. He will keep your foot from being caught in a trap.

PROVERBS 3:25-26

HOW ABOUT YOU?

How and from whom do you get your sense of feeling safe?

CONSIDER THIS . . . The earth goes through seasons as we tilt toward, and then away from, the sun that keeps us warm. Spring and summer are warmer because we tilt toward the sun, while autumn and winter are colder as we tilt away from our source of heat. Some of us think of seasons not according to the weather but in terms of holidays—for those of us in the United States, Christmas is in the winter, Easter in the spring, Fourth of July in the summer, and Thanksgiving in autumn. We can also think of seasons according to the school calendar; a school year typically starts in autumn and ends in early summer. For most of human history, people thought about the seasons in terms of planting (spring), growing (summer), harvesting (autumn), and rest (winter). Their ability to eat depended on their thinking that way!

In autumn, the time of harvest, there are two special moons that mark the season. In September there is the harvest moon, and in October there is a hunter's moon. These full moons last longer, shine brighter, and show more color than full moons at other times of the year. People came to think it was to allow those picking crops and hunting animals a few extra hours of light so they could provide food for the long winter ahead.

In some ways, the passing of one season and the start of a new one, year after year, is comforting. God has made the world and everything in it, and they all tick along according to plan, month after month, year after year.

HOW ABOUT YOU?

Have you ever seen the harvest moon or the hunter's moon? Find the days this year that they will be visible and make a plan to view them. How does the passing of seasons show that God is a God of order?

GOD SAYS . . .

You made the moon to mark the seasons, and the sun knows when to set. PSALM 104:19

Dear God, Why are some girls nice one day and then mean the next day?

CONSIDER THIS . . . What happens when a gardener plants a lemon tree? It grows up and soon produces lemons. First, only one or two lemons appear. They might even look like limes or oranges at first, from a distance. As the tree gets more and more established, more lemons grow. Soon the tree is covered with lemons, and it's clearly a lemon tree.

When you first get to know someone, you assume the best. She's probably nice. She wants to be kind. You do a few things with her. Maybe one or two lemons pop out, but overall, good things are happening. However, as you spend more and more time with her and watch her in action, you see more lemons. Even if she tries to fake being nice, it won't work very long. Why not? Because she's growing lemons in her heart, not just in her actions.

Jesus said that whatever is in the heart of a person comes out through his or her mouth. A lemon tree can't fake being a sweet orange tree by painting its fruit orange. Soon enough you'd take a bite and know it was a sour lemon. In the same way, a truly mean-hearted person can fake good words or deeds when it benefits her, but she can't cover up her true feelings forever. What's in her heart will always come out.

Don't waste your time trying to change this person from a lemon tree to an orange tree. Only God can do that. Don't waste your time wondering *why* this person is a lemon tree. Instead, look around you and find a nice apple, pear, peach, or cherry tree to befriend. Until she allows God to change her heart, a mean person is always going to grow lemons.

GOD SAYS . . .
A good person produces good things from the treasury of a good heart, and an evil person produces evil things from the treasury of an evil heart. MATTHEW 12:35

HOW ABOUT YOU?
Who are some sweet girls who can be your friends?

Dear God, Why don't you just get rid of all the bad people in the world?

September 23

CONSIDER THIS . . . There is a certain kind of tumor that can grow deep within a brain. Even when it's small, it causes symptoms like headaches and blurry vision. Technology can help find this kind of tumor, but if it's found while it's small, it can't be removed. To take it out then would cause brain damage. You have to wait till it's big enough to be cut out without damaging the brain around it.

Do you think the person who had that tumor would be nervous letting it grow? Of course! While the person waited for the tumor to grow large enough, she'd still have those headaches and the blurry vision. But there'd be nothing to do except wait till it was big enough to remove safely—a priority!

Just like that, God has a perfect timing for everything that might not seem to make sense at first, and can cause some pain during the waiting. One of the stories Jesus told was about a farmer who planted good seed in his fields. While his workers were sleeping, an enemy came in and planted weeds among the farmer's good crops. The weeds and plants grew up close together. If the farmer's workers would have pulled out the weeds while the good plants were still young, the good plants might have come out as well.

God knows who the good plants are, and who the weeds are. Even though we feel some pain with bad people still in the world, we can trust that God knows just the right time to wait and just the right time to weed.

HOW ABOUT YOU?
When things hurt and don't make sense, can you trust God's timing? What's a situation that requires you to trust God's timing?

GOD SAYS . . .
"Should we pull out the weeds?" they asked. "No," he replied, "you'll uproot the wheat if you do. Let both grow together until the harvest. Then I will tell the harvesters to sort out the weeds, tie them into bundles, and burn them." MATTHEW 13:28-30

Dear God, I want to become more like you. What characteristics will grow in my life as I get to be a stronger Christian?

CONSIDER THIS ... The Iroquois people, a nation of Native Americans, believe that squash, beans, and corn are three sisters who can't be separated if they are to grow and thrive. The three types of seeds must be planted together, or else each of them will die.

When you plant those three seeds—squash, beans, and corn—in the same mound, they help one another out as they grow. The corn provides a tall pole for the beans to grow on. Beans are vines—they need something steady to wrap around! Once they do, they act kind of like a rope, making the thin little stalks of corn stronger till they grow thick enough to resist the wind. Squash plants have prickly leaves and stems. No animals want to risk getting scratched and scraped, so they avoid nibbling on not only the prickly squash but also the growing corn and bean plants. The beans and corn help the squash by providing nutrients that the squash needs to grow.

There are three "sisters" in our Christian life that work together too—in fact, where you find a lot of one, you're likely to find a lot of another. Why? They help each other grow strong. Scripture tells us that these three things—faith, hope, and love—will last forever.

Each of us has a little more of one or two of these than the other. But if you carefully water and weed your heart, you'll find that the third sister can grow tall and strong too. Faith, hope, and love need one another to thrive.

GOD SAYS ...

Three things will last forever—faith, hope, and love—and the greatest of these is love.
1 CORINTHIANS 13:13

HOW ABOUT YOU?

Do you have more faith, more hope, or more love? How can you feed and water the one or two that need a little boost to grow?

> Dear God, I don't really like going to church. It's so boring to me. Can't I stop going to church with my family?

September 25

CONSIDER THIS . . . A favorite kind of diary is called *All about Me*. In it you get to write down all of the things you like best—favorite colors, favorite foods, what you want your house to look like when you grow up. You can even mark down how many kids you want. In the back is a section about hopes and dreams—including what you want your future husband to look like—and also secret fears! Anyone can spend a lot of time doodling about herself. But the downside is that it keeps us really focused on *me*.

Church, as it turns out, is *not* all about me. First and foremost, church is all about God—learning more about him, worshiping him, serving him, and most important, loving him and getting to know him better. After God, church is all about God's people. If you're a Christian, you're one of them. God tells us to love one another, learn the Scriptures so you won't be ashamed, and use your gifts to help others. Rather than focusing on what you are *getting* from church and the *All about Me* mind-set, switch your focus to the *All about Him* book—the Bible—and those he's placed you with in Sunday school or in the chair right next to you. That's not just entertainment!

HOW ABOUT YOU?

What can you do to make sure you focus on God while you're at church? How does changing the focus from *me* to *him* or *them* change your feelings about church?

GOD SAYS . . .

Let us not neglect our meeting together, as some people do, but encourage one another, especially now that the day of his return is drawing near. HEBREWS 10:25

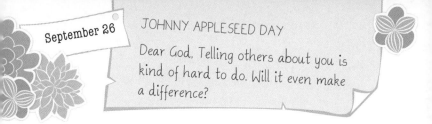

JOHNNY APPLESEED DAY

Dear God, Telling others about you is kind of hard to do. Will it even make a difference?

CONSIDER THIS . . . Johnny Appleseed was a famous American who lived around the time of the American Revolution. He was a good, nice man, but he was kind of a wanderer. He believed in treating people and animals well—and in planting apple trees! Many of the apple orchards in the United States today are there because Johnny Appleseed planted them. He couldn't stick around long enough to see the trees grow into fruit producers because he had other places to go and more seeds to plant. He just knew that if he did the right thing, the fruit would come.

That's how it is when you share your faith. You may not see the "fruit" right away, but if you're planting good seeds, someone else will come along and water those seeds. God is the only one who can cause something spiritual to be born in anyone's heart. So you do your part, let someone else do theirs, and God will, for sure, do his! Then there will be fruit for everyone in the world to share.

Johnny used to sing a song as he traveled across the country:

Oh, the Lord's been good to me.
Oh, and every seed I sow
Will grow into a tree.
And someday there'll be apples there For everyone in the world to share.
Oh, the Lord is good to me!

GOD SAYS . . .

I [Paul] planted the seed in your hearts, and Apollos watered it, but it was God who made it grow. It's not important who does the planting, or who does the watering. What's important is that God makes the seed grow. 1 CORINTHIANS 3:6-7

HOW ABOUT YOU?

Where can you plant good seeds?

Dear God, My best friend is having a hard time in class even though she studies hard. She wants me to let her read my answers during a test. Should I?

CONSIDER THIS . . . Do you remember the fairy tale about Rapunzel? A man and a woman waited a long time to have a baby . . . and finally their dream was about to come true! One day, the woman looked outside her window and saw some beautiful plants growing nearby. She desperately wanted to eat some. And her husband desperately wanted to help her. So he sneaked into the garden and stole some plants for his wife. A few days later, the evil woman who owned the plants caught him and made him promise, in order for him to go free, that his soon-to-be-born baby would belong to her.

There is a similar tale in the Bible, about two brothers. One was very hungry, and the other had just prepared some stew. The hungry brother gave away his birthright—all the property and privilege he would inherit from his father as the firstborn—for a bowl of stew.

Although we might say, in both cases, "I would never do that!" the fact is that all of us are tempted to exchange something precious in the future for what seems like a pressing need at the time. By letting your friend cheat off you, you're denying her the help she'll get when your teacher sees what a hard time she's having. And you'll be giving away your good reputation for honesty, something very hard to get back.

HOW ABOUT YOU?

When were some times when you were tempted to do something wrong because you needed or wanted something at the moment?

GOD SAYS . . .

"Look, I'm dying of starvation!" said Esau. "What good is my birthright to me now?" But Jacob said, "First you must swear that your birthright is mine." So Esau swore an oath, thereby selling all his rights as the firstborn to his brother, Jacob. GENESIS 25:32-33

Dear God, I'm having problems worrying about what other people think about me. What can I do?

CONSIDER THIS . . . Everyone wants people to think well of them. We dress carefully when we're going to meet people for the first time; we prepare for a speech by practicing over and over. Sometimes it all pays off—and we do things perfectly. Sometimes, well, let's just say life interferes!

The truth is, people will form ideas about you as they get to know you better. They will learn what you are really like, and they have the choice to like you or not. But your value does *not* depend on what other people think of you. Your great value is in what God thinks of you. He thinks you are pretty special. He made you just as you are. He loves you, and Jesus died for you so you could be with him forever. He must have thought you were okay to want to do that! You could do the right thing over and over again, and some people still won't like you. You could do the wrong thing over and over again, and some people will still think you're great. You can't win by being a people pleaser!

Guess what the best cure is for worrying about what other people will think? If you try it, it will work. Every time you worry about what someone else is thinking about you, change the subject in your brain. Think of something kind or nice to say or to do for the people you are with, and then do it—right then! Instead of focusing on *you*, focus on them. Ask how they are, what their day was like, if they want to do something together. Compliment them. Then do something together. Soon enough you'll find that you are loving others and not worrying so much about yourself.

GOD SAYS . . .
Obviously, I'm not trying to win the approval of people, but of God. If pleasing people were my goal, I would not be Christ's servant.
GALATIANS 1:10

HOW ABOUT YOU?
In what situations do you worry too much about what others think of you? What can you do about it?

Dear God, When I look at pictures of other girls in magazines, I feel fat. What should I do?

September 29

CONSIDER THIS . . . Sadly, we live in a culture that tells women, and girls, that the most important thing about them is how they look. And how are they supposed to look? They're supposed to have perfectly shaped bodies (is there such a thing?) and perfect hair and perfectly straight, white teeth. Just like the girls in the magazines. Except . . .

Those girls don't exist!

A recent study showed that all—that means 100 percent—of women and girls in magazines have been Photoshopped and airbrushed. Not only do you not look like women in a magazine, but the models don't even look like that in real life! So love yourself just as you are.

Now, you still have to take good care of the body you were given. Part of taking care of your body is to not overeat. Overeating means to take in more food than your body needs to run properly. If you do that for too long, your body will begin to store everything it doesn't need to use that day, which is what we think of as fat. A lot of times we eat too much when we're bored, or sad, or scared, or worried. The Bible says that food was made for the stomach, but it definitely does not say that it was made for the brain (which is what you're "feeding" when you're bored or confused) or for the heart (what you're "feeding" when you're feeling sad or upset). Instead, activities and people were made to meet those needs.

Are you hungry? Well, then, eat something! Sad? Get a hug. Bored? Do something . . . just don't page through magazines wishing you could look like those Photoshopped girls!

HOW ABOUT YOU?

Do you have a realistic sense of what typical girls look like and what you, at your natural state, look like?

GOD SAYS . . .

You say, "Food was made for the stomach, and the stomach for food."

1 CORINTHIANS 6:13

Dear God, I like wearing some clothes that are black. My sister barely wears any black, but people ask if she's emo. Why would people ask that?

CONSIDER THIS . . . It's true that the clothes we choose to wear give people a clue about us. If you wear track pants and T-shirts, people may think you're sporty. Do your clothes have a lot of flowers or ruffles? People may assume you're a girly girl. People tend to associate black clothing and nail polish and heavy makeup with being emo. And they usually associate emo with being depressed.

Now, clothing is only one clue we send out to others. Our attitudes usually serve as another hint. If you're wearing black clothing but you're bubbly and active and cheerful, especially if you partner your dark clothes with some brighter accessories, people aren't likely to think that something may be wrong. But if you wear black and purple and you're withdrawn and are having a hard time in other ways, they might be concerned. Your sister may not wear black clothes, but if she seems sad or depressed all the time, people might assume that she's emo.

Jesus told us that we are to be concerned not only with ourselves, but also with others. That means looking at the clues people are giving about themselves to see if they need help. If people are rude or nosy about your sister, well, then, that's not right. But if they're politely inquiring if she's all right because they're concerned about her well-being, they're loving others like they love themselves. And we're supposed to do that, so it's okay!

GOD SAYS . . .

Jesus replied, "'You must love the LORD your God with all your heart, all your soul, and all your mind.' This is the first and greatest commandment. A second is equally important: 'Love your neighbor as yourself.'"
MATTHEW 22:37-39

HOW ABOUT YOU?

Do you know anyone who looks or acts like they might need help? Can you offer to help or share your concerns with a parent?

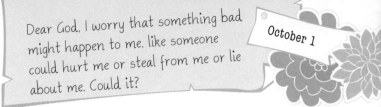

Dear God, I worry that something bad might happen to me, like someone could hurt me or steal from me or lie about me. Could it?

October 1

CONSIDER THIS . . . Try this experiment: focus on an object across the room. Stare at it. You'll notice, out of the corner of your eye, the other things in the room, but everything will be centered on what you're focusing on. It's not that it is bigger—it's just getting all the attention. Whatever you focus on will take over your thoughts.

There are bad people in this world, and some of them do bad things. Mostly, though, there are kind people. One woman lost her debit card and worried that someone else would use it before she got it back. But the person who found the debit card didn't use it before giving it back.

Out of 365 days in a year, maybe five of them have really bad weather. If people prepare themselves and their homes, though, most are perfectly safe inside while the storm whirls around them. They don't spend the other days worrying about possible bad weather. In the same way, there are bad things and bad people in this world. Scary things happen to everyone from time to time, many of them hurtful. However, worrying won't help. What can you do?

Take some safety precautions—don't walk alone, always be in before dark, follow your parents' instructions. Listen when people at home, school, or church teach you about protecting yourself. Ask questions when something feels uncomfortable. After you've done all you can do, though, set it aside. Focus on God and his ability to protect you from evil and restore you if something does happen, not on potential problems. Focusing on his peace will help you stop worrying.

HOW ABOUT YOU?

What do you fear? What steps can you take to act wisely to protect yourself from that?

GOD SAYS . . .

Don't worry about anything; instead, pray about everything. Tell God what you need, and thank him for all he has done. Then you will experience God's peace, which exceeds anything we can understand.
PHILIPPIANS 4:6-7

Dear God, I'd really like to trust you more. How can I do that?

CONSIDER THIS ... When you first meet a new friend, you don't know very much about each other. You might chat and find out you have a lot in common. After you spend time together, you trust her more and more. You might tell her some secrets because now you know she won't blab them. You might ask her for help with something because now you know she won't laugh at you. You've spent enough time with her to know she can be trusted.

So how do you get to know God better? The same way you get to know your other friends—by hanging out together. You read about him in the Bible. You discover that he is dependable. Talk to other people about him. Read books about him. When it's praise and worship time at church, close your eyes and spend time singing to him. The Bible says God is right there in the middle of our praise, so you're really close to him when you're praising him. Then tell him your secrets like you would your other friends.

When you've spent some more time with God, you'll know him better. So the next time trouble rolls around (and it always rolls around, doesn't it?), you can take a deep breath and say, "Okay, Jesus, I trust you with this." And then you do trust him. You do what you know is right. You talk to people who give you godly answers. You pray. You keep doing those things until the Lord shows you what to do next or shows you that the problem is solved.

Trusting someone is like riding a bike—you can't learn how to do it without actually doing it! The more you ride, the better you get!

GOD SAYS ...
[Jesus said,] "Don't let your hearts be troubled. Trust in God, and trust also in me." JOHN 14:1

HOW ABOUT YOU?
What problems or concerns do you have right now, this week, in your life? Will you pray, tell the Lord you trust him, and ask him to show you what to do?

Dear God, How do I know which music is okay to listen to and which is not?

October 3

CONSIDER THIS . . . Have you ever looked at a fish tank? Maybe you have one, but even if you don't, you've probably seen one at the doctor's office, at a pet store, or even at an aquarium. At the top or to the side of each fish tank is a filter. The filter runs all the time, making sure that all of the gunk and goop that would accumulate in the tank is strained out so the fish can swim in—and breathe—clean water. If the filter is broken, or not cleaned often enough, a thin layer of green slime starts to cover the rocks, the walls, and the lid of the tank. You can practically hear the fish gasping, "Help! Someone clean out this tank!"

In kind of the same way, you need to filter what goes into your ears. When you're listening to music that you haven't heard before, you need to have your filter turned up high and pay attention. What are the words saying? Do they lift you up or bring you down? Do they use language that you would be embarrassed to sing along with in front of your grandma? Do they make fun of people? If so, it's time to turn off that song and, when you come across that group again, make sure your filter stops the music before it reaches your ears.

Scripture tells us that we need to taste what we eat to make sure it's good, and listen to what we hear to make sure it's healthy. If you took a bite of an apple and found a worm, would you bite again? No way! Just like that, test what you listen to, too!

HOW ABOUT YOU?

Are there bands or groups that you or someone you know listens to that you sense might be "iffy"? Which bands or groups could you listen to instead?

GOD SAYS . . .

The ear tests the words it hears just as the mouth distinguishes between foods. JOB 12:11

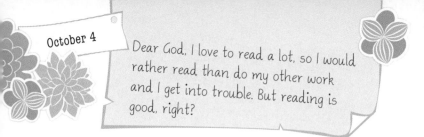

Dear God, I love to read a lot, so I would rather read than do my other work and I get into trouble. But reading is good, right?

CONSIDER THIS . . . Yes, reading is good. Reading is educational, but reading is also entertaining. Just like anything else you do for fun, reading has to have its proper place.

We all need to sleep. In fact, people who don't get enough sleep start having trouble in their everyday lives! They can't concentrate, speak well, or think straight. However, if people get too much sleep, that's not good for them either. They grow lazy, the Bible says, and eventually don't work, so they don't have enough to eat. You know that you need to eat each and every day. Your body uses food for fuel to think and work and keep running. If you eat too much, though, it will be bad for your body, not good. That's called gluttony, and it will slow your body down and cause it to work too hard.

When you neglect your schoolwork or chores for reading, it's really not choosing to spend time doing something good. First, it's disobedience, because you're not doing the things you've been asked to do. Next, it's spending time doing something fun rather than work, which will lead to laziness. Ouch! There should be a certain amount of time set aside each day and each week for you to do what you please. If you don't feel that you have time for that, speak with your mom and dad about helping you set a time for fun. Then, if you choose to read or play or draw or watch TV during that time, it'll be truly *free* time because you'll have met all of your obligations first.

GOD SAYS . . .
Whoever fears God will avoid all extremes.
ECCLESIASTES 7:18 (NIV)

HOW ABOUT YOU?
Do you make sure your work is completed on time? What stands in your way, if anything?

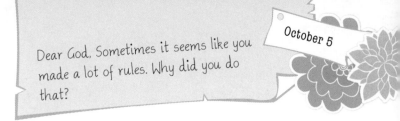

Dear God, Sometimes it seems like you made a lot of rules. Why did you do that?

CONSIDER THIS . . . One of the most fun things to do with family and friends is to go bowling. You get to hang out at a bowling alley (what other place do you get to go to that's called an alley?) with shiny floors, great music, lots of great lighting, and snacks. Once you get there, you put on your stylin' bowling shoes and pick a large bowling ball. The best ones? Pink and green marble. And then you're set to go.

Except, if you haven't been bowling in a while, you can throw that pretty pink ball right into the gutter long before it has a chance to knock down any pins. If you do that too many times, it can be frustrating and not so much fun anymore. That's why the best bowling alleys have bumper guards.

Bumper guards are like long skinny balloons that fill up the gutter on each side of the lane. If your ball hits one of them, the guard bounces that ball right back into the lane and down toward the pins. A guard won't guarantee that you'll get a strike, but it helps your ball to stay in the lane long enough to have a chance.

This is what God's rules are like. They aren't meant to cause you harm or steal your fun—they're meant to keep you in the lane long enough to win the game!

HOW ABOUT YOU?

What are a couple of rules, either from the Bible or from your mom or dad, that might annoy you but actually keep you in your lane?

GOD SAYS . . .

The LORD says, "I will guide you along the best pathway for your life. I will advise you and watch over you." PSALM 32:8

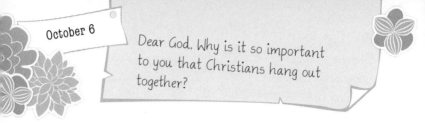

Dear God, Why is it so important to you that Christians hang out together?

CONSIDER THIS . . . Well, first of all, it's important to remember that God is a parent. And what parent doesn't want his children to get along together? Have your parents ever said, "Be nice to your sister!" or "Help your brother out with that"? Of course they have . . . or something just like it.

But it's also true that when people work together, they get a lot more done than when they work on their own. And Christians working together are hopefully getting God's work done and having a good time while they are at it.

Emperor penguins are just about the cutest creatures on earth. They waddle when they walk, and their slick black-and-white skin is just adorable. But besides being cute, they have an important lesson to teach us. When it gets cold out (and it's cold a lot of the time where these penguins live!), they all huddle together, really close to one another. When it's time to move, they shuffle along together, leaning on each other as they do. There's barely a breath's space between them! As the group moves, it churns around and around, the birds on the outside working their way in while the birds on the inside work their way out. Crowding together helps keep them warm, and everyone has a turn on the outside—and the inside!

It's great to have friends from every background, including people who aren't Christians too. But be sure to save your closest relationships for those already in the huddle—and then invite the others in where it's warm.

GOD SAYS . . .
Make me truly happy by agreeing wholeheartedly with each other, loving one another, and working together with one mind and purpose. PHILIPPIANS 2:2

HOW ABOUT YOU?
Who are your best buddies? Who needs to be invited into the huddle?

Dear God, My friend is totally boy crazy. Every week it seems she has a new boyfriend. How can I show her that there is much more to life than boys, boys, boys?

October 7

CONSIDER THIS . . . Two girls had been best friends forever when one of them got a crush on a boy named Mike. Pretty soon, she was passing notes to him, trying to get her friends to sit by him too, talking about him all the time—even if people tried to change the subject. She always wanted to call him on the phone. Finally, when she kept writing Mike's name all over the bottom of her sneakers, her buddy spoke up.

It's not that her friend thought being interested in boys was totally wrong. In fact, there were some boys that *she* thought were interesting too. She talked about them and even to them sometimes. It's just that they didn't take over her life. She thought about other things, talked about other things, and had a good time without them.

Tell your friend how you feel. Tell her that every now and then it's interesting to talk about boys and that you don't mind doing that sometimes. But you miss talking about the other things you used to discuss too. You miss giggling about clothes and talking about what job you want to have when you grow up or where you want to live. You miss her company! If you feel that she's boy crazy, other people probably do too. But they might not be brave enough to say something. A good friend will tell you if you're doing something wrong or something that pushes others away. It doesn't feel good to be confronted (and it might be uncomfortable to confront her), so she might feel hurt at first. A true friend will tell the truth, though, because she knows it's the best thing for her friend. And just think of the reward—you could get your best buddy back!

HOW ABOUT YOU?

Do you have a friend who is doing something that makes you uncomfortable? What can you say to her about it in a kind, loving way?

GOD SAYS . . .

Wounds from a sincere friend are better than many kisses from an enemy. PROVERBS 27:6

Dear God, How should we think about sin?

CONSIDER THIS . . . If you've been around "Christian talk" your whole life, sometimes it's easy to kind of pass over words you hear a lot without really stopping to think about what they mean. *Sin* is one of those words. We know sins are bad things we're not supposed to do, from "big" ones to "little" ones. Because we know that we can confess them, and ask God to forgive them, we sometimes don't see how really serious they are.

The truth is, sins are our enemies. They hurt us and others around us, and they steer us in the wrong direction. They lead us to do things that make us weaker, not stronger. We get worse, not better. Even "little" sins can do great damage. "Little sins" are kind of like the tiny worms called heartworms that truly harm and even kill dogs. Those worms are so small that they live inside mosquitoes. And you know how small mosquitoes are! When a mosquito bites a dog, it passes some of those worms into the dog. The worms wiggle their way all the way to the lungs and heart of the dog, and small as they are, they can kill a very big dog if they aren't stopped.

Sin is something to take seriously, for sure, because it can work its way into our hearts too. The Bible says that after God pardons our sins, he tramples them and throws them into the ocean. Did you know that mighty elephants trample their enemies? After an elephant tramples something, you had better believe there is not very much left. Maybe just enough to . . . throw into an ocean!

GOD SAYS . . .

You will trample our sins under your feet and throw them into the depths of the ocean! MICAH 7:19

HOW ABOUT YOU?

Do you take sin seriously enough?

Dear God, Is it unfair that there are a few rich people in the world who have everything easy when most people have everything so hard?

October 9

CONSIDER THIS . . . When you or someone you love is going through a tough time, it can be easy to get angry at those who seem to live on "Easy Street." It seems so unfair. Why don't they have it as hard as you do? Or why don't you have it as easy as they do? But remember, Christianity is sometimes the "upside-down" faith. Jesus says the first shall be last, and the last shall be first (Matthew 20:16). Sometimes that means putting off now what we're going to get later.

The year is moving toward the end, and it's getting colder out. Plants are going dormant, kind of like hibernating. They don't grow at all over the winter. This time of year, you might be mowing your lawn for the last time before winter comes. Think about those grass clippings. Are they worth much? Could you sell a bag of them for one hundred dollars? Probably not. They might be good in a compost bin, but that's about it. That's what God says will eventually happen to all of the achievements of those who depend on their riches for their value. Later on, they won't be worth much at all.

When you think of crowns, though, you think of gold and jewels. Those are definitely worth a lot! Way, way more than one hundred dollars. And that's what is promised to those who patiently endure temptation and trials. A trial is a difficulty you have to get through, and not having much money feels like that sometimes.

It's better to have a crown later than dried grass now.

HOW ABOUT YOU?

What is something that doesn't seem fair to you? Do you believe, deep in your heart, that everything will work out fairly in heaven?

GOD SAYS . . .

The rich will fade away with all of their achievements. God blesses those who patiently endure testing and temptation. Afterward they will receive the crown of life that God has promised to those who love him.
JAMES 1:11-12

Dear God, What's the best way for me to know the right things to do, especially when everyone has a different opinion?

CONSIDER THIS . . . There's a lot of "noise" in our lives, isn't there? Chatting from people we like a lot . . . and those we're not crazy about. Talking from TV. Music from the radio or from MP3s or YouTube. We read different kinds of books and listen to different teachers, and each of them has something different to say. So how's a girl to know which to listen to and which person says things God would agree with? That's who you want to follow.

Think about a radio station you like, or maybe a show you enjoy. If you want to listen to a selection of music on that station, you have to first turn the radio on. Then you have to tune it to the right channel. And you can't stay put for just five minutes, or you won't hear many songs. If there's a certain show you want to watch, you have to be in the right place (in front of the TV) at the right time (when it's on). Otherwise, you'll miss it!

Where are the places you can "hear" wise advice? Good counselors would be people like your parents, grandparents, Sunday school teachers, and schoolteachers who offer biblical advice. You have to be present to listen to what they are saying, though, tuning in when they talk (and not tuning out what you don't like)! To grow in your faith each week, you've got to be at church—the right place—every Saturday evening or Sunday morning—the right time.

A couple of times each week, turn down the noise for a couple of minutes and listen to the good things people around you have to say.

GOD SAYS . . .

Listen as Wisdom calls out! Hear as understanding raises her voice! PROVERBS 8:1

HOW ABOUT YOU?

What do you do if someone is saying something you don't want to hear? Do you mentally check out? Or do you listen?

Dear God, Some of my friends start talking to me at school when I'm doing my work, so then I talk with them and get in trouble. What can I do?

October 11

CONSIDER THIS . . . Talking with friends is fun. Sometimes it's so much fun to talk that we have a hard time stopping! Soon, though, the trouble it causes isn't worth it anymore. It sounds like you're at that point. You don't get your work done on time, so you have to bring it home. You get corrected in front of everyone—even if you don't start the conversation. That can ruin a whole day! Even worse than the trouble you cause yourself is the trouble you can cause other people by chatting in class. Your friends can't get their work done, either, and it's disrespectful to the teacher.

Can you and your friends make a plan to chat during breaks, free time, lunch, or after school? If you agree to concentrate only on your work during the study times, you'll have so much more time after school that the world will open up for you. One idea is to keep a piece of paper on the top of your desk, and if you think of something interesting you want to talk about with your friends, jot it down. That way you won't forget it by free time. It can even be exciting to see what other people have written on their papers. It's almost like a game, looking forward to what your friends have written down to chat about later.

The main thing is, you're in school to learn, even though it's fun to talk. If you work hard, your knowledge will show it. You'll have something to be proud of and friends to hang out with—later!

HOW ABOUT YOU?

Do you talk or text in school when you're not supposed to? What can you do about it?

GOD SAYS . . .

Work brings profit, but mere talk leads to poverty!
PROVERBS 14:23

Dear God, What is the most important part of my Christian life?

CONSIDER THIS . . . There are many important parts to living life as a Christian girl, but without a doubt, one of the most important things is faith. It's by faith, after all, that we are saved. Faith in Christ is what started our Christian lives. And it only makes sense that we will live by faith too, once we become Christians.

Think about a body—if you only ate, say, dandelion fluff, would you have much energy to get done what you needed and wanted to do? No way! How far would your car get if you filled the tank with water? Not far at all, and it might even get damaged. Bodies are created to run on food, and cars are made to run on gas or electricity. In the same way, Christians are designed to live by faith.

Once you figure out the right kind of "fuel," you have to make sure that you're taking in enough. There's no sense eating three cherries and nothing more on the day you need to run a marathon. And you wouldn't make it out of town if you only put a gallon of gas in your car. You can't just read your Bible once a year, or pray once a month, or trust God with the things that don't matter too much if you want to live by faith.

The good things you do definitely count, and the Bible study you do is important. So is worship and giving and living and growing and learning. But in the end, you need to make sure you're filling your tank with faith. It's the only thing that will help you get done what you need and want to do.

GOD SAYS . . .

It is clear that no one can be made right with God by trying to keep the law. For the Scriptures say, "It is through faith that a righteous person has life." GALATIANS 3:11

HOW ABOUT YOU?

What are some things you can do to live more by faith?

Dear God, My breasts are growing, and it feels uncomfortable. What can I do?

October 13

CONSIDER THIS . . . Have you ever wondered how an oak tree can grow from a tiny acorn? The acorn shell is so hard. How does the plant burst out? In the same way, your body grows from a tiny body at birth to the larger body you will have when you're a fully grown woman. One of the truths about growth of any kind is that it can hurt!

Your breasts are growing from those of a young girl into those of a woman. The same hormones that cause them to grow can also cause them to feel tender. Wearing a well-fitting bra that keeps your breasts closer to your body will help. Recognizing that the pain may come and go in monthly cycles will help too. Part of the discomfort might be emotional. You feel differently about your body as it becomes a woman's body. You might draw more attention. You're not used to looking that way. All of that is uncomfortable. But it's all normal, too. It's the way your body was designed to be. God designed your body with the greatest care. Of all of his creations, humans are most important to him. The growth that you are experiencing was all planned by him, and he plans only for your good.

Be gentle with yourself. Talk with your mom or an aunt about your feelings as your body grows. Wear comfy clothes that make you feel good about yourself. Most of all, be proud that you're becoming a woman. Read a helpful book like *A Growing-Up Guide: What Girls Like You Want to Know*, and learn more about the what, why, when, and how of growing up. Then enjoy. It's who God designed you to be!

HOW ABOUT YOU?
What part about growing up is uncomfortable—either physically or emotionally—right now?

GOD SAYS . . .
We, out of all creation, became his prized possession.
JAMES 1:18

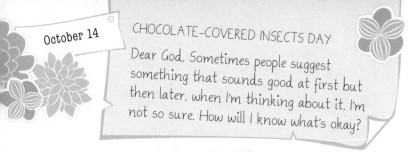

CHOCOLATE-COVERED INSECTS DAY

Dear God, Sometimes people suggest something that sounds good at first but then later, when I'm thinking about it, I'm not so sure. How will I know what's okay?

CONSIDER THIS . . . People all over have different tastes—that's one of the beauties of living in a diverse world. Sometimes we try new things, but other times we have to draw the line and just say no.

Take, for example, eating bugs. Most of us prefer to keep little critters out of our food. But what if those bugs were covered in chocolate? Would it be worth it to eat, say, an ant to get the little bit of chocolate on top? How about a handful?

Putting something sweet over something wrong is a way to hide what's bad under something that's good. But it doesn't get rid of what's bad—you still swallow it. The chocolate only makes it easier to eat something icky. If you saw a small plate of little pieces of chocolate that looked different from what you were used to, it might be better to examine them carefully and ask the person who was serving them what was inside before making a decision to eat them. In the same way, if someone suggests that you try something new, or read something new, or change the way you think about your faith, you might want to find out more about it before you agree.

The Bereans in the Bible were given a shout-out because they tested every teaching that came their way to make sure it lined up with the truth before they "swallowed" it. You, too, can test new thoughts or ideas with what you know to be good and right. Some will be great new thoughts and ideas, and some will be tossers. Better to spend a little time figuring out if what's being suggested is good than finding out later that it's a cocoa crispy cockroach.

GOD SAYS . . .

Test everything that is said. Hold on to what is good.
1 THESSALONIANS 5:21

HOW ABOUT YOU?

Has anyone ever tried to tempt you to do something wrong by promising something sweet, too?

Dear God, Why do Christian parents think their kids have to have the same religion as them?

October 15

CONSIDER THIS . . . When a mother and father find out that they are expecting a baby, all sorts of things happen. They begin to plan ahead. They buy a crib and tiny clothing, and they go through their home to make sure that everything is safe. They put covers over electric plugs and move glass lamps out of the way. They buy medicine that is just the right strength for babies. They want everything to be ready for their child to be happy, warm, and safe.

Think, for a minute, about an airport. There are dozens and dozens of planes taking off and landing at practically all hours of the night and day. And many precious souls are on those planes. If one of them goes off course and veers into an area where another plane is landing or taking off, both planes could crash. Because of that, there are airport employees who work in a tower, and also on the ground, to make sure that every plane stays in its own lane. Staying in the right lane keeps everyone safe.

As important as it is to keep your body safe, it's even more important to protect your soul. A Christian parent's most important responsibility is to teach you how to stay in the right "religious" lane. A Christian parent's job is to teach you how to develop a relationship with Christ on your own. But part of that responsibility is yours, too. Your mom and dad can help from the tower and on the ground, but you have to keep steering yourself on the right path!

Christian parents want their kids to know Christ so their kids are happy and safe, both now on earth and for eternity.

HOW ABOUT YOU?

Do you have parents who help you to know God? If not your parents, who else can help keep you in the right "lane"?

GOD SAYS . . .

Direct your children onto the right path, and when they are older, they will not leave it. PROVERBS 22:6

Dear God, How do I know you exist? I mean, I can't see you.

CONSIDER THIS . . . Sometimes it's hard to believe the things right in front of us—like a surprise party. Believing in things we can't see is even harder. We live in a world that wants us to "prove it," and proving that God is there isn't easy. God knows this is hard. Believing in him when we can't see him with our eyes is part of our faith. Hebrews 11:1 says, "Faith means . . . knowing that something is real even if we do not see it" (NCV).

How do you know someone is real even when you don't see him or her? One way is to look for other evidence. You've probably never met your favorite author, for example, but you know that person exists because you can plainly see his or her work: your favorite book. When you look at the world and the amazing way it all works, or see your body and the way everything is put together just right, that is proof of God, the Creator. Romans 1:20 says, "There are things about [God] that people cannot see— his eternal power and all the things that make him God. But since the beginning of the world those things have been easy to understand by what God has made" (NCV). God lets you know in other ways that he is here. Have you ever prayed about something and then gotten an answer—just sensing the Holy Spirit guiding you, speaking to you through your heart, through your parents, or maybe through a book or a song? The Holy Spirit helps you understand when God is talking to you.

Ask the Lord to open your eyes so that you may see him, his love, and his work all around you.

GOD SAYS . . .
Then Jesus told him, "You believe because you have seen me. Blessed are those who believe without seeing me." JOHN 20:29

HOW ABOUT YOU?
When you look at the world around you, what does it teach you about God? When have you heard the "still, small voice" of God speaking to your heart?

Dear God, I know I'm supposed to memorize Bible verses, and I really want to. But it's hard to remember them. What can help?

October 17

CONSIDER THIS . . . People have always had cool ways to help themselves remember what is important. Some people put a string around their finger, or even wrap a finger with a piece of tape to help them remember something. A lot of kids write stuff on their hands and their arms, which is okay, too, as long as you wash it off (and don't use it to cheat!). Little yellow sticky notes are a great help—you can write down an assignment or a Bible verse on one and then stick it to your computer, your mirror, your bedpost, or anywhere else you hang out a lot. How about putting a sticky note with a Bible verse on your refrigerator door? Families often have bulletin boards or whiteboards to help them schedule sports and other activities—could you write a Bible verse on one of those?

Back in the Bible times, they didn't have sticky notes or bulletin boards, but they still tied stuff onto their hands (like those strings and tape) and wrote them on papers that they attached to their bodies (foreheads instead of hands and arms) to make sure they recalled what was important. Find creative ways to keep God's Word in front of your eyes night and day, and then you'll be certain to find it written in your mind right when you need it. Scripture is a tool that the Holy Spirit uses to help us in times of trouble, when we need to make a decision, when we're tempted, when we need to learn something, and even when we feel bad and we just want to feel good again.

HOW ABOUT YOU?

What are two creative ways that can help you (and your family) memorize Scripture?

GOD SAYS . . .

Always remember these commands I give you today. . . . Talk about them when you sit at home and walk along the road. . . . Tie them on your forehead to remind you, and write them on your doors and gates. DEUTERONOMY 6:6-9 (NCV)

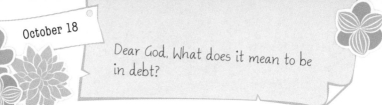

Dear God, What does it mean to be in debt?

CONSIDER THIS . . . Being in debt means to owe somebody something. You can owe them money, a favor, or work. Have you ever heard someone say, "I'll do this for you, but you owe me big-time"? That means she will do something for you, but she expects you to do something for her the next time she asks.

The problem with debt, whether it's money or love or favors, is that you're not free. If you owe people money, you have to pay them back before you can spend the money on other things. Those things might be something you want or something you'd like to give to others. People who owe a lot of money to credit card companies can't give as much to godly causes or even take care of their needs. They are, in a way, servants to their debt.

One way to stay out of debt with money is to not spend more than you have, starting when you're young. Do you get an allowance? Do you spend it all ASAP, or do you spend some, save some, and give some?

One way to stay out of relationship debt is to make sure that when you do something for or with someone else, there are "no strings attached." That means if you invite someone to your house, it's because you want to spend time with her, not because you expect her to invite you to her great pool the next week. On the other hand, don't ask someone to help you with something if you'll have to pay her back. Ask someone only if she'll help you freely and allow you to do the same. Don't become indebted to anyone you don't want to serve.

GOD SAYS . . .
Just as the rich rule the poor, so the borrower is servant to the lender. PROVERBS 22:7

HOW ABOUT YOU?
Do you ever do things for people expecting them to pay you back? Have you asked someone for help, but then she expected you to pay her back?

Dear God, Why can't I have a new phone when all of my friends have one? I need one.

October 19

CONSIDER THIS ... Recently there were two pictures next to each other in the newspaper. One was a picture of a couple of children with very thin arms. They were clearly poor, had worn-out clothing on, and tried to smile even though they were obviously troubled. The other picture showed a long line of teenagers and adults waiting to get the latest smartphone—which wouldn't be released for two days.

Now—there is nothing at all wrong with having a phone. You can keep in touch with people you love, make plans, and even use it for memorizing Bible verses. But in our world, where there are so many "toys" calling out to us, it's important to remember what a need is and what a want is.

The things we need are those things that keep us alive—food, shelter, clean water, clothing, medical care, education. People should do whatever is necessary to take care of their own needs and their kids' needs. But almost everything else is mostly a want. It's okay to want things, and to get some of the things we want. But when people start doing everything they can do to get all of their wants, they can get into trouble. They spend too much and get into debt, or they work too many hours, which takes them away from friends and family. They get crabby when others have stuff they don't, and they become bitter. Sometimes they are even tempted to steal what they want.

If your parents have said no to a new phone, they've likely decided that you don't need one. Since they work hard to provide the things you need, can you hold off on some of the stuff you want?

HOW ABOUT YOU?

Do you have a good sense of what the difference is between a want and a need? What is something in your life that you want, rather than need?

GOD SAYS ...

If we have enough food and clothing, let us be content. But people who long to be rich fall into temptation and are trapped by many foolish and harmful desires that plunge them into ruin and destruction.
1 TIMOTHY 6:8-9

Dear God, How can I be an example to a Christian adult who isn't acting like a Christian?

CONSIDER THIS . . . If you're learning a new concept in school, or trying to remember one you've forgotten over the summer, sometimes an example can really help you to understand and remember what you've learned. For example, a teacher can give you the rules for solving a math problem and explain what it means, but unless she gives you an example of a math problem to show you what she's talking about, it can be really hard to make it all click.

As a kid, you have some limitations. You can't go around schooling adults, because it's disrespectful. And, even though it's wrong, adults sometimes do not listen to kids. However, you can do something very powerful to make it all click for the adults you want to encourage. You can be a living example.

Do the adults around you swear? Keep your lips pure. Do they tell bad jokes? Don't laugh, and just quietly walk away when you can. Get "caught" reading your Bible, or offer to pray for someone you love. Invite them to your church. Whenever they are with you, offer a healthy serving of your fruit of the Spirit: love, joy, peace, patience, kindness, goodness, faithfulness, gentleness, and self-control. It will be much tastier than the sarcasm, anger, bitterness, and greed they're served elsewhere.

Do you like and learn best from the teachers who lecture or the teachers who show you how to do it? That's right. Be that kind of teacher to the adults around you too!

GOD SAYS . . .

Lead them by your own good example. 1 PETER 5:3

HOW ABOUT YOU?

Which adults in your life could you be an amazing example to?

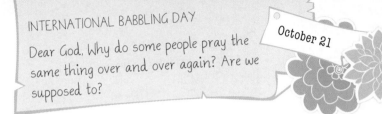

INTERNATIONAL BABBLING DAY

October 21

Dear God, Why do some people pray the same thing over and over again? Are we supposed to?

CONSIDER THIS . . . Have you ever been in the grocery store and listened to a kid beg his mom for something he wanted? It probably sounded something like this: "But I want it I want it I want it." And if Mom said no, you likely heard, "Why not? I want it I want it I want it." Most of the time, moms don't seem too persuaded by their children repeating that they want something over and over again. However, that doesn't mean that you're supposed to ask once and give up. A much better approach is to respectfully ask for something you'd like, listen carefully to the response, and move on. Later, if that's something you still want, you can approach your parents again, until they either agree or ask you to stop asking!

God says two things in the Bible about praying over and over. First, he does tell us to never stop praying (1 Thessalonians 5:17), and he gives us parables that show people persistently asking for things they need and want. So it's okay to ask more than once, unless God has told you not to ask for it again. But those requests need to be made respectfully, over time, and you need to be listening for God's response.

Scripture also tells us just saying something over and over does not move God to action any more than the little kid in the grocery store. God knows what our needs are, and he likes to hear from us, but in a way that brings honor to him. God isn't counting how many times we ask for something, so we don't get points for repetition. He is looking at the heart of the asker, though!

GOD SAYS . . .

When you pray, don't babble on and on as people of other religions do. They think their prayers are answered merely by repeating their words again and again. Don't be like them, for your Father knows exactly what you need even before you ask him!
MATTHEW 6:7-8

HOW ABOUT YOU?

Are you respectfully persistent in your requests to your parents, to your teachers, to your Lord?

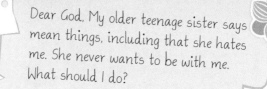

Dear God, My older teenage sister says mean things, including that she hates me. She never wants to be with me. What should I do?

CONSIDER THIS . . . One of the very first poems we learn as little girls is "Sticks and stones will break my bones, but words will never hurt me." Ouch. It's not true, is it? Sticks and stones cause bruises you see, but they go away in just a few days. Words cause wounds you can't see, but they don't go away for a long time.

When your sister says she hates you, that's gotta hurt. As you probably already realize, you face bigger challenges when you grow older. It's not just about what kind of lunch box you have anymore; it's about who your friends are. It's not about your clothes feeling good; it's about your clothes *looking* good. Your sister is probably facing even bigger challenges. Boys. Peer pressure. Body pressure. Grade pressure. Kermit the Frog sang, "It's not easy being green." It's not easy being a teen, either.

Just knowing that it's the pressure around her that causes her to say and do the things she does—and nothing you yourself are doing—can help ease the hurt. You might talk to her and say, "I really like to spend time with you. When you have some time, or when there's something you want to do with me, let me know." Then let her pick the time and place. Let *her* come back to *you*. Try hard to let those words stop at your skin and not dig into your heart. Be kind, and go out of your way to do something nice for her once in a while to show your love. Then be patient. If she invites you to do something, enjoy the time together. If not, spend your free time with people who treat you, and speak to you, kindly.

GOD SAYS . . .
It takes wisdom to have a good family, and it takes understanding to make it strong. PROVERBS 24:3 (NCV)

HOW ABOUT YOU?
What helps you to be patient and kind toward people who are being difficult to you?

Dear God, What if I forget to ask you for something or don't know what to say? Will you help me anyway?

October 23

CONSIDER THIS . . . There's a funny joke about a boy who was always connected to his earbuds. One day, his friends found him lying outside on the sidewalk, passed out. They tried to wake him up and shook him, but they couldn't get him to wake up. One of his friends picked up the earbuds, which had slipped out of the boy's ears. When the friend listened to what was playing, she heard, "Breathe in. Breathe out."

"Hey!" she told the others. "Without these in his ears, he doesn't know how to breathe. No wonder he passed out!"

Not breathing is funny as a joke, but we know that we don't need to tell our lungs how to breathe, we don't instruct our hearts to beat, and we don't have to ask our brains to think either. They were created to do those things automatically, and unless there's a medical emergency, they do them perfectly without our intervention.

It's terrific to talk to God, to tell him what you need and want and fear, and to ask him to be with you throughout the day. But he doesn't need your instructions to do what is right, which is to care for you every minute of the day. Just like your lungs bring you air and your heart pumps your blood, your God has your back without you even thinking about it.

Feels good, doesn't it?

HOW ABOUT YOU?

How do you feel knowing that Jesus has got you covered whether you think to ask him about it or not?

GOD SAYS . . .

[Jesus said,] "Don't let your hearts be troubled. Trust in God, and trust also in me." JOHN 14:1

Dear God, Sometimes bad things happen and destroy everything that I've been working for. Why?

CONSIDER THIS . . . A few years ago, in Colorado, the people of a small farming town stood outside of their houses and watched as a giant black cloud moved closer and closer. Suddenly, the buzzing cloud dropped to the ground and millions of grasshoppers began munching on any living plant—stalks of grass, dandelions, and worst of all, the carefully tended wheat crop. Imagine the juicy hum of all of those jaws devouring a year's worth of the farmers' work. The roads were so covered with bugs that the pavement seemed to move. The insects would only part—like the Red Sea—when a car with its windows tightly rolled up drove by.

As quickly as they came, the bugs flew away, but only when there was nothing left to eat. The farmers had no harvest that year. They were sad, scared, and broke.

The next winter, however, was cold, which meant many grasshopper eggs did not survive. When summer came, the crops grew thick, and that autumn the farmers had their best harvest ever—enough to make up for everything that had been lost the year before. No grasshoppers came to destroy their plants, and because there had been a shortage the year before, the prices were higher, which meant more profit for the farmers.

Sometimes things happen that seem awful. You work hard on a group project only to see it ruined by someone else's poor work. You try hard to earn a spot on a team, but you don't make it. You pray, but you don't receive what you'd hoped for.

There are years of grasshoppers in everyone's life. But hold on, because God promises a year of harvest will soon follow.

GOD SAYS . . .
The Lord says, "I will give you back what you lost to the swarming locusts, the hopping locusts, the stripping locusts, and the cutting locusts."
JOEL 2:25

HOW ABOUT YOU?
What hard things have happened in your life that you are discouraged about? Is God willing, and able, to restore them when the time is just right?

Dear God, I am worried that I'm not really a Christian. I keep acting like one because I know people think that I am, but I'm not sure. What should I do?

October 25

CONSIDER THIS . . . A big problem in our society is stolen identity. Someone will steal another person's name and social security number, which everyone in this country gets when they are born. This criminal can order credit cards in the other person's name, or write online in the other person's name, or even commit other crimes with the other person's name! By stealing someone else's identity, they get all the benefits of the other person's good name. But each time they use the other person's name, they have to worry that they're just about to get caught. That would be worrying! It's so much better to use your own name.

If you're pretending to be someone you aren't or you aren't sure that you're a Christian, you're kind of using a borrowed identity. It's not stolen, because you didn't take it from someone else to do wrong, but somehow, you're not sure if it's you, either. It can be worrying. Who are you?

Sometimes girls who grow up in Christian homes aren't always sure if they have asked Jesus to be their Savior on their own. Girls who are not raised in Christian homes aren't always sure how to do that. It's easy. Becoming a Christian is the same path for each girl. You ask the Lord to forgive you of your sins, confess that he is the Son of God and the only path to forgiveness and eternal life, and ask him to be the Lord of your life here and now, too.

When you become a Christian, you get a new identity. You are born again, and although God doesn't assign you a number, he does make a place for you in his family. No more faking, no more worrying about if you belong or not, no more borrowed identity. You're set for life as a child of God.

HOW ABOUT YOU?

Are you certain of your identity in Christ? If you're not sure, there's no harm in asking!

GOD SAYS . . .

Once you had no identity as a people; now you are God's people. 1 PETER 2:10

Dear God, Is there such a thing as a little white lie that doesn't hurt anyone?

CONSIDER THIS . . . Remember the story of the Boy Who Cried Wolf? He was a shepherd, and he thought it would be interesting to see if the villagers would come running if he shouted for help.

"Help! Wolf!" he shouted, and people in the nearby village dropped what they were doing and ran to the boy's aid. When they arrived, they found that there was no wolf threatening the boy and his sheep. He laughed and told them it was a joke. It worked so well that another day, when he was bored, he told himself that he would try it again.

"Help! Wolf!" he cried. Some people didn't move at all, but a few of the villagers did drop their work to see if, perhaps, this time the shepherd boy really did need help. Once again, he laughed at those who had come running, thinking them stupid for falling for his joke again.

On a clear, cold night a few weeks later, the boy was nodding off, when suddenly he heard his sheep bleating. The boy awoke and found three ferocious wolves prowling around his camp. "Help! Wolf!" he shouted. But, of course, no one came to help the boy this time. He had lied so many times before that no one believed him when he really did need help protecting his lambs.

A person becomes known for her character, mainly by what she does over and over again. If she's always honest, even when it might cause her some discomfort, she becomes known as someone who is honorable and tells the truth. If she lies when it's convenient, or fun, or easier on her, she becomes known as someone who can't be trusted.

Even if no sheep are at risk—it's always best to tell the truth!

GOD SAYS . . .
Don't lie to each other, for you have stripped off your old sinful nature and all its wicked deeds. COLOSSIANS 3:9

HOW ABOUT YOU?
What kind of girl do you want to be known as?

Dear God, It seems like I get used to something—my friends, a sport, a church—and then it changes. How can I deal with it when that happens?

CONSIDER THIS . . . This time of year, the leaves begin to fall off the trees. The leaves that made the trees thick, bushy, and green from spring till summer now begin to turn gold, red, and orange. One by one they let go of the branches and flutter to the ground. The days get shorter and cloudier in many places. The temperature cools down. Before, when you'd been thinking about lunch, you might have wanted a salad. Now, soup sounds good.

These things are clues that a season is changing. This time, it's from autumn to winter. Changes can sometimes be surprising—for example, you wake up one day to a few inches of snow—but normally we have clues and change comes little bit by little bit. When you open your eyes to these changes, it's easier to see what's going on around you. It might not make that change easier to handle if you don't want change, but it can make it less surprising. And that helps you to deal with it.

If your parents have been talking about a new job, you might have a clue that you'll be moving. If they have been talking about visiting different churches, you might see the possibility of attending a new church. If your coach isn't playing you as much, or homework takes more and more time, these are clues that change might be ahead.

Change can sometimes be scary, but mostly, it leads to good. If the leaves didn't fall off the trees, there would be no Christmas season just ahead! If you don't leave a church that isn't teaching the right things, you can't find one that is. Don't fear change, and don't be surprised. When the leaves start to fall, pay close attention.

HOW ABOUT YOU?

What are three good things about changing seasons, both those in the natural world and those in your personal life?

GOD SAYS . . .

For everything there is a season, a time for every activity under heaven.
ECCLESIASTES 3:1

Dear God, No matter how hard I try to be a good example for my friends, I just keep on doing bad things.

CONSIDER THIS . . . There's a word that Christians use sometimes, and it's a mouthful. It's *sanctification*. Sanctification means becoming more and more like Jesus as you grow as a Christian. Of course, that means you are *not* just like Jesus when you first become a Christian. And you won't be sinless until after you die. So you're stuck in an imperfect world doing both bad and good things. How can you win?

The first thing is, the people around you know that you aren't perfect. Don't you hate it when someone is fake and pretends that she has no problems? It makes you feel as if she's not being real. But when someone admits that she *does* have problems and is working on them, you respect her. The people around you, the ones you want to shine for, are watching you. They're not expecting you to be perfect. They want to see what happens when you're not.

Even the apostle Paul said, "I don't really understand myself, for I want to do what is right, but I don't do it. Instead, I do what I hate" (Romans 7:15). So what can you do? You keep trying. You pick yourself up and dust yourself off when you do something wrong. You apologize if you need to and ask God to forgive and help you. The next time, you'll be a little bit stronger, a little bit more in control. The fight against doing wrong things—evil itself—is a war. You can't win every battle, but you will win the war. Your friends will see you're not perfect, but that you're growing more like Jesus every day. *That* is something they can admire and copy. You shine more than you know.

GOD SAYS . . .
Don't let evil conquer you, but conquer evil by doing good.
ROMANS 12:21

HOW ABOUT YOU?
What do you do after you sin? Who is watching you to see how you respond?

Dear God, I got put on a school project with someone I don't really like. How can I work together with her and still get a good grade?

October 29

CONSIDER THIS . . . It can often be hard to work on a project with people you *do* like, because you know your grade is at stake. Working on a project is much harder with people you don't like. What if they don't do their fair share? What if they slack off and you have to pick it up by doing more work? What if they don't do their work the way you want them to? Because they aren't you, they probably won't!

But working together with different people can have benefits, too. Each person brings her own knowledge, insight, and ideas to the project. Since everyone has a different background, what they have to share will be different. In the end, it will make your project better, richer, and more well rounded than it would have been if it had only come from one perspective. Yours!

Have you ever smelled cookies baking? Of course you have! That delightful scent that perfumes your house is mostly from vanilla. Have you ever tasted vanilla on its own? Of course you haven't! But if you did, you'd find it to be bitter and not tasty at all. Vanilla needs to be blended with all of the other ingredients to bring out its best. God made us that way too. When we work together, with each of us doing our own special work but adding up to a whole, our work is absolutely delightful. It's so much better than being bitter!

HOW ABOUT YOU?

Have you ever had to work with someone who you didn't like at first? What did you learn about yourself and about him or her?

GOD SAYS . . .

He makes the whole body fit together perfectly. As each part does its own special work, it helps the other parts grow, so that the whole body is healthy and growing and full of love. EPHESIANS 4:16

Dear God, How does the devil work to hurt us?

CONSIDER THIS . . . The devil has a whole pack of evil tricks, but one of the ways he works to hurt Christians is to separate us from other believers.

Consider some of the nature shows on television. You'll see that a lot of animals travel in packs. There are many reasons they stick together in packs:

1. They can help one another get food.
2. They can help one another keep warm.
3. They can take care of one another and the babies.
4. They can face an enemy more safely with their pack.

If the pack of animals is on the move, sometimes one of the animals that is sick, or young, or tired drops farther and farther behind. If you watch carefully, that's the one that the predator starts to track. It works hard to separate that member from the rest of the pack so it can pick the weak animal off when it's alone. A predator knows that it can't take on the whole team, but if it can separate one member, it can attack that one pretty easily.

You, too, are a member of a "pack" or a team: Christians! Christians are all members of one body. We need to move together, stick together, care for one another, and keep one another safe when the enemy is trying to attack. Stay in church, stick with your believing buddies as well as those who don't know God, and make sure you don't fall further and further away from the tribe. The team needs you, and you need the team!

GOD SAYS . . .
Stay alert! Watch out for your great enemy, the devil. He prowls around like a roaring lion, looking for someone to devour. 1 PETER 5:8

HOW ABOUT YOU?
Are you running with the pack? How can you make sure you are?

Dear God, So how will I recognize the devil? Does he really have a pointed tail and horns?

October 31

CONSIDER THIS . . . The Bible calls Satan, also known as the devil, by many titles. It says he is a tempter, that is, someone who tries to persuade other people to do wrong things. He's an accuser of innocent people. He tells other people, and even God, that God's people deserve blame and punishment for things they did not do or have been forgiven for. Satan is an enemy—he wants to hurt others. He's a bad-mouther and a liar, and he is happy when others believe his lies about people who are innocent. He's a robber and a thief. You know what those are.

Does this sound like someone you want to put on your friends list? No!

So the devil doesn't want to make his evil obvious. The Bible says that he disguises himself as an angel of light. He's a dark angel, but he presents himself as someone who is good and wholesome. If he really wore a pointed tail and horns, you'd know to stay away. Instead, he makes himself look loving, kind, and helpful.

When people wear disguises, it can be hard, at first, to tell who they really are. But if you look at them long enough, study their actions, and ask some wise people around you, you'll realize that the disguise is, literally, a cover-up. God's Spirit will help you too. So be sure to tune in all day and listen for God's whispers!

HOW ABOUT YOU?

Have you ever considered that Satan may wear a lovely, kind-looking disguise to trick you? What ways can Satan trick you?

GOD SAYS . . .

I am not surprised! Even Satan disguises himself as an angel of light.
2 CORINTHIANS 11:14

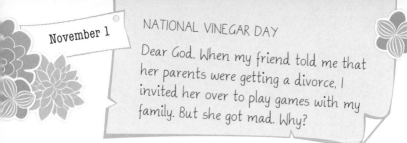

November 1

NATIONAL VINEGAR DAY

Dear God, When my friend told me that her parents were getting a divorce, I invited her over to play games with my family. But she got mad. Why?

CONSIDER THIS . . . Sometimes when our friends share sad news, our first idea is to rush and tell them that things will be okay. Or maybe we want to plan something fun to cheer them up and distract them. Although it's kind to want to help your friend when she's sad, pretending that bad things aren't happening isn't always the best way to help.

If you don't let her talk about her sad feelings or the things she's going through, she might feel like she was wrong for bringing them up at all. That will make her too embarrassed to share those feelings in the future. And she hasn't had anyone tell her that it is okay to feel hurt when bad things happen. Maybe inviting her over to your house right away, especially if your family is happy right now, reminded her of things she doesn't have.

When you get a bad scratch or a burn, for a little while the best thing to do is put a Band-Aid over it to protect it from infection. But within a few days, you have to take the Band-Aid off and let some light and air get on the skin in order for it to heal. When your friend brought up her parents' divorce, she was trying to bring the topic, and the wound, into the light and air. If you can let her talk it over for a while, and share your thoughts and love with her, you can let her wound heal even faster than slapping another Band-Aid on it—even a great one, like a fun day out.

Don't worry. She'll be back to herself one day soon, and then the game night will be a perfect solution.

GOD SAYS . . .

Singing cheerful songs to a person with a heavy heart is like taking someone's coat in cold weather or pouring vinegar in a wound. PROVERBS 25:20

HOW ABOUT YOU?

Do you feel awkward when someone shares bad news, or are you able to let her talk about bad things as well as good? How can you help your friends when they're sad?

Dear God, Sometimes people make fun of me because I seem to know a lot. What can I do?

November 2

CONSIDER THIS . . . Have you ever been in a neighborhood where every single house was exactly the same? Every house was the same style, with the same kind of roof, the same color paint, the same little patch of grass with one little tree in the yard. It's boring. Most neighborhoods have lots of different kinds of places to live—big houses, small houses, apartments, town houses.

God made the human race like that. Some people are short and others are tall. All people have different shades of skin. Most people think differences are cool—God is very creative, after all. But some feel uncomfortable when people are different from them. They are threatened when they feel they are less pretty or less smart than someone else. Maybe some kids are making fun of you because they think you are a threat to them.

When God blesses us with something, no matter what it is, it is not his intention for us to be too proud about it. God has blessed you with intelligence. Make sure you are using it wisely—not raising your hand every time you have an answer, not correcting others all the time. Try to ignore the people who are making fun of you, knowing that in their hearts they are feeling bad about themselves, not you! Pray and ask God if there is someone you could use your smarts to help. You'll need to do this quietly, so as not to embarrass the person. The Bible says people will see our good deeds and praise our Father in heaven (Matthew 5:16). How can you use your smart brain—or anything else he has blessed you with—to bring glory to your Lord?

HOW ABOUT YOU?

Who in your life could be blessed by something you have but they don't?

GOD SAYS . . .

If you are wise and understand God's ways, prove it by living an honorable life, doing good works with the humility that comes from wisdom. JAMES 3:13

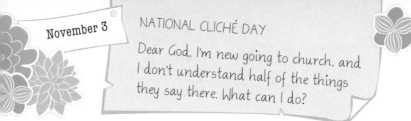

November 3

NATIONAL CLICHÉ DAY

Dear God, I'm new going to church, and I don't understand half of the things they say there. What can I do?

CONSIDER THIS . . . Every nation has its own language; even if they speak English, their English might sound different from other nations that speak English. Their French or Spanish may sound different from other nations' French or Spanish. Then when you get into those countries, you'll find that people have both accents and certain words that people in their area understand but outsiders might not. Cliques at school even have code words—it's all a part of being in a group. That's not a problem—unless you don't speak the language and can't understand what's being said!

Christians often use phrases that sound strange to ears that are unused to hearing them: "washed in the blood of the lamb" or "backsliding" or "convicted" or maybe even "being saved." And what's the difference between a disciple and an apostle? It can all be very confusing, and if you're a new Christian, it can make you feel like you're not really "in" the group. Even worse, you won't be able to learn and worship if people are using terms that make no sense to you.

If you're new to church and confused about some of the words people use, write down the words or phrases that don't make sense to you and ask a good friend or the person who brought you to church. If you've been a Christian for a while, be careful not to use clichés and odd terms when talking about your faith. Your goal is to explain the concepts of your faith, and your Savior, in the everyday language that the people around you use. That's how they know who Christ is and what he came to earth to do.

You want everyone to understand the code, right?

GOD SAYS . . .

His disciples said, "At last you are speaking plainly and not figuratively. Now we understand that you know everything, and there's no need to question you. From this we believe that you came from God." JOHN 16:29-30

HOW ABOUT YOU?

If you're new to Christianity, are there words you don't understand? If you've been around Christianity a lot, have you started using "Christianese" that people outside of your tribe can't understand?

Dear God, Whenever I watch the news, something scary has happened, and it makes me worried. What can I do?

November 4

CONSIDER THIS . . . The news headlines seem to focus only on the negative stories. People getting hurt, natural disasters ruining towns, and criminals breaking the law are always there in bold print. People helping others or enjoying life with their families are nowhere to be found—or else buried on the back page.

The fact of life is that bad news is scary, so bad news sells. Whenever something bad happens, it's on the television hour after hour. Whenever something really fantastic happens, like thousands of people accepting Jesus Christ at a crusade, it barely makes a minute or two. So which do you think you hear more of, bad news or good? Bad, of course!

When we hear so much bad news, it can make us feel like the world is extra scary. There *are* scary things happening around us from time to time. But there are many, many more wonderful things happening, like See You at the Pole, which happens at thousands of schools each year. Because we mostly hear the bad news, the world seems scarier than it really is.

God does not take us out of the scary things in this world. In fact, he wants us to be the lights that shine brightly for him during dark times. But he does promise us something even better: his peace. His peace is something we can't make ourselves have. It's something he gives us. When does he give it to us? After we give thanks. How does he give it to us? Through prayer.

Your Father doesn't want you to worry. He wants you to rest easy in him. Try it and see how faithful he is.

HOW ABOUT YOU?

What are you worried about right now? Pray about it, right now. Okay. How do you feel?

GOD SAYS . . .

Don't worry about anything; instead, pray about everything. Tell God what you need, and thank him for all he has done. Then you will experience God's peace. PHILIPPIANS 4:6-7

Dear God, What does it mean to be faithful to you?

CONSIDER THIS ... People have long called dogs "man's best friend." You don't have to be a man to know that dogs love their owners, their masters, even . . . their pet families. Most people who have a dog understand the kind of love and devotion a dog gives to the people it lives with.

Why are dogs called our best friends? They are always with us. No matter if we've been gone for ten minutes or ten weeks, when we return they're right there at the door, eager to see us, greeting us with wagging tails or wiggles on the floor. Dogs guard us—they don't let anyone threaten us, and they "speak" right up, loudly sometimes. Somehow, dogs know when their owners are sick or sad, and they stay particularly close during those times. Or they may do funny things to try to cheer us up. They stick near us no matter what.

Pet dogs are called domesticated, which means they are made for, and want to serve, their masters. They get happiness and fulfillment out of being loyal to those to whom they belong. They cannot be bribed away to a new master. They are faithful: devoted, trusty, and true to whatever is best for their masters.

Now, we are people, of course, and not dogs. We are made in the image of God, our master, which gives us an honor our beloved pets don't have. But we can still learn from puppies something about being a faithful companion and follower of our master.

Ruff!

GOD SAYS . . .

I will search for faithful people to be my companions. PSALM 101:6

HOW ABOUT YOU?

Are you as faithful of a companion to God as your pet is to you?

Dear God, The world seems a little darker. What can make it lighter?

CONSIDER THIS . . . This time of year it gets light later in the morning and dark earlier in the evening. Even though we have the same twenty-four hours in every day, we say the days grow "shorter" because we have fewer hours of light. That means it can seem like night at the beginning of your day, and it can feel like night comes earlier at the end. For some reason, when the days are shorter, they seem to be filled with less joy. We were made to live in the light.

But the truth is, we can't have summer all year long—there are four seasons, remember? So what do we do? We make our own light. In our homes, we turn the lights on in the rooms we're going to be reading, chatting, or eating in. We might light a fire in a fireplace to make the room warm and cozy. We use reading lamps in bed or turn a light on over a piano before we play. Even our TVs and computer screens make light for us.

Sometimes, our lives can seem a little darker too. Things don't turn out the way we wanted them to. We're sick or hurt or worried. Someone we loved rejected us or a friend moved on. The days seem shorter and darker. We can't always be in a summer season in those parts of our lives either. But we can "turn the lights on" in our lives. How?

Studying the Bible. Turning on praise music. Praying. Laughing. Reading a Christian book. Talking to a friend who loves us at all times— Jesus. He is our lamp in all seasons, those with sunny mornings and those when it's foggy all day. He will light up our darkness.

HOW ABOUT YOU?

What makes you feel foggy inside? How can you invite God to bring some light to that?

GOD SAYS . . .

O LORD, you are my lamp. The LORD lights up my darkness. 2 SAMUEL 22:29

Dear God, What is the right kind of boy for me?

CONSIDER THIS . . . Although you're many years from marrying, and even several years away from dating, it's not too early to think about what kind of boy, and eventually man, is right for you. You're probably already crushing on some boys. So it's good to know what kind of boy you eventually might want to date and marry.

When God created man, he decided that it wasn't right for the man to be alone. So he created a woman, too. The Lord said that he would make someone for the man who was just right for him. Eve was just right for Adam.

We know that God tells Christians that it's not good for them to be partnered with people who do not believe in Jesus like they do, so the right kind of boy for you is one who will share your strong faith. That means he will also show the fruit of the Spirit, like you do. He will treat you well. God tells us that a man is to treat his wife like Jesus treats the church. If a boy makes fun of you, or doesn't treat you respectfully, or doesn't speak to you kindly, he is not the right kind of boy for you.

Right now, you're just dreaming of the man who will someday be your best friend and husband, and that's okay. You can pray for him now, too, and hope that he is praying for you. It's all right to dream in the right direction, thinking about the boy, or the man, that God would approve as just the right one for you.

GOD SAYS . . .
The LORD God said, "It is not good for the man to be alone. I will make a helper who is just right for him." GENESIS 2:18

HOW ABOUT YOU?
What is important to you in a close friend?

Dear God, How do I know you want to be close to me? I mean, you're God. And I'm a human.

November 8

CONSIDER THIS ... From the very beginning, the Lord God wanted his people to know that he was not a God who lived very far away from them, sternly looking down upon them and pronouncing judgments from afar. In the book of Exodus, after God freed his people from the Egyptians, the Israelites were living in tents in the desert. God wanted them to know he was always close, so he instructed Moses to build a Tabernacle, kind of like a fancy tent, in the middle of their camp.

When God lived among them, in the middle of them, he was close to them all the time—even though they couldn't see him. God wanted his people to know that he was there. He told them to bring sacrificial food to him two times a day—at breakfast and at dinner. He not only wanted to be thanked for providing the meals, but he wanted to be included at them!

Later, Jesus came to earth and lived among us in very much the same way that God the Father had in the Tabernacle. Except Jesus was even closer—he lived in homes like we do, ate his meals like we do, laughed and cried like we do. When Jesus left, he said that the Holy Spirit would come and make things even better. And they are. Why? Because now God the Holy Spirit lives as close to us as possible—inside us. He's with us 24-7.

People who do not know or understand God feel like he is miles away in heaven, watching to see what we do wrong so he can correct us. Instead, he lives inside us, as close as possible, so he can guide and love us all day and night.

HOW ABOUT YOU?

How does it make you feel to think about God loving you so much that he wants to be where you are, live where you are, all the time?

GOD SAYS ...

Have the people of Israel build me a holy sanctuary so I can live among them.
EXODUS 25:8

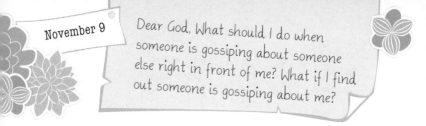

Dear God, What should I do when someone is gossiping about someone else right in front of me? What if I find out someone is gossiping about me?

CONSIDER THIS ... There is almost nothing worse than finding out that someone has backstabbed you—told your secrets or made up lies about you. The only thing worse is when someone spreads them around. Proverbs 11:13 tells us that a person who gossips can't keep secrets but a trustworthy person can. If someone shares a secret with you, she has trusted you with a little part of herself. If you break that trust and tell someone else, you are proving that you can't be trusted and that gossiping is more important than your friend.

Proverbs 26:20 says, "Fire goes out without wood, and quarrels disappear when gossip stops." Once people stop talking about an issue, other people lose interest and forget about it. Once they forget about it, it's not causing trouble anymore.

What should you do when someone is gossiping in front of you? Think of how awful it is when someone blurts your secrets to a crowd. You hate it! So protect the person who is being gossiped about. Be brave—speak up and say it's not a nice thing to talk about. Change the subject. Stopping the gossip in that way will be like pouring water on the fire. If someone gossips all the time, that person is not to be trusted. Is that really the kind of friend you want? You might think again about hanging out with people who enjoy gossip.

What should you do when someone gossips about you? If you hear about it, you might privately tell that person it hurt your feelings when you heard about it. Then say nothing more and let the fire die out.

GOD SAYS ...
A troublemaker plants seeds of strife; gossip separates the best of friends. PROVERBS 16:28

HOW ABOUT YOU?
Do you know anyone who has a problem with gossip? Who? What can you do to help stop gossip?

Dear God, I'm the youngest person in my family. By the time I speak up, people are done with whatever they were talking about. Can my family forget me?

CONSIDER THIS . . . It can be difficult to be the youngest. When it's your first day at middle school, all of your older brothers and sisters have already "been there" and "done that." When you learn something new, they've already mastered it. And by the time you get to form a thought in an argument, the older ones might have already pushed past it. When you're the smallest, it does seem like you can be overlooked.

If you feel like you are being forgotten in your family, it might be a good idea to talk to each member of your family separately. Tell your brothers and sisters that you like being their sister, but you don't feel like stuff is divided fairly sometimes. You could also talk to your mom or dad and ask them to referee discussions and choices so you get a fair chance too. Even if you are the youngest, you're just as important as anyone else in your family. Some people even feel that the youngest, as the baby, is the most loved and most special member of the family.

Even when you feel you're being talked over and elbowed out in conversations, God is always listening. None of his children are more important than any of the others; he loves them all, from the youngest to the oldest. In good times and bad, noisy days and quiet nights, you are always on God's heart and mind.

HOW ABOUT YOU?

Are there times when you feel your family or friends forget about you? How do you feel? What can you do?

GOD SAYS . . .

Can a mother forget her nursing child? Can she feel no love for the child she has borne? But even if that were possible, I would not forget you!
ISAIAH 49:15

Dear God, I've seen pictures of Jesus with sheep and a long stick that looks like a candy cane. I have no idea what that means, though. Is it important?

CONSIDER THIS . . . God tells us that his thoughts are not like our thoughts and that his ways are far beyond anything we could imagine (Isaiah 55:8). In fact, his thoughts and ways are very different. But he wanted us to be able to clearly understand what he was saying, to know about him, and to be able to relate to him. One way he helped his followers understand him better was by telling stories, called parables, so they could "get it" in a story format. Another way he helped his followers to understand things was by describing himself in ways that his followers could relate to. For instance, because the Bible was written during a time when there was a lot of animal care, he used the idea of his being a shepherd to help listeners understand him.

A shepherd is in charge of the sheep. He watches over them night and day to make sure that wolves don't come and kill his sheep. The shepherd moves his sheep from pasture to pasture so they always have fresh grass and water. If they get hurt, he cares for them. He watches over them so they don't wander off and get lost. When one does, he makes sure the other sheep are safe, and then he goes and finds the lost sheep, even if it's dangerous or difficult for the shepherd to do so.

Even though no one has a picture of what Jesus actually looked like, people have made paintings like the one you talked about that shows a man as a shepherd, or sitting with little children all around him, because that's how Jesus talked about himself.

Now that you understand that Jesus is a shepherd, how do you feel about being a fluffy, beloved sheep?

GOD SAYS . . .
[Jesus said,] "I am the good shepherd; I know my own sheep, and they know me."
JOHN 10:14

HOW ABOUT YOU?
How does Jesus lead and protect you?

Dear God, Why can't I talk to my parents without being embarrassed?

November 12

CONSIDER THIS . . . When we're little, we have easy things to talk about with our parents. Can we play with a certain toy? May we please be excused from the table? As we grow older, our concerns are different. A lot of the things we want to discuss with our parents can be embarrassing or hard. On top of it all, we're not sure how our parents will answer. Do they still think we're little girls, or do they realize we are growing up?

Many girls have questions about their bodies, about their feelings, about scary things they think about but never tell anyone else. All of those topics are normal even though you don't hear anyone else talk about them. Perhaps you tried to talk with your parents about these at one time, and they were rushed or for some other reason didn't recognize how important it was to you. If they gave you a quick answer or brushed you off, you may feel afraid to bring the subject up again. Maybe you just think that the stuff you want to say is weird.

Be brave and speak up! God gave you parents to love you and guide you. He gives them wisdom to do it. Chances are, the topics won't be as embarrassing to them as they are to you. After all, they had questions when they were your age. If you feel more comfortable talking with one parent than the other, wait until you have some time alone. Ask for it. Pray and ask the Lord for the right words, then dive right in. The hardest part will be opening your mouth and getting the first sentence out. The Lord will help you with the rest.

Remember, the only silly question is the one that goes unasked!

HOW ABOUT YOU?

What questions do you have that you've been too embarrassed to ask your parents? When will you be brave enough to ask?

GOD SAYS . . .

Now go! I will help you speak, and I will teach you what to say. EXODUS 4:12 (NCV)

Dear God, If you love us so much, why do you let hard things come into our lives?

CONSIDER THIS . . . There are many reasons why difficulties come into everyone's lives. First of all—we're not in heaven yet. There are still bad people and hard situations going on right here on planet earth, and that's how it will be till we're in heaven. Second, hard times make us stronger sometimes; we learn from them and we grow from them. Later, when someone we know goes through a tough time, we're able to encourage her and remind her that she can make it through, just like we did.

As Christians, we're told to live by believing, not by seeing (2 Corinthians 5:7). That means we have to trust God and do what he asks us to do, or what we know to be right, even when we can't see how it's all going to work out. That trust is called faith, and God says our faith is precious to him.

What if your mom told you the only way you could make her happy was if you played the piano for her, but then she refused to buy a piano and would not let you take lessons? She'd be setting you up to fail, wouldn't she? So when the Lord tells us that the only possible way to please him is by our faith, would it be right of him to take away every possible chance for us to show that faith?

Showing faith means believing he is taking care of you, even when it doesn't look that way. Next time something hard comes up, put on your believing glasses and don't rely so much on your seeing glasses; and know that, as you do, you're pleasing God very much.

GOD SAYS . . .

It is impossible to please God without faith. HEBREWS 11:6

HOW ABOUT YOU?

When have you had to live by believing and not by seeing?

Dear God, Is it okay to be quiet around some people and hyper around others?

November 14

CONSIDER THIS . . . God created you with a unique personality. You will have likes and dislikes. When you have those things in common with others, you will often be friends. If you and another girl like softball, enjoy reading the same kinds of books, and hate history, you'll probably be friends. When you're friends with someone, you find it easier to talk with her. If you have little in common with others, you'll have less to talk about. Sometimes our friends mean different things to us. A friend on a sports team might bring out a competitive nature in you. A friend who loves to talk may spend hours chatting with you on the phone. A zany friend can free you to be zany too!

No matter what your unique likes and dislikes are, a girl who wants to be like Jesus still has some requirements. You must be kind to all. You must be gentle. You must be honest. If you squeeze a tube of toothpaste, what's going to come out? Toothpaste! Whatever is inside you is what is going to come out in your words and your deeds. You might want gel candy to come out, but if toothpaste is inside of you, that's what's going to come out. Jesus said that whatever is in a person's heart comes out of his or her mouth (Luke 6:45). The more time you spend with God and the more you allow the Holy Spirit to direct you, the more fruit of his Spirit you'll show.

It's okay to be more comfortable with some people than others. In fact, it's wise! Just make sure that what's inside you is juicy fruit and that whatever you do share with others is sweet.

HOW ABOUT YOU?

Who are five people you are comfortable with?

GOD SAYS . . .

The Holy Spirit produces this kind of fruit in our lives: love, joy, peace, patience, kindness, goodness, faithfulness, gentleness, and self-control.
GALATIANS 5:22-23

Dear God, How is Christianity different from other religions?

CONSIDER THIS . . . There are many religions in the world. Most people on earth understand that there is a bigger power that is truly good. But they disagree about who that being, or god, really is.

Christians believe that there is one God who exists in three persons: God the Father, God the Son (Jesus), and God the Holy Spirit. (This is called the Trinity.) Christians also believe that while all persons are made in God's image, it's only those who trust in Jesus for salvation who will receive his power here on earth and eternal life with him in heaven.

Jewish people, God's original chosen people, believe in the same God the Father that Christians do. But they are still waiting for the Messiah, whereas Christians understand that Jesus is the Messiah promised to the Jewish people, and that he has already come. Hindu people believe in many different things; they don't all agree on all of the same beliefs, kind of like a bush with many branches that sometimes overlap but have no main trunk. Muslims hold Allah to be their god. They believe that Jesus was a prophet but that he is not the Son of God.

Although many people say that the God of Christians and the god of Muslims is the same, that cannot be true. Christians understand God to be the Father of Jesus and part of the Trinity with him. Muslims disagree with that. Therefore, their god cannot be the same God.

God wants us to treat all people with respect, no matter what their religion. But he also wants us to boldly hold on to and speak the truth. It's tough, but he helps us to do both.

GOD SAYS . . .

Jesus told him, "I am the way, the truth, and the life. No one can come to the Father except through me."
JOHN 14:6

HOW ABOUT YOU?

Do you understand that all religions are different, but that Scripture says that Jesus is the only way to the Father?

Dear God, What does it mean when people in the Bible call you Rabbi?

CONSIDER THIS . . . In the Bible, the word *rabbi* is used to speak to or about a teacher, especially a male teacher. The word means more than teacher, though. It might be something more like "Honorable Teacher" or "Great One" or even "Master."

In our culture, we don't value teachers as much as we should—and perhaps as much as other cultures do. Many other cultures treat their teachers with great respect. They understand that there is only one way to pass information on from one generation to the next, and that is through teachers. If you don't have good teachers, you cannot go forward in your education, your career, or your spiritual life. We could learn a lesson from the cultures that still treat teachers honorably.

Master is a word we're more familiar with. There's the kind of master we use to describe a dog and its master, but the other kind is someone who has "mastered" something, like being the very best violin player, basketball player, or math student. *Great One* needs no explanation, right? It means the best, the top of the top, and worthy of admiration.

We get used to thinking of Jesus as Savior, but we don't often think of him as our teacher. He teaches us through Scripture, through stories, through his own life and the choices he made, and the direct commands he gives us. He even instructs us by the situations he lets us go through. More than any other master, he is worthy of our time, attention, and respect.

Remember, he called us his disciples, and the word *disciple* really means student!

HOW ABOUT YOU?

What are five ways that Jesus has taught you something this year?

GOD SAYS . . .

Peter remembered what Jesus had said to the tree on the previous day and exclaimed, "Look, Rabbi! The fig tree you cursed has withered and died!" MARK 11:21

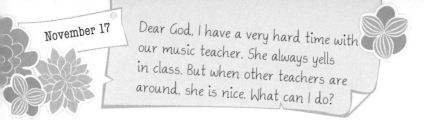

November 17

Dear God, I have a very hard time with our music teacher. She always yells in class. But when other teachers are around, she is nice. What can I do?

CONSIDER THIS . . . Each snowflake God created is made of the same material—snow. Each has a similar shape to other snowflakes. They all melt. But they are all different. People are the same way. God made all of us, and we look alike. But we are all different, too. Because of this, we don't always automatically get along with everyone—because other people see things differently than we do. We each have different backgrounds and different goals and different ways of dealing with things. Your teacher might handle problems differently than you do. Not very well, it seems.

But, just for a minute, try to see things from the teacher's perspective. She might have other classes that are really disobedient. She could be stressed from that and overreact to your class. It's not fair, but it happens. Maybe she *is* just acting sweet in front of others, or maybe she's sweet to other adults because she's more comfortable with them. Maybe someone in your group laughed, and she thought you were laughing at her. Maybe someone said something disrespectful to her, and now she thinks all of you are disrespectful. Maybe you did *nothing* wrong, but she's dealing with a difficult situation away from school.

For now, your teacher is an authority over you. You can try to win her—change her actions by doing what is right. Don't goof off in her class, and if your friends are giving her dirty looks or whispering, move away from them. Make an extra effort to be kind and helpful, even if you haven't been doing anything wrong. Try this for a few weeks, and see if she lightens up. If not, talk with your parents about the situation. Maybe they will need to step in and help.

GOD SAYS . . .
For the Lord's sake, respect all human authority.
1 PETER 2:13

HOW ABOUT YOU?
Is there a teacher you don't get along with? What can you do to help the relationship be a little smoother?

Dear God, I'm pretty popular this year. My old friend from last year, who isn't popular, still wants to be friends. How do I tell her we're not friends anymore?

November 18

CONSIDER THIS . . . It sounds as if you think you're moving up the social ladder—you have places to go, and you don't want anyone to hold you back. It's nice that you are popular and enjoying your new friends. But are you the kind of girl who leaves friends in the dust?

The Bible is clear that Jesus was not popular. Some people picked on him. Some people made fun of him. He didn't have a big house for people to admire—in fact, he didn't have a house at all. His friends were, for the most part, not the rich and famous and powerful. They were the people that other people left in the dust.

If we are Christians, we should become a little more like Jesus every day. The Bible says that God does not look at the outward appearance of a person: what kind of clothes she wears, whether she's pretty, whether she has a lot of cool things. God looks at what is inside a person—for example, if she is more interested in people or power, or if she is giving or selfish (1 Samuel 16:7). If you are a Christian, ask yourself, "Am I becoming a little more like Jesus each day?"

Have you heard the song that begins, "Make new friends, but keep the old; one is silver and the other gold"? Your new friends are fine—enjoy them! But they're silver. The friends who stay with you a long time and love you for yourself are gold. Cherish them, too.

HOW ABOUT YOU?

How could you become a little more like Jesus every day? Pick two ways and start right away.

GOD SAYS . . .

Live in harmony with each other. Don't be too proud to enjoy the company of ordinary people. ROMANS 12:16

Dear God, Am I supposed to forgive everybody for everything? What if someone really hurts me and I don't want to? How is this supposed to work?

CONSIDER THIS . . . Everyone has been hurt. Even Jesus was called bad names, spat upon, and beaten before he was crucified. Some people who said they were his friends turned out to be his worst enemies. But because unforgiveness hurts the person who was hurt even more by keeping that pain alive (kind of like roasting a marshmallow on a stick and turning it on the fire over and over again), Jesus has given us an example of how to forgive based on his forgiveness of our sins.

In order for forgiveness to be given, the person who has sinned has to repent first. When we ask God to forgive us for our sins, we must first admit to them. And that means without giving excuses for our bad behavior. Repenting from sin doesn't mean sharing the blame. It means taking responsibility for your own part without concerning yourself about what others did or didn't do. God expects us to repent, admit to our sin, and then show fruit of that repentance by a changed life. That means we don't do those things anymore. Once we admit we're wrong, turn away from that kind of wrong, and see if we can repay in goodness those who we have done wrong to, God is willing to forgive us.

God tells us that we should forgive others in the way that he has forgiven us. That means we can reasonably expect that those who harm us must repent, turn away from that sin, and make things right with us. Once they do those things, we must be ready to forgive too. When we forgive others as God forgave us, it allows us to be obedient and whole but also doesn't make us pretend that bad things didn't happen to us.

GOD SAYS . . .

If another believer sins, rebuke that person; then if there is repentance, forgive. LUKE 17:3

HOW ABOUT YOU?

Is there anyone you need to forgive? Has she repented, said and shown she was sorry, and asked your forgiveness?

Dear God, Once a person repents, what happens next? Does she get to keep hurting me just because she said she was sorry?

November 20

CONSIDER THIS ... There's nothing worse than a person being forced to say she's sorry when she doesn't mean it at all. But if she means it, you need to forgive. Jesus tells us that if we forgive those who sin against us, God will forgive us. But if we don't, he won't forgive us, either. Ouch!

If a person has hurt you, but she shows by her actions that she is truly sorry, you must forgive her. Not forgiving someone leads to stewing over it. Do you know how stew is cooked? All the ingredients are put into a pot, and the cook goes back to the stove over and over again to stir things up until it's well mixed and hot. That's what happens when you go over and over what a person has done to you. You mix it up till it grows hot inside you. And you have no peace.

Forgiving that person does not mean giving her permission to hurt you again. It means you don't hold a grudge and you give all the consequences to God. He promises he will take care of it.

Once you let go of your anger, you can decide if that person is someone you still want to be around or not. If not, it's okay to go your way in peace and end the friendship; that does not mean that you have not forgiven, it means that person has taken advantage of your kindness too many times. If you choose to be friends still, it's okay to be cautious till she proves herself trustworthy again. You may find that, like all of us, she made a couple of bad choices for which she is sorry and wants to do things differently next time—just like you!

HOW ABOUT YOU?

Is there anyone you need to forgive? Is there anyone you need to ask forgiveness from?

GOD SAYS ...

If you forgive those who sin against you, your heavenly Father will forgive you. But if you refuse to forgive others, your Father will not forgive your sins. MATTHEW 6:14-15

Dear God, Why won't my parents let me listen to the music I want?

CONSIDER THIS . . . Just a few years ago, if you wanted to listen to music you either

1. turned the radio on or
2. popped in a tape or played a CD.

Now there are so many options! You can listen to music on the computer, stream music through your phone or your MP3 player, or turn on a music channel on the TV. Instead of having just a few choices for how to listen and what to listen to, there are hundreds of options. It's almost like eating a huge buffet with many items to offer your ears . . . and your mind.

And that's where the problems come in. If you feed your body junk day after day, it can cause health problems, some of which you might not see right away. A few months or years later, though, you'll see that years of bad eating habits caused bad health. The same is true for music selections. You might not see that some of the things you're choosing are bad for your heart, your mind, or your soul, but your parents can. Why? They're a few years down the road from you, and they are able to see what happens over time.

It might not be fun to avoid buying, downloading, or listening to music you really like but your mom and dad have said no to. But with so many options on the musical buffet, do you think you can poke around a little bit to find something both fun to listen to and good for you, now and later?

GOD SAYS . . .

I am young and you are old, so I held back from telling you what I think. I thought, "Those who are older should speak, for wisdom comes with age." JOB 32:6-7

HOW ABOUT YOU?

What have your parents ever said no to you about? Were you glad later that they did?

CONSIDER THIS . . . Dogs love "people food" much, much more than they like dog food. Say the word *treat* and any dog is ready to do an about-face, go running, and do whatever you say.

Stand on her hind legs? *No problem.*

Roll over and play dead? *I'm a goner.*

Lay on the floor? *You won't see me move.*

It's fun to watch them, and it's fun to give them treats—as long as the treats are okay for them. But some foods that are delicious and safe for humans, like grapes and chocolate, are poisonous for dogs. If dogs eat them, or eat enough of them, they will get very sick and possibly die. Since chocolate smells good to dogs, and they see you eating it, they'll want it too. If they sometimes get a little piece of whatever you're eating, of course they're going to beg for it. Their eyes will be on your every move. But you know you can't give in. Instead, you might turn them away from it, distract them, say no, or give them something else.

This is the way it is with our temptations, too. Sometimes we know right away that they are not good for us. But sometimes, well, we're just not sure. Or we convince ourselves that it will be okay. But sin leads to sickness and death. The way out is to keep your eyes on the Lord. He will show you when traps are laid for you so that you can step around them. He'll turn you away, distract you, say no, or give you something else that's good for you. Because he loves you, he's always willing to show you the way out of temptation.

And you won't even have to roll over and play dead.

HOW ABOUT YOU?

Have you ever given in to a temptation, only to feel sick about it later? How can that help you to keep your eyes on the Lord, and then follow his lead the next time a temptation comes along?

GOD SAYS . . .

My eyes are always on the LORD, for he rescues me from the traps of my enemies. PSALM 25:15

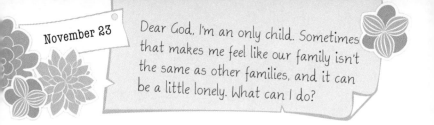

Dear God, I'm an only child. Sometimes that makes me feel like our family isn't the same as other families, and it can be a little lonely. What can I do?

CONSIDER THIS ... It may feel as if your family is different from other families, but the truth is that families are made up of all kinds of wonderful combinations. Although we get used to thinking about families as having a mom, a dad, and several kids, that's really not a "typical" family anymore. Some families are like that, of course, but some families have a mom and kids, or a dad and kids, or only one kid (like your family!) or stepparents and stepsiblings. Other families have grandparents and kids. Some have a mom and a dad and foster kids that will live with them for a little while. There are many ways that families can be put together.

Families don't have to be made up of only people who are related to you either. The Bible calls other Christians our brothers and sisters for a reason. Because we have the same Father, God, we are all siblings. That means you have millions of brothers and sisters all over the world. (Aren't you glad you don't have to buy each of them a birthday present?) In this way, you get to choose some brothers and sisters of your very own. You might even have more in common with them, and enjoy more fun with them, than you would with siblings who had been born in your family.

You don't have to stay lonely—adopt a sister or a brother or two from the family of God. By doing this you can add to your family in a way you'll all enjoy.

GOD SAYS ...
A real friend sticks closer than a brother.
PROVERBS 18:24

HOW ABOUT YOU?
Do you have a friend who is like a sister to you? Would you like to add more "sisters and brothers" to your family?

Dear God, What does it mean to take the Lord's name in vain?

CONSIDER THIS . . . Taking the Lord's name in vain means using his name in a disrespectful way. People take the Lord's name in vain, using it as a curse word, when they see something they like, or call out in surprise. Because many people probably live in families where people talk that way, they don't see anything wrong with doing that. But to people who love the Lord, it can be painful to hear.

What should you do if your friends are taking the Lord's name in vain? Most of the time, your friends won't even know that they're offending you. If they did, they would probably stop. Pray about how you should talk to your friends about it, and ask the Lord for a humble and gentle spirit. Then talk with your friends in private, one by one, so they don't feel attacked. You could say, "You might not know this, but whenever I hear you say 'God' or 'Jesus Christ,' and I know you're not talking to him, it hurts my feelings. It's just like if someone said something bad about your mom or dad. Would you mind saying something else when I'm around?"

Most times the person will be embarrassed, and you might be too. But good friends can overcome that. They will probably try to stop saying these things in front of you, but don't be angry if they slip up or don't realize it from time to time or even if they don't stop at all. They might laugh at you and keep on saying it. The important thing is that you took a stand to honor the Lord's name, even though it was a risky thing for you to do. Jesus says that when we stand up for him before other people, he stands up for us before his Father.

HOW ABOUT YOU?

Do you know anyone who uses the Lord's name in a disrespectful way? What can you do about it?

GOD SAYS . . .

[Jesus said,] "Everyone who acknowledges me publicly here on earth, I will also acknowledge before my Father in heaven." MATTHEW 10:32

Dear God, What if everyone is watching something on TV that I'm not supposed to, and kids are making fun of me because I'm trying not to watch it?

CONSIDER THIS . . . It's never easy to be made fun of, especially when you know you are doing the right thing. It's even harder if you are the only one who is going to speak up about not watching the TV show. When you speak up, the others might think you are judging their TV shows. In a way, you are. You're saying that something they watch isn't good for them. This might make them defensive. And when people are defensive, they can get angry. You might be afraid of that. Or maybe you're afraid of being embarrassed because you're different.

In Philippians 1:10, Paul says to the early Christians, "I want you to understand what really matters, so that you may live pure and blameless lives until the day of Christ's return." What you watch on TV really matters, so remember that speaking up about a TV show that you shouldn't be watching is part of living a pure and blameless life. It may be difficult to defend your values, but you are doing the right thing.

If you don't want to make a big deal, just say, "I'm not allowed to watch this, and a TV show isn't worth getting in trouble about." Ask your friends to do something else. If your friends still want to watch the TV show, you might try leaving the room or concentrating on a book or something. If your friends keep watching, you might suggest that you leave and come back another time. People might make fun of you, but you can just tell them that you don't make the rules. You can tell them why your family decided that, or say nothing at all. You make the call.

GOD SAYS . . .
May you always be filled with the fruit of your salvation—the righteous character produced in your life by Jesus Christ—for this will bring much glory and praise to God. PHILIPPIANS 1:11

HOW ABOUT YOU?
What TV shows are you not allowed to watch? Why does your family have this rule?

FAIRY TALE DAY

November 26

Dear God, Sometimes when I speak out about things that are right, people make fun of me. I feel stupid. Should I just stop?

CONSIDER THIS . . . It's never easy to be the one voice that says something different from what everyone else is saying, even if it's the right thing. Remember the story of the emperor's new clothes?

There was once a ruler in a land, a high and mighty man who was filled with pride. He thought so much of himself that he absolutely believed he could never be wrong. But he was very unwise, and people took advantage of that. The emperor's tailors made him a very expensive suit of clothing, but the clothing was made out of . . . nothing! In order to cheat the king and take advantage of his pride, they told him that the clothing was magnificent and could only be seen by the wisest people of all.

When the emperor looked into the mirror he only saw . . . his naked body! Afraid to admit it, lest he be seen as unwise, he pretended to see grand clothing. The word went out that the emperor's new clothing could only be seen by the wise, so everyone else faked that they could see it too. Until one kid said, "Hey! The emperor has nothing on. He's naked!" When that kid was brave enough to speak up and say the truth, everyone else began to agree. It wasn't easy for that kid to be the first one to say what was right, but eventually, everyone else was able to see the truth.

Sometimes you'll speak up and there will seem to be no one to back you up, and sometimes you'll speak up and there will be people who support you. No matter what, you'll be acting on wisdom—ready to say what is right even if everyone around you is scared to.

HOW ABOUT YOU?

Have you ever been afraid to speak up with the truth? What can help you be brave enough to do so next time?

GOD SAYS . . .

God chose things the world considers foolish in order to shame those who think they are wise. And he chose things that are powerless to shame those who are powerful.
1 CORINTHIANS 1:27

Dear God, I know Jesus came to earth once already, but is he coming again?

CONSIDER THIS . . . All throughout history, God has been leading his people toward himself, toward truth, and toward holy and right behavior. First he gave the law to Moses, to share with the people and to show them how to live. Then Jesus came, and he became a human just like us to show us the right way to live. Jesus also died for us so that through his sacrifice we would be able to be holy and right, even though we do not always follow God's laws. The good news is that Jesus is indeed coming back again a second time. This time, however, he will not come back meekly as a baby born in a stable, but he will return powerfully, on a great horse.

The second coming of Jesus will be the time when everyone who has ever lived will be judged for the good and bad that they have done in this world. Those found faithful will be given new bodies (Long legs! Perfect hair?) and will head toward eternal life with the Lord in heaven, while those who have rejected Christ here on earth will head toward punishment. All evil, sin, sickness, and suffering will finally come to an end.

The second coming of Christ is a serious subject, isn't it? Because the Lord says that no one knows the time he will come (he says it will happen unexpectedly, like a thief coming in the night), he urges everyone to be ready today, tonight, right now!

GOD SAYS . . .

The Lord himself will come down from heaven with a commanding shout, with the voice of the archangel, and with the trumpet call of God. . . . Then we will be with the Lord forever.
1 THESSALONIANS 4:16-17

HOW ABOUT YOU?

Are you ready in case the Lord returns today?

Dear God, My best friend has been hanging out with someone else. I want to tell that other girl to back off and not steal my best friend. Should I?

CONSIDER THIS . . . Whenever you have a best friend, it's like you've given her a little piece of yourself. You share secrets about the boys you like. You giggle about inside jokes. You count on her in times of trouble when you need someone to talk to. If that friend pulls away, it's scary! You might think, *Who will be my special friend now?*

You know what? It's healthy—and fun—to have more than one friend! Sometimes being with only one friend is like eating only one kind of fruit. Apples may be tasty, but bananas are too. Or it's like reading only one kind of book when there are lots of other great stories out there. Your friend might want to see what other friends have to share, and you might want to see too.

Don't say anything mean about your friend's new pal—and try not to think anything mean about her, either. It won't help your friendship, and it will only hurt people—including you. Instead, tell your best friend, "I've missed being together. Do you want to come over this weekend?" And *you* make some new friends too! Think about a girl you'd like to know better. Be brave! Ask her, "Want to be my partner on this assignment?" or say, "Sit here!" at Sunday school and pat the seat beside you. Then you'll have several special friends to share your life with.

HOW ABOUT YOU?
What could you say and do if your best bud wants some other friends too? Name at least one person you would like to be better friends with.

GOD SAYS . . .
May the words of my mouth and the meditation of my heart be pleasing to you, O LORD, my rock and my redeemer. PSALM 19:14

Dear God, How am I supposed to pray? Some people want me to pray out loud, but I'm kind of embarrassed to do that.

CONSIDER THIS . . . Prayer is having a conversation with God, just like you would have with anyone else. It's important that you remember who it is that you're talking to. Be respectful, but besides that, you can talk just how you normally would with a friend. Do you need help? Ask God for advice. Are you sad? Tell him about your feelings. Are you excited? Share your joy.

When someone speaks to you, or shares an idea with you, you show respect when you include that in the conversation with him or her. When you include whatever you've been learning in the Bible in your prayers, it shows God that you care about his Word, and it brings honor to him. When you praise him for what he has done, you're telling him that you're grateful.

Praying by yourself, either in your head or quietly in a room, at your desk, or anywhere else is just fine. But when you pray with others, you grow closer with them in a special way. Jesus says that when two or three people are gathered together in his name, he is there with them (Matthew 18:20). That means it's you and your friends and family and the Lord. Don't be afraid about sounding dumb or silly or wondering if anyone will be judging your prayers. Just try to concentrate on what you'd be saying to him if you were alone with him. And then when others pray, you can quietly pray along with them, urging the Lord to listen to their pleas.

The master of the universe has his ear and his heart bent toward you all day and night, no matter if you pray quietly or out loud. Isn't that amazing?

GOD SAYS . . .

If I had not confessed the sin in my heart, the Lord would not have listened. But God did listen! He paid attention to my prayer. Praise God, who did not ignore my prayer.

PSALM 66:18-20

HOW ABOUT YOU?

Do you speak freely with God, by yourself or among others, or does prayer feel like a foreign language you're still trying to learn?

Dear God, So, after I start this conversation with you, what should I do next?

November 30

CONSIDER THIS . . . A good conversation is kind of like playing tennis or Ping-Pong. One person speaks, and then it's the other person's turn. If you are praying in a group with other people, like around the dinner table or at Sunday school, each person takes a turn praying and then is silent, listening to what the others have to say. It's no different with God.

Have you ever been in a group where someone was a talk-hog? She talks, talks, talks, and doesn't slow down long enough for anyone else to have a turn. If someone speaks up, she starts in about how the same thing happened to her—but worse! Or it reminds her of a time when she . . . You get the idea. A good conversationalist is someone who knows how to listen as well as speak. After all, we learn much more by what we hear than by what we say.

After you get done speaking to God, be sure to save as much time for listening and hearing as you did for talking. This can be hard. You have to focus on what he might be saying, on how he speaks to your heart. He might remind you of a Scripture verse, or a situation you were once in, or a time when he told you something else. He might gently whisper in your heart. You might wait respectfully for a while, and if he doesn't speak up, he might do so later.

Good listeners have many friends, and you'll have a strong friendship with God if you're a good listener. The more you listen, the more you hear. The more you hear, the more you understand.

What does the Lord have to whisper to you today?

HOW ABOUT YOU?

Has God recently told something to you? What was it? How did you know it was him speaking?

GOD SAYS . . .

Pay attention to how you hear. To those who listen to my teaching, more understanding will be given. But for those who are not listening, even what they think they understand will be taken away from them.
LUKE 8:18

Dear God, One girl at school copies my work all the time, and it really annoys me. How can I solve this problem?

CONSIDER THIS . . . Of course it annoys you—and it should! You've worked hard to study, and someone who didn't is trying to take advantage of your hard work. It's not fair for you. She's not helping herself by copying you either. She can't copy you for the rest of her life. She will have to know how to spell, write, and do math.

The hard thing—but the thing you're going to have to do—is to speak up. That girl is doing something wrong, and you caught her. Until someone corrects her, she's going to keep doing it. You might take her aside and gently say, "Please don't copy off of my paper anymore. It's not fair to either of us." If she tries to look on your paper, cover it up with your hand and look her straight in the eye so she knows that *you* know what she's trying to do. If she keeps copying your work or someone else's, it would be wise to tell your teacher in private. Teachers are there to help you learn, and the teacher can't help this girl learn if she doesn't know she's not answering the questions on her own.

The Bible tells us to speak up when we have any problem. Speaking up can be one of the hardest things in the world. It's much easier to keep quiet and not have trouble. But the real trouble comes when we don't tackle a problem. Since you know she's cheating, you need to be part of the solution whether you want to or not! Don't worry, though. The Lord will give you strength to say what needs to be said. He can work this situation out to be good for both of you.

GOD SAYS . . .

If someone in your group does something wrong, you who are spiritual should go to that person and gently help make him right again. GALATIANS 6:1 (NCV)

HOW ABOUT YOU?

What problems do you have right now that could be helped by speaking up?

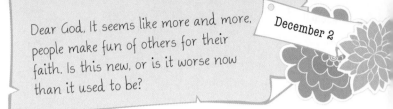

Dear God, It seems like more and more people make fun of others for their faith. Is this new, or is it worse now than it used to be?

December 2

CONSIDER THIS . . . Have you ever noticed that when you have a red car, you see a lot more red cars on the road? Or if your dad has migraine headaches, do you notice when commercials come on the television for migraine medicine? We are naturally tuned in to what is happening to and around us, and to the people we care about. It can make things seem like they are happening more often, when really what's going on is we are noticing it more often!

Faith is a difficult thing for people to explain and to understand because it's not tangible. That means you can't touch it, see it, smell it, hear it, or taste it. Faith in God is a mysterious thing, and it is better seen by other people who have faith than by people who don't. Jesus said that only people who have ears to hear and eyes to see will understand some of the things he did (Matthew 13:16-17). People who don't have faith don't yet have those kinds of ears and eyes, so things of faith can seem foolish to them.

People made fun of Elisha in the Old Testament for his faith. People laughed at Jesus for his faith. But when they saw the things that faith in God actually did, they stopped laughing. They wanted some of that faith. They worshiped the living God!

A Christian is called to speak up for her faith sometimes, and once in a while God will open the eyes of the people around her, and they will see and be amazed. It will be worth all the other times being made fun of to be present just then.

HOW ABOUT YOU?

How do you feel knowing that people laughed at even Jesus for his faith?

GOD SAYS . . .

"Get out!" [Jesus] told them. "The girl isn't dead; she's only asleep." But the crowd laughed at him. MATTHEW 9:24

Dear God, There are some hard parts about being a Christian. I didn't know about that, but as I get older, I see more and more of them. Is that normal?

CONSIDER THIS . . . In December, many people begin to plan for and buy their Christmas gifts. They write out a list of who they'll need to buy for, and then they look at their money to see how much extra they'll need to spend. Sometimes people divide their money up—for example, twenty-five dollars for each person. Then they look over their budget to make sure they have enough money to spend before buying any gifts.

There are some people who don't do that. They just head to the mall with a card and start shopping. In that case, sometimes an embarrassing thing happens. They get to the cashier with their haul of Christmas gifts and the cashier has to say, "I'm sorry, but there is not enough money in your account to pay for all of these." The gifts have to go back, and the shopper slinks out to her car, humiliated.

In anything we decide to do, it's important to count the cost before we start on it. You might want to sign up for a new sport, but do you have the time? You might want a pet bird, but do you have the ability to care for it? This is true for your Christian faith, too. Now that you're old enough to understand that there are both gifts and costs to being a Christian, you have to decide for yourself if it's the life you want to live. Jesus asks you to do just that. That way, when the hard times come up, you won't be surprised or angry. You will have already added things up and know you'll come out ahead, anyway.

GOD SAYS . . .
Don't begin until you count the cost. For who would begin construction of a building without first calculating the cost to see if there is enough money to finish it? LUKE 14:28

HOW ABOUT YOU?
What things in your Christian life have surprised you?

Dear God, I know that I need to listen to you, but can you tell me how to know it's you speaking?

CONSIDER THIS . . . The phone rings, and you answer it. "Hello?" you say. "Hello," the voice says on the other end of the line. "How are you?"

Who's on the other end? If it's your grandma, your best friend, or your mother, you probably recognize the voice right away. If it's someone you don't talk to very often, like an aunt or one of your dad's friends, you might recognize the voice—or you might not. If it's a stranger, you won't recognize the voice at all.

This is the way it is with the Lord. When you spend a lot of time with him, you learn to recognize his voice more often and more easily. It can be a bit tougher to recognize than your friends' voices at first, because you don't hear an out-loud voice. But you definitely can learn to recognize his voice through the ways he *does* speak to us. God always speaks to us when we read the Bible. When he tells us about a situation with someone in the Bible, he is telling us about ourselves, too. He shows us what happens to someone who doesn't obey—and he is telling us we must obey too. He tells us he loves us through his stories of sacrifice and rescue.

Sometimes God speaks to us through people who give us godly advice or who simply reach out an arm to hug us. God sometimes speaks to us through ideas that pop into our minds after prayer. God can speak to us through songs, books, and nature. God speaks to us through our circumstances. Pray and ask the Lord to help you to recognize his voice. You will because you belong to him.

HOW ABOUT YOU?

When is it easiest for you to hear God's voice? What can you do to hear his voice more clearly?

GOD SAYS . . .

After [Jesus] has gathered his own flock, he walks ahead of them, and they follow him because they know his voice. JOHN 10:4

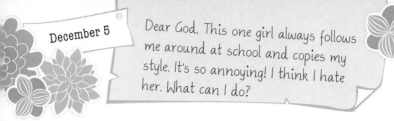

Dear God, This one girl always follows me around at school and copies my style. It's so annoying! I think I hate her. What can I do?

CONSIDER THIS . . . Words can be powerful weapons. Remember the saying "Sticks and stones may break my bones, but words will never hurt me"? Well, that's a lie. The hurts caused by words are stronger and last longer than almost any hurt to your bones. When you say you hate someone, it's like kicking her in the heart.

But your feelings matter too. Your feelings of hate come from your anger at not being left alone and from your helplessness to stop her from trailing after you. You don't feel like you have any control. It's understandable that you'd want some time to yourself and with your friends. If you can get some control over this situation, you'll feel less angry and less likely to say or do something you'll regret later.

Does this mean you have to be best friends with the girl who follows you? No. Does it mean you have to be friends with her at all? No. Does it mean that you have to treat her gently and with respect? Yes. If you have a problem with someone, talk with her. Chances are, she feels really insecure and doesn't have many friends of her own. That's why she's following you around. She's copying you because she admires you. If you are nice to her, it will show Jesus' kind of love. Now, *that* would be something for people to copy! If you are unkind, it will only harden your own heart and change you from the person you are into a person you don't want to be. Being mean can destroy you.

Quietly ask her to please stop following you around. If she keeps doing it, ask a teacher or parent for help.

GOD SAYS . . .
Your kindness will reward you, but your cruelty will destroy you.
PROVERBS 11:17

HOW ABOUT YOU?
How can you deal with a friendship issue? Who can help you with this?

Dear God, It bugs me when people don't respect their leaders. Why don't they?

December 6

CONSIDER THIS . . . Everyone, and everything, needs a leader. In the animal world there are leaders. The alpha dog is in charge of the pack. Bees have a queen bee. Geese fly in the form of a letter V. The leader stays at the front and takes the brunt of the wind for a time, and the other geese follow.

Humans need leaders too. We have laws, most of which are based on laws God set up, and we need to follow them. Leaders help us do that. We need to make new, good laws from time to time to address our world. Leaders help us do that. Sometimes wars or disasters happen. Leaders help us respond to that. God set up his universe to be one of order. Leadership helps keep the order.

Sometimes people don't like the leaders over them. They don't agree with their decisions or their plans or the way they live their lives. As Christians, we might disagree with certain things that our leaders do. But we are to respect the position that the leader has, even when we don't respect the person. When Christians bad-mouth other people, it just makes Christians look bad. That's different from honest difference of opinion. Honest difference of opinion is offered with respect. It's okay to disagree with a leader, but it needs to be done with respect. It's okay to wish the rules were different, but until they are, we need to obey them or work to change them. Keep in mind that, like geese, human leaders take on the brunt of the wind in the world around them. They need our prayers till it's their turn to fall to the back of the flock and let someone else take over.

HOW ABOUT YOU?

Do you ever talk disrespectfully about those in leadership around you? If you have an honest difference of opinion, what can you do?

GOD SAYS . . .

Pray for rulers and for all who have authority so that we can have quiet and peaceful lives full of worship and respect for God. This is good, and it pleases God our Savior. 1 TIMOTHY 2:2-3 (NCV)

NATIONAL PUPPET DAY

Dear God, If you're a Christian, is it okay to have different opinions from other Christians?

CONSIDER THIS . . . Have you ever been to a puppet show, or seen a puppet in a movie? Maybe you've watched the Muppets—which are really puppets! Puppets, of course, are not alive. Hand puppets have someone's hand inside of them making them move and making them talk. Some puppets are moved by strings. When the puppet master moves his or her hand and lifts a string, the puppet moves in the very same way.

Puppets are fun to watch in a movie or a show. But they don't really think or move for themselves. Humans have to do that for them!

All Christians have some very important things in common—basic tenets, or beliefs, of our faith, starting with the fact that we believe Jesus to be the Son of God and the only Savior. But we also differ in many ways. We look different from one another, come from different nations, and like different kinds of music, clothes, and books. Some of us like sports, and some do not. Some like science and math, and some love language arts and history. There are Christians in nearly every political party, and while they see some things very differently, because their lives are based on their faith, they agree to disagree in love.

It's not only okay to have different opinions from other Christians, but it's also one of the things that makes the body of Christ so interesting. Self-control means that you get to control yourself; you are not a puppet only able to do and say what other people tell you to do. As cute as Kermit and Miss Piggy are, Jesus came to save people—not Muppets!

GOD SAYS . . .
Think clearly and exercise self-control. 1 PETER 1:13

HOW ABOUT YOU?
Do you feel confident respectfully sharing an opinion that is different from the one others have?

CONSIDER THIS ... Well, they were celebrating his birth, right? Perhaps this is when bringing people gifts for their birthdays started!

The wise men knew that Jesus was the King of the Jews and God, and they set out to worship him. Worship is reserved for God, or in pagan religions, gods. The wise men wanted to bring gifts to Jesus that were worthy of both a king and God. So they chose gold, frankincense, and myrrh. Although those were gifts that any rich person might bring to a king during that time, God often has a richer spiritual meaning for the things he causes people to do. Like these gifts!

When the wise men came to look for Jesus, they first stopped to ask evil King Herod where they could find Jesus. When Herod heard that people thought of Jesus as a king, he was fearful that Jesus would take his kingdom. So he instructed the wise men to come back and tell him where he, Herod, could find Jesus after they located him. The wise men found Jesus, but they did not tell Herod. Jesus' dad, Joseph, was warned in a dream that he needed to take Jesus and his mom, Mary, to Egypt, where they would be safe. How could they pay to live in a strange country, where Joseph had no job?

Why, the gold of course! Gold back then was very valuable, and it could be used anywhere as money.

Although there were bad people after Jesus and his family, it was no surprise to God. He planned, way in advance, to take care of his Son through the wise men and their generous gift.

HOW ABOUT YOU?

When you give a gift to someone, do you think in advance how it will be special or helpful to him or her?

GOD SAYS ...

[The wise men] entered the house and saw the child with his mother, Mary, and they bowed down and worshiped him. Then they opened their treasure chests and gave him gifts of gold, frankincense, and myrrh. MATTHEW 2:11

Dear God, Did Joseph sell the frankincense in Egypt, too, then?

CONSIDER THIS . . . He might have, because frankincense was very valuable when Jesus was a young boy. We don't know how much of each gift the wise men gave to Jesus and his family. We do know that the wise men were both rich and generous and that Jesus and his family stayed in Egypt for two years. So they needed a good amount of money!

But besides how much it was worth, the gift of frankincense was very special in other ways. All throughout the Bible, starting from the very beginning with the sons of Adam and Eve, God has asked his chosen people to offer sacrifices to him. Sometimes the sacrifices were grains, and sometimes they were animals. The gifts were *to* the Lord, of course, but they were *for* the good of the people. The sacrifices helped people to remember that God is the giver of everything. The people worshiped God by offering back to him a bit of what he'd given them. Sacrifices were payment for sins that the people had committed, instead of God's punishing the wrongdoer.

Frankincense was one of the important spices that was sprinkled on the sacrifices to make them sweet smelling. The final and most important gift to God's chosen people was Jesus Christ. He came as the giver of everything and offered himself as the sacrifice for everyone. For the wise men to have given him frankincense, a spice sprinkled on sacrifices, was a special way for God to point to the birth of the most important offering of all.

GOD SAYS . . .
Put some pure frankincense near each row to serve as a representative offering, a special gift presented to the LORD. LEVITICUS 24:7

HOW ABOUT YOU?
Had you ever considered why the wise men gave certain gifts? Do they now make more sense in a wonderful way?

Dear God, So myrrh must have a special meaning too. Right?

CONSIDER THIS . . . Myrrh does have a special meaning too. Have you heard the word *bittersweet*? It's something that's both bitter and sweet at the same time. It might be like a sweet candy covered in sour powder, or a sour lemon drop covered in sugar. It's also like when people you love come to visit, but you know they'll have to leave soon. It's sweet that they're coming to be with you but bitter because it will be sad when they go.

Myrrh is a bittersweet gift.

In order to get myrrh, a person has to wound a special kind of prickly, thorny tree. He takes a sharp object and drives it into the tree, scratching and scarring it until some of the sap bleeds out. When the sap bleeds out from the tree, it eventually gets hard, making a pasty kind of "Band-Aid" for the tree. That sticky paste is the sweet-smelling resin called myrrh. In Bible times, people used myrrh when they were preparing a body for burial in order to keep it sweet smelling. Some of Jesus' followers did just that for him after he was crucified.

The gift of myrrh was bittersweet because it was a reminder that Jesus would be harmed by sharp objects driven into him, causing him to bleed, and prepared for burial with the sweet perfume.

The gift of myrrh was bitter because Jesus would be hurt and die, but it was also sweet because he would come once as a baby, rise from the dead, and come back again!

HOW ABOUT YOU?

Does thinking about the wise men's gifts remind you that God knew all about and planned for the Crucifixion right from the beginning?

GOD SAYS . . .

[Nicodemus] brought about seventy-five pounds of perfumed ointment made from myrrh and aloes. Following Jewish burial custom, they wrapped Jesus' body with the spices in long sheets of linen cloth. JOHN 19:39-40

Dear God, I'm worried that someone I know will pick our names from the angel tree at church. I don't want people to know we don't have money.

CONSIDER THIS ... Have you heard of Saint Nicholas? He was a famous Christian who lived more than a thousand years ago, not too long after Jesus was born. He was a man who was kind to everyone, and one of the things he was famous for was giving gifts to people in need—in secret! He'd give to almost anyone, of course, but he especially delighted in giving to children. Sometimes, after everyone in a household had gone to bed, he'd slip coins into their shoes. When they woke up in the morning and put their shoes on, they'd find a shiny, delightful surprise. Money!

It can be hard to be the person who needs to find those coins in her shoes, or whose name has to be on the Angel Tree, though. It hurts our pride a little, and perhaps our feelings, wondering why we need to have others donate to us when they have enough. But the Bible tells us that we are to encourage other people, in the same way that we ourselves have been encouraged (1 Thessalonians 5:11). It very well might be that the people who take your name off of the tree had their names on that tree, or received other help, at a different time. This is their way of being obedient and encouraging you.

Some year, you will have enough left over at Christmas that you can help someone in need. You won't do it with a snobby or self-righteous attitude, because you'll know exactly how that person feels. Instead you'll do it secretly and kindly because you'll understand the feelings of the person in need. Christmastime is the perfect season, after all, to love one another as Jesus loves us.

GOD SAYS ...
Tell them to use their money to do good. They should be rich in good works and generous to those in need, always being ready to share with others. 1 TIMOTHY 6:18

HOW ABOUT YOU?
Do you feel embarrassed when you receive help from others? How do you feel about those whom you help?

Dear God, Why won't my mom let me get my ears double-pierced?

CONSIDER THIS . . . Your parents have an awesome responsibility. They have to explain to God why they made the choices they made as your parents. They love you very much. They want to do everything they can to make sure you grow up happy and healthy. They want you to be the best young lady you can be. It's not always easy to figure out how to do that!

Have you ever done those pencil mazes? You start from one side and then try to find your way out. Along the way you might take a wrong turn, but then you go back and retrace to the place you went wrong. If you take a wrong path, you may find your way out of the maze, but it won't be the exact place you wanted to end up.

Your parents are walking through a maze with you. They are making choices for and with you every day. They want those choices to help you end up in a good place. They are raising you to be a godly young woman. Sometimes they make decisions you don't agree with. Sometimes they might even make mistakes. When they do, good parents turn around, backtrack, and start over. Why are they willing to do this? Because they want you to come out right! They know if they show you the right path now, you're going to stay on that path later, too.

Smart girls like you try hard to be patient with the decisions their parents make for them, even if they don't agree. Almost everything your parents do, they do because they love you. When you end up a beautiful, Christlike woman, you can thank them. You can double-pierce your ears, if you still want to, when you're an adult!

HOW ABOUT YOU?

What mazes are you walking through right now?

GOD SAYS . . .

Train children to live the right way, and when they are old, they will not stray from it.
PROVERBS 22:6 (NCV)

Dear God, I'm in the Christmas play, and I'm afraid I'm going to forget my lines. What should I do?

CONSIDER THIS . . . In a recent poll, in which people were asked what they were most afraid of, more people said they were afraid of speaking in public than they were of dying! So it's no wonder that you might be concerned about something like that. The good news is that millions and millions of people speak in public and do it well, and you can succeed too. What's the secret?

Practice!

Saying the lines to your play is kind of like a piano or violin performance. When you practice the same piece over and over, so many times, it gets into your muscle memory. That way, when you're on stage ready to perform and tempted to panic, your muscles say, "Relax! We'll take over from here." When you practice your lines many, many times, the same thing happens. You say the same thing over and over, in the same tone of voice, and with the same body movements. Later, when you're in the play, your mind and body will say, "Relax! We'll take it from here."

Doing something over and over again sinks it deep in our hearts and minds. This is true for reading your Bible, too. When you make a habit of reading the Word over and over, the words are filed away in your spiritual muscle memory. At just the right time, the Holy Spirit can pull that up into your heart and mind, reminding you of what the Lord said. No rehearsal required!

GOD SAYS . . .
When the Father sends the Advocate as my representative—that is, the Holy Spirit—he will teach you everything and will remind you of everything I have told you. JOHN 14:26

HOW ABOUT YOU?
Has the Holy Spirit ever brought something to your mind, or your lips, just as you needed it?

Dear God, What do I do when a teacher makes jokes about Christians?

December 14

CONSIDER THIS . . . The way that you defend your beliefs starts way before a teacher makes a joke or tears your faith down. And it starts with you, not your teacher. How? Your attitude in class, the quality of your work, your tone of voice, and your word choices all tell your teacher what you're like. Your actions might be saying, "I'm responsible. I'm kind. I do thorough work." Or, if you haven't been doing so well in class, your actions might be telling the teacher, "I don't like this subject, so I'm not trying. I would rather talk with a friend or pass notes than listen to you." Whatever you've been "telling" your teacher, using words or not, is going to play a big role when an important moment comes.

And it will come.

While some teachers are sensitive to matters of faith, others are not. At some point a teacher may say something that goes against your Christian beliefs. At that moment all the things you've been "telling" the teacher are going to go before you. Approach your teacher, ask him or her if you can talk privately, and then share your concerns like this: "I'm really learning a lot in your class. Thank you. I wanted to tell you that I'm a Christian, and when you make fun of Christians, it troubles me. I know you wouldn't want to hurt my feelings, so I wanted to let you know. Thanks." Sound hard? It is. Even most adults avoid conflict. But when you lovingly speak the truth to someone, you show him or her respect. You will walk away from that feeling stronger. You will have made an impact for Christ in your world. That rocks!

HOW ABOUT YOU?

Do you know anyone who tears down your faith or makes fun of your beliefs? How can you lovingly speak the truth to him or her?

GOD SAYS . . .

Always be ready to answer everyone who asks you to explain about the hope you have, but answer in a gentle way and with respect. 1 PETER 3:15-16 (NCV)

Dear God, If someone gives a gift to me, am I supposed to give a gift back to her?

CONSIDER THIS . . . The beauty of a gift is that it is freely offered—given out of love with nothing expected in return. If your neighbor offers to pay you five dollars to shovel her driveway, that five dollars isn't a gift. It's pay for work you've done. If your friend offers to swap you one of her old books for one you've already read, that's not a gift either. It's a trade. So the idea of a gift is that you give it to someone without expecting anything in return.

However, if a person does a kind thing for you, it's nice for you to do a kind thing in return sometimes. It doesn't have to be right away, but maybe you could find some way to show your love and affection later on. It doesn't have to be a present—it might be an invitation or a compliment. But it might be a gift, too!

Sometimes people give things to other people as a way of forcing them, subtly, to give something back to them or do something the way they'd like. That's not a gift. That's pressure! Whenever someone gives anything to you with an expectation that you'll do what she wants, she's trying to control you. When you give a present of any kind to someone because you feel you owe her, that's not really a gift either. It's paying a debt. One you might not owe!

Be kind, be generous, and give cheerfully. But only give "gifts" to people you really want to.

GOD SAYS . . .
You must each decide in your heart how much to give. And don't give reluctantly or in response to pressure. "For God loves a person who gives cheerfully." 2 CORINTHIANS 9:7

HOW ABOUT YOU?
Is it more fun to give a gift to someone because you want to or because you have to?

Dear God, Is it okay to give someone a gift that I already got from someone else? Or is that tacky?

December 16

CONSIDER THIS . . . Well, it all depends. If you're giving shampoo to someone after you used half the bottle, or you're giving a mug that has a crack in it, or you spilled on one of the pages of the book, then—yup—it's tacky. There's an old joke that you should never eat a fruitcake if someone gets you one for Christmas. Why not? It's probably been passed around for many years because no one likes fruitcake!

If, however, you are trying very hard to give a present to someone, but you have very little money and are offering something of your own, sacrificially, then no, it's not tacky. Oftentimes people will "regift" something that was offered in love to them but doesn't fit, either their size or their style. If it's something you truly believe that a friend would enjoy, there's nothing wrong with giving it. And if you received something that you absolutely loved and want to share the same thing with a friend, then go ahead!

The best thing to "regift" at Christmas, of course, is the Good News that Jesus Christ was born! You can pass along something that is good for everyone, and you don't even need to give it up to do so. It's the gift that, as they say, keeps on giving!

Whatever you give and share, remember that you will be blessed for doing so, because it shows the generous, God-shaped heart inside you.

HOW ABOUT YOU?

Have you ever received exactly the right gift? How much do you think about the gifts you choose for others?

GOD SAYS . . .

You should remember the words of the Lord Jesus: "It is more blessed to give than to receive." ACTS 20:35

Dear God, We're going to visit some relatives, but I'm afraid to fly. What should I do?

CONSIDER THIS . . . Flying can be crazy fun, exhilarating, boring, or . . . scary. In the winter, when the weather is sometimes iffy, the scary part tends to kick in more often. You put your headphones on, open a book, and try not to complain about the kid sitting behind you who is kicking the back of your seat!

We often pray for smooth air when we're flying. Mostly we don't really believe we're going to crash, but flying can be so uncomfortable and out of our control. We can actually get a lot more praying done in the air than we ever do on the ground! As great as it is to be praying for so long, is it a good idea to simply ask God, over and over, to make the air smooth? What we really want is comfort and the reassurance that nothing is going to worry or harm us!

Isn't that how it is in life sometimes too? Instead of praying for other people, or for our friends to draw near to Christ, or any of a thousand other great things, we pray for "smooth air," which means we pray for all of our bumpy problems to disappear. No money worries, bullies, fights with our friends, or disagreements with our siblings!

Go ahead and slip those headphones on and get out a good book when you fly. Make sure you take time to pray along the way—both for a safe flight and for the many things that will matter to you and those you love after you land, too!

GOD SAYS . . .

[Jesus said,] "I am leaving you with a gift—peace of mind and heart. And the peace I give is a gift the world cannot give. So don't be troubled or afraid." JOHN 14:27

HOW ABOUT YOU?

What do you pray for? Is your prayer time divided between praying for yourself and praying for others?

Dear God, I love going to the movies with my family, but do I have to wear those geeky 3-D glasses?

December 18

CONSIDER THIS . . . There are a lot of new 3-D movies out now, and to see them right, you have to have special 3-D glasses. When you put them on, you can see the movie screen come alive in a whole new way! But if you don't—maybe because you don't think they're stylish—you're going to miss a lot of the movie, perhaps the main point. The movie, after all, was made to be seen through the right lenses.

Sometimes, contests are held using 3-D glasses, or only red cellophane, kind of like the thin plastic film that you pull over a tray of Christmas cookies to keep them fresh. If you hold up the contest picture behind the sheet of red plastic, the plastic blocks out most of the picture, which is in red. Then you can see the true picture underneath, magically revealed!

So often we girls think about how we fail and what we do wrong: sins we struggle with, bad decisions we've made, choices we regret, parts of our bodies that we don't like. If we let them, these kinds of sad thoughts will drag us down, and that's not at all what God wants for us.

When you catch yourself thinking like that, remember that God looks at you through a set of "red glasses," that is, the red blood of Christ. When he sees you, he doesn't see the sins he's forgiven and forgotten or the troubles you wrestle with. He sees the true, extra-beautiful you, without all of the distractions that block out the true picture!

HOW ABOUT YOU?

Do you see yourself through eyes of failure or eyes of love?

GOD SAYS . . .

Long ago the LORD said to Israel: "I have loved you, my people, with an everlasting love. With unfailing love I have drawn you to myself." JEREMIAH 31:3

Dear God, Why is everything red and green at Christmas?

CONSIDER THIS . . . No one knows exactly when the red and green colors first became associated with Christmas, but most people agree on what the colors mean. Green is almost always considered to be the color of life. Christmas trees are green, mistletoe and other plants are green, and even though people aren't green, most people think of living things when they think of that color. Red is also a color that has a connection with life, except that it's often associated with blood. Without our blood, we wouldn't be able to live! Blood isn't red when it's inside our bodies, but once we are hurt in some way and the blood comes out of us and is exposed to the air, it turns red.

Many people believe that the red and green colors of Christmas started with the holly bush. Have you ever seen a holly bush, or symbols of it, during Christmas? Holly has pointy, poky little leaves and red berries. The holly vine and leaves, when they dry, look very much like the crown of thorns that the Lord wore at his crucifixion. And the berries look like drops of blood.

Christmas is, as they say, the most wonderful time of the year! So even though we don't want to dwell on the sad parts for very long, it's good to remember what the green and red colors of Christmas represent: Jesus was born to eventually die for our sins. But then he rose from the dead and will live forever!

GOD SAYS . . .
For God presented Jesus as the sacrifice for sin. People are made right with God when they believe that Jesus sacrificed his life, shedding his blood. ROMANS 3:25

HOW ABOUT YOU?
What other symbols during December do you think hold a special meaning for Christians? Angel on the treetop? Stars? Lights on the tree? Cookies?

Dear God, Why does everything seem quiet in winter? Even "Silent Night" says, "All is calm."

CONSIDER THIS . . . Each season has its own charm. Spring is bursting with energy—baby birds and baby squirrels, new plants, and spring fever! Summer is a string of long, hot days full of vegetables continuing to grow and ripen, fun trips to places like the zoo and amusement park, lazy afternoons at the pool, and exciting family vacations. Autumn is when everyone must buckle down to work again. Kids go back to school, farmers harvest their crops and prepare their fields for winter, and other adults get focused on finishing projects for the end of the year. And what season is that end of the year? Winter!

Winter is a time of rest. Trees go dormant, meaning they don't grow for a little while. They're kind of like the animals who hibernate, or sleep, during the cold winter months. They're storing up energy for the season that comes next: spring, with its crazy burst of activity.

Winter is a time for people, like plants and animals, to slow down and rest too. You likely have a couple of weeks off from school around Christmas, so you can spend your days off sleeping in a little, reading more, and hanging out with your friends and family. Because most of us live in cooler climates, winter is a good time to have a bowl of tomato soup or to take a nap under a warm blanket.

Just like plants, maybe even more so, people need seasons of rest. Can you take some downtime this week?

HOW ABOUT YOU?

Do you make time in your life for rest? When? (And not just in the middle of the night!)

GOD SAYS . . .

Jesus said, "Let's go off by ourselves to a quiet place and rest awhile." He said this because there were so many people coming and going. MARK 6:31

Dear God, Why do people sing Christmas carols?

CONSIDER THIS . . . Have you ever tried to keep a secret that you were really excited about? Did you spill the beans about someone's surprise party or Christmas gift? Have you ever had to wait to share good news, very good news like an upcoming trip to Disney World, with your sister or brother? When you're happy about something or someone, it's hard to keep that inside without bursting.

That's exactly what praise is. Scripture tells us that even if men and women and boys and girls don't shout about God's goodness out loud, the very rocks will cry out and praise him (Luke 19:40). God fills you up so much inside that, like an overfilled balloon, you just have to let some praise out or you'll pop!

The word *carol* means "a song with a dance." People often danced in the Bible when they were praising or celebrating God. We may not think of dancing to Christmas carols, but they help us praise God during this time of the year. Christmas carols tell mostly, of course, about Jesus coming to earth as a humble human baby and the eternity-shaking effect that had on history. Christmas carols are also some of the few songs about Jesus that are played in public—in grocery stores, at the mall, in restaurants. Thanks to Christmas carols, we can praise God when we're shopping or eating out.

When you hear a Christmas carol, be happy and sing along. Maybe you could host a caroling party at your house with hot cider and warm cookies. Enjoy celebrating the birth of your Lord in public. It's hard to keep that kind of good news to yourself!

GOD SAYS . . .
Everything on earth will worship you; they will sing your praises, shouting your name in glorious songs.
PSALM 66:4

HOW ABOUT YOU?
What is your favorite Christmas carol? Why?

Dear God, What should I say to people who say that all religions lead to heaven and that it's selfish to think only Christians go there?

December 22

CONSIDER THIS . . . This is a tricky thing because we want to consider other people's thoughts and beliefs to be as important as our own. Nobody likes someone who insists that it's "my way or the highway" all the time. It seems selfish, and thoughtless, and maybe bossy. And honestly, that is exactly the right way to think when it's a matter of style or choice or opinion. But not everything can be the truth. When things are either true or false, we can't pretend that they are equal.

Someone may say that he does not believe in gravity, but it doesn't matter what he believes when he jumps off a cliff. He'll still fall down. We may wish to believe that 2 + 2 does not equal 4, but it does, no matter if we agree with it or not. Jesus says that he is *the* way to the Father. He's not just one way. He's the only way to the Father. Sadly, if someone does not agree with that, he or she will not get to heaven.

One thing that helps when people disagree with your beliefs is for you to say that it's not what *you* believe, but it's what *God* teaches. You're not asking everyone to follow you or to agree with you. You're asking them to follow God and to agree with him. That way, if they disagree, it's not you they have to take that up with. It's the Lord. You can share that you respect them and their right to disagree, but you can't in good faith agree that all religions are the same. If you treat others kindly, even when you disagree, they will respect you for being true to your beliefs.

HOW ABOUT YOU?

What is your answer when others ask you what you believe and why you believe it?

GOD SAYS . . .

Jesus told him, "I am the way, the truth, and the life. No one can come to the Father except through me."
JOHN 14:6

Dear God, Are other religions not true then?

CONSIDER THIS . . . There is a saying that all truth is God's truth. And little bits, and sometimes even large chunks, of his truth have found their way into many other religions. In the Bible, Paul tells us that from the earliest time, people could look around them and know that there is a God (Romans 1:20). Most of the world's religions have parts of the truth in them; the problem is, they mix in things that are not true or are tradition, or they interpret the Bible in an inappropriate way. Some religions take what the Bible says and then add to it. God forbids us from doing that, and he promises consequences to those who do. Other religions take much of what the Bible says as true, but then they take away the most important part, the heart. They say that Jesus is not the Son of God or that he did not die or rise again. The Bible tells us that people who believe that are not on the right path.

We live in a world where people would like everyone's beliefs to be of equal value. The thought behind that is not all bad. It's good to take people's feelings into consideration. However, that same kindness isn't always extended back to people who believe that Jesus is the only way. For Christians, there can only be two choices: either we believe exactly what Jesus said about himself, that he is *the* truth, or we choose not to.

When discussing other people's religions or faith, be sensitive to the fact they and people they love very much believe a certain way and will be naturally defensive and protective of that. Speak softly and act lovingly, but share the truth. There's only one absolute truth.

GOD SAYS . . .
You will know the truth, and the truth will set you free. JOHN 8:32

HOW ABOUT YOU?
Can you treat people of other faiths with respect, without having to agree that their view of God is the same as what the Bible teaches?

Dear God, Why did you choose Bethlehem to be the place where Jesus would be born?

CONSIDER THIS . . . God doesn't do anything by accident or surprise. Nearly 750 years before Jesus was born, the Old Testament prophets announced that the one who would be King of Israel would be born in the little town of Bethlehem.

The name *Bethlehem* means the "town of bread." Back then, and even today in many parts of the world, the biggest part of people's diets was bread. Bread was the most important food people ate every day. It was the main part of every meal, and other things were added.

Before Jesus was born, everyone was told to travel to their hometowns so they could be counted in what is called a census. Mary and Joseph traveled from where they lived in Nazareth to Bethlehem. The journey must have been difficult because Mary was very pregnant. When Mary and Joseph finally arrived in Bethlehem, just in time for their baby, Jesus, to be born, they found nowhere to stay. Instead of a nice inn, they had to stay in a stable, which is a type of barn. After Jesus was born, Mary laid him in a manger because they didn't have a crib. What is a manger used for? Why, it's a feeding trough, used to hold animals' food!

God tells us that man does not live by bread alone, but by every word that comes from him (Deuteronomy 8:3). The most important Word that came to earth was, of course, our Savior, Jesus Christ. He calls himself the Bread of Life. Is there a more fitting place where he could have been born?

No way!

HOW ABOUT YOU?

Would you go a part of any day without eating? Your soul needs "food" each day too! Today, a day of feasting, remember to thank God for the Bread of Life that feeds your true life!

GOD SAYS . . .

Jesus replied, "I am the bread of life. Whoever comes to me will never be hungry again. Whoever believes in me will never be thirsty." JOHN 6:35

CHRISTMAS DAY

Dear God, What is the real reason Jesus was born?

CONSIDER THIS . . . From the very beginning, when God created the first man and woman, he knew everything that was going to happen. He understood that they were going to sin and that they would be separated from him because he could have no relationship with sin.

From the start, God made a way to "cover" man and woman's sins. The first way was an animal that was killed in the Garden of Eden in order to make clothing to cover Adam and Eve. Then there were sacrifices of grain and animals, which "paid" for sin. There were also "scapegoats." Everyone would put their hands on a goat to transfer their sins from themselves to the animal, and then the animal would have to be sent away. But all of these solutions were temporary.

Remember the story of when Abraham took his son Isaac up a mountain and God asked Abraham to sacrifice Isaac? (If you don't remember the story, you can read about it in Genesis 22:1-19.) Abraham was prepared to sacrifice his son, but God called out to him and told him to stop before the boy was hurt. And then God provided a sacrificial animal for Abraham to use instead. Many years later, however, God did allow his own Son to be crucified. The death of Jesus on the cross was the final, holiest sacrifice. Since then, there has been no need for any other kind of sacrifice. Jesus is the lamb who takes away the sins of the world.

We can't pretend to understand how all of this works. It takes faith to believe in the sacrifice Jesus made for us. But we do know that because Jesus came, died, and rose again, we can be saved. He is our Messiah!

GOD SAYS . . .

The Savior—yes, the Messiah, the Lord—has been born today in Bethlehem, the city of David!
LUKE 2:11

HOW ABOUT YOU?

Take a couple of minutes today, maybe by the Christmas tree, to thank Jesus for coming, for dying, and for rising again.

Dear God, I don't have very much money, so I can't give much to my church for you. What else can I do?

CONSIDER THIS . . . One of the most beloved of all Christmas stories is the one about the little drummer boy. The little boy had a hard life. His parents were killed, and he was left with only a sheep for a friend and his drum. By chance, he happened to catch up with the wise men as they were on their way to visit Jesus. Once they arrived, the little drummer boy was dazzled by the Lord and by the gifts that the wise men had to offer. Do you remember what they were? Gold, frankincense, and myrrh. The little drummer boy had nothing except for a wounded lamb. When his lamb was miraculously healed, it only added to the boy's gratitude and the hope that he had. But what could he give as thanks, compared to what the others had brought?

A song.

Psalm 33:3 tells us to offer to the Lord a new song, and that's just what that little boy did. He played his drum for Jesus, Mary, and Joseph. He took what he loved and what he was good at and made that his offering. Do you write poems? Write a poem for the Lord. Do you draw? Paint? Play the piano? If you love babies, you can work in the nursery. Think about what you love most, something that is special to you, and then figure out a way to make that your offering. It's not the size of the gift but the size of the love behind it that matters.

HOW ABOUT YOU?

What do you have to offer to God that's uniquely you?

GOD SAYS . . .

This poor widow has given more than all the others who are making contributions. For they gave a tiny part of their surplus, but she, poor as she is, has given everything she had to live on. MARK 12:43-44

December 27

Dear God, I got a new phone for Christmas. Some people haven't returned my calls yet. Do you always answer when we pray?

CONSIDER THIS . . . How fun that you got a new phone for Christmas! The new ones are so cool, with all their updated and improved features. Some phones even offer enjoyable background music to people calling you before you pick up the line! Most people usually answer the phone on the second or third ring, but sometimes it's not the right time for them to answer, so they will let your call go to voice mail instead of answering the phone. Usually they'll call you back in a few hours or by the next day.

It's sometimes like that when we "call" God in prayer. He's always there, and he's never too busy to listen to us, but it might not be the right time, in his plan, for him to answer. Sometimes he "picks right up" and we hear back from him either through impressions or words in our hearts and minds, through what another person says, or through what we read in Scripture. But oftentimes we have to wait for an answer.

And while we wait, life goes on. But the days, weeks, and months spent waiting usually include good meals, fun times, and cool stuff to do with our families and friends. Like those fancy phones, God has provided us some enjoyable background music until it's the right time for him to answer.

GOD SAYS . . .

This is what the LORD says: "At just the right time, I will respond to you." ISAIAH 49:8

HOW ABOUT YOU?

Even if God doesn't answer you right away, do you believe that he will at just the right time?

Dear God, I got some perfume for Christmas. Am I too young to wear it?

December 28

CONSIDER THIS . . . Usually girls are just about your age when they first start wearing perfume or cologne. Perfume is fun on so many levels. The bottles are pretty, and the scents are delicious. Because you are young and lovely, you will want to start by wearing a perfume with a light fragrance. Some people find a fragrance that they love, and it becomes their "signature scent." If you choose a signature scent, when anyone smells that particular perfume, they'll think of you right away!

Perfume played an important role in the Bible, too. Just before Jesus was to be crucified, a woman poured an alabaster jar of very expensive perfume over him as a way of giving him honor (Matthew 26:7). Another time, Mary, a follower of Jesus and the sister of Lazarus, spread expensive perfume on Jesus' feet and wiped them dry with her hair to honor and thank him (John 12:3). The sweet fragrance of the perfume spread through the house.

Later in the Bible, God tells us that the knowledge of Christ is actually like a sweet perfume, and that we, his followers, are to spread that wherever we go (2 Corinthians 2:14). In a sense, speaking about Jesus is the "signature scent" of a Christian.

You are definitely old enough to enjoy that lovely gift of perfume given to you. Wear it with pride. Soon enough, people will welcome both you and your fragrance!

HOW ABOUT YOU?

Is there anyone in your life who wears a special perfume, and when you get a faint whiff of it, it reminds you instantly of her?

GOD SAYS . . .

Thank God! . . . Now he uses us to spread the knowledge of Christ everywhere, like a sweet perfume.
2 CORINTHIANS 2:14

Dear God, I would like to serve you and other Christians with my special gifts. How do I do that?

CONSIDER THIS . . . Whenever we think of leaders, we think of people who are in the front, the ones who go first. Who is the line leader? The person at the head of the line. Right? But things in the natural world are not always the same as things in the spiritual world. In the spiritual world, the ones who lead are often doing it most quietly, and sometimes not in the very best of jobs.

Sometimes the strongest messages are the quietest ones. A soft touch on the forehead and a gentle kiss on the cheek when you're sick say "I love you" much better than a loud announcement. Serving others and God quietly, persistently, and without drawing attention to yourself is the way Jesus modeled. In his culture, people wore sandals almost all the time, if their feet weren't bare. The roads were dusty and muddy. One of the very worst jobs for household servants—sometimes slaves—was to wash not only the family's feet, but also the feet of the guests. When Jesus bent down to wash his disciples' feet, they were at first a little embarrassed. Peter protested, but the Lord insisted. He wanted to leave a strong message. No job is too lowly for God, and therefore not for us, either.

In this next year, find someplace to serve your brothers and sisters in Christ, and know that no matter what the job, you're following the example of your Lord.

GOD SAYS . . .
After washing their feet, he . . . asked, "Do you understand what I was doing? . . . Since I, your Lord and Teacher, have washed your feet, you ought to wash each other's feet." JOHN 13:12, 14

HOW ABOUT YOU?
How can you plan to serve others in the new year?

Dear God, Were you born or made? Will you die?

December 30

CONSIDER THIS . . . For everything and everyone we know, there is a birth, a life, and a death. Humans are born, grow up, and eventually die. It's the same with pets, plants, fish, and even insects. Each may have a different length of life cycle, but they all have a beginning and an end. There is only one exception: God.

God, by his nature, is different and set apart. He tells us that he has always existed. God hasn't just been here since the beginning; he *is* the beginning. And he is now, and he is still to come. Have you ever noticed bookends on a bookshelf? One is on the left holding up the books, then the books are all lined up, and then the second bookend holds everything up on the right. When something completely surrounds other things, we say they are "bookended." History is bookended by God.

Although it's difficult to understand how God has no beginning or end, in some ways, it's comforting. Nothing can surprise him. Nothing can overpower him. Nothing can move or change him. He is in charge of all, and he is caring for you and everyone you love.

Although we have a beginning (all of us were born), if we are Christians, we will not have an end. Oh, sure, our earthly bodies will die. But our spirits will live forever with God and his other people. He made us in his image in that way too. So take heart! You've already had your beginning, and in him, you will have no true end!

HOW ABOUT YOU?

How do you feel knowing that God is the beginning and the end? His great and mighty hands hold everything.

GOD SAYS . . .

"I am the Alpha and the Omega—the beginning and the end," says the Lord God. "I am the one who is, who always was, and who is still to come—the Almighty One."
REVELATION 1:8

December 31

Dear God, Should I be making New Year's resolutions?

CONSIDER THIS . . . Every year, people make New Year's resolutions—things they are going to do differently in the new year. No more eating junk food! Getting homework done on time! Reading the Bible every day! We get a makeover, a do-over, and a new to-do list with New Year's resolutions!

The beauty of a January 1 in each year, or a Monday in each week, is the chance to start fresh. But sometimes in our excitement to begin again, we try to do too much too fast. Then, when we aren't perfect with our new goals, we're discouraged and slide back into old habits.

But the good news of Christianity has always been the good news that we don't have to make a fresh start on our own. We can't give ourselves a spiritual fresh start—we have to be born again by the Spirit—and we can't make new growth along the way. Only God can do that. And he will!

Jesus said, "Yes, I am the vine; you are the branches. Those who remain in me, and I in them, will produce much fruit. For apart from me you can do nothing" (John 15:5).

The Bible also says, "Forget all that—it is nothing compared to what I am going to do. For I am about to do something new. See, I have already begun! Do you not see it?" (Isaiah 43:18-19).

If we remain in him, God will bring the "fruit." If we watch, we can see that he is doing the new things—not us. We just need to open our eyes and then follow his leading. Betcha can't wait to follow!

GOD SAYS . . .

And the one sitting on the throne said, "Look, I am making everything new!" REVELATION 21:5

HOW ABOUT YOU?

What are you excited to see God doing with, through, and for you in the new year?

Scripture Index

Luke 14:28   *December 3*
Luke 17:3   *November 19*
John 1:1-3   *August 2*
John 6:35   *December 24*
John 6:66-67   *February 10*
John 8:32   *December 23*
John 10:4   *December 4*
John 10:11   *February 14*
John 10:14   *November 11*
John 10:28-29   *July 13*
John 11:33-35   *March 12*
John 13:12, 14   *December 29*
John 14:1   *May 23*
John 14:1   *October 2*
John 14:1   *October 23*
John 14:3   *September 18*
John 14:6   *April 9*
John 14:6   *November 15*
John 14:6   *December 22*
John 14:16-17   *January 30*
John 14:26   *December 13*
John 14:27   *December 17*
John 15:1-2   *June 13*
John 15:15   *July 14*
John 16:13   *August 19*
John 16:29-30   *April 23*
John 16:29-30   *November 3*
John 19:39-40   *December 10*
John 20:29   *October 16*
Acts 1:8   *June 2*
Acts 2:21   *March 30*
Acts 4:32   *August 23*
Acts 17:22-23   *March 10*

Acts 17:27   *April 5*
Acts 20:35   *December 16*
Acts 26:17-18   *February 23*
Romans 1:20   *September 10*
Romans 3:25   *December 19*
Romans 5:5   *February 24*
Romans 8:7   *May 9*
Romans 8:28   *July 27*
Romans 8:29   *January 26*
Romans 8:29   *July 23*
Romans 8:38   *July 3*
Romans 10:16   *January 31*
Romans 10:16-17   *June 23*
Romans 12:2   *May 7*
Romans 12:9-10   *September 13*
Romans 12:16   *November 18*
Romans 12:21   *October 28*
Romans 14:14   *January 25*
Romans 15:4   *March 27*
1 Corinthians 1:27   *November 26*
1 Corinthians 3:6-7   *September 26*
1 Corinthians 3:7   *September 4*
1 Corinthians 4:2   *September 17*
1 Corinthians 6:13   *September 29*
1 Corinthians 6:19-20   *June 12*
1 Corinthians 10:13   *July 12*
1 Corinthians 10:23-24   *May 10*
1 Corinthians 11:1 (NCV)   *August 5*
1 Corinthians 11:14-15   *July 25*
1 Corinthians 13:4   *January 18*
1 Corinthians 13:4   *February 26*
1 Corinthians 13:4-5   *April 29*
1 Corinthians 13:4-5   *August 25*

About the Author

After earning her first rejection letter at the age of thirteen, bestselling author Sandra Byrd has now published more than three dozen books, including London Confidential, the Tyndale House series for tweens. Her contemporary adult fiction debut, *Let Them Eat Cake*, and her historical fiction debut, *To Die For: A Novel of Anne Boleyn*, are both Christy Award finalists. Sandra is passionate about helping new writers develop their talent. She has mentored and coached hundreds of new writers and continues to coach dozens to success each year. Sandra resides in Washington state with her husband, Michael, a chaplain; their two children; and a circus dog named Brie.

Please visit Sandra online at www.sandrabyrd.com.

Fiction series by Sandra Byrd, author of *The One Year Be-Tween You and God*

Join fifteen-year-old Savvy and her family as they adjust to the British way of life after moving from the States. Experience the high-fashion world of London and learn about life in England— all while journeying with an all-American girl and budding journalist.

Along the way, you'll probably learn the same lessons Savvy does: it's better to just be yourself, secrets can be complicated, and popularity comes with a high price tag!

Giving advice to others is one thing.
It's another thing to find out that God expects
you to live out those lessons yourself. . . .

Read the entire series!

Book #1: *Asking for Trouble*
Book #2: *Through Thick & Thin*
Book #3: *Don't Kiss Him Good-Bye*
Book #4: *Flirting with Disaster*